Women in Ancient Rome

BLOOMSBURY SOURCES IN ANCIENT HISTORY

Women in Ancient Greece: A Sourcebook
Bonnie MacLachlan

Greek and Roman Sexualities: A Sourcebook
Jennifer Larson

Women in Ancient Rome

A Sourcebook

Bonnie MacLachlan

B L O O M S B U R Y
LONDON · NEW DELHI · NEW YORK · SYDNEY

Bloomsbury Academic

An imprint of Bloomsbury Publishing Inc

50 Bedford Square
London
WC1B 3DP
UK

1385 Broadway
New York
NY 10018
USA

www.bloomsbury.com

Bloomsbury is a registered trade mark of Bloomsbury Publishing Plc

First published in 2013
Reprinted 2013

© Bonnie MacLachlan 2013

British Library Cataloguing-in-Publication Data
A catalogue record for this book is available from the British Library.

ISBN: HB: 978-1-4411-7749-0
         PB: 978-1-4411-6421-6
      epub: 978-1-4411-4242-9
      epdf: 978-1-4411-5385-2

Library of Congress Cataloging-in-Publication Data
A catalog record for this book is available from the Library of Congress.

Typeset by Fakenham Prepress Solutions, Fakenham, Norfolk NR21 8NN
Printed and bound in the United States of America

Contents

Introduction

For many years now the field of Classics has moved on from the study of artifacts and texts in a hermetically sealed time capsule to consider the material in its broader context. The resources for Ancient Greece and Rome date from the second millennium BCE until the dissolution of the Roman Empire in the fifth century CE, and while our interpretations are still in large measure informed by their historical context, we are now free to engage in an examination that is both diachronic and synchronic, incorporating cross-cultural evidence and noting common features in human behaviour and expression across a span in time and space. Not infrequently one of the consequences of this is the fresh insight we gain about our own social interactions. Nowhere is this clearer than with the study of texts and artifacts that tell us something about Greek and Roman gendered behaviour.

This makes the teaching of *Women in Classical Antiquity* a lively enterprise, and this book is intended to play a part in the unveiling of features of modern as well as ancient gender interaction. I have translated a variety of Latin and Greek texts that address the situation of women in ancient Rome from its legendary beginnings in the eighth century BCE until the fourth century CE. This is a compilation of historical, legendary, philosophical and inscriptional texts, as well as others drawn from a variety of literary genres. They are presented for the most part in chronological sequence, with a brief running commentary situating them in their context. I anticipate that fuller contextualization and interpretive guidance will be supplied by instructors, as there remains the challenge of finding an authentic portrait of the life of women in a patriarchal culture where most of the texts are composed by men. I assume also that in this study a fuller array of texts will be consulted as needed, taking advantage of such resources as *Women's Life in Greece and Rome: A Sourcebook* (1982/1992/2005), *Women in the Classical World* (1994), *Reading Roman Women* (2001), *Roman Women* (2007), and others supplied by the general bibliography at the end of the book. More specialized bibliographies are found at the end of each chapter. It is most certainly the case that these bibliographies will quickly be out of date, but it is equally clear that students will have immediate access to new titles as soon as they appear.

The first part contains largely legendary material, covering the two and a half centuries during which tradition held that Rome was governed by kings (between the conventional dates of 753 BCE and 509 BCE). From the outset, several patterns are clear that can be traced throughout the history of Rome, such as the fact that women's capacity to reproduce was closely guarded and often exploited by men. With the emergence of the Republic at the end of the 6th century BCE, the historical material can be read with a greater degree of confidence, but as with historical accounts of any age, readers must be prepared to recognize the ideological assumptions that frame them. Part 2 covers the Early and Middle phases of the Republic, exposing the ways in which gender and class intersected when the patrician and plebian orders were in conflict. Where possible, I have tried to include evidence for the activities of lower class and slave women, despite the fact that the historical record is preoccupied with the elites. The third part covers the turbulent century of civil wars in Rome that ended with the victory of Octavian/Augustus over Mark Antony in 31 BCE; this therefore includes excerpts detailing the effect of war on women's lives. Part 4 contains material from the first six decades of the Empire launched by Augustus, with the effects on women (of all classes) of relative political stability and affluence for the privileged governing and elite groups. "The Later Empire" is the final part, presenting a broad selection of excerpts from various genres and contexts composed over roughly four centuries, ending with the effects of the clash between polytheistic religion and the monotheistic cult of Christianity that left female martyrs from both traditions.

This book would not have been possible without my being able to consider, and in many cases include, texts already selected by authors/editors of books in this field – most notably *Women's Life in Greece and Rome* and *Women in the Classical World*, mentioned above. In addition, there are certain individuals whose help has been crucial to the project: Dwayne Meisner, a doctoral student in my home department, who provided a careful reading of my translations and verified the numerical references; Elaine Fantham, my former teacher and dear friend, who offered many important suggestions about the selection of texts and the historical commentary; Paul Potter and Beate Gundert, who provided helpful comments on the passages quoting ancient medical writers; my colleagues Beth Greene and Alex Meyer who assisted with interpreting material from Vindolanda and Pompeii and Kelly Olson, who supplied important contributions for the bibliographies. Particular thanks go to Nicholas Horsfall, who was always prepared with professional suggestions for my textual queries and to Carol Agocs, for her assistance with proof-reading. My thanks also go to Charlotte Loveridge, Kim Storry and Dhara Patel of Bloomsbury Press, for competent handling of the manuscript. Of course I hold none of these individuals responsible for errors that may be discovered.

The translations are all my own. Material in parentheses within the translations is explanatory; that in square brackets supplements the text. With the numerical references, which can vary considerably because of a range of established texts, I decided to follow those used by the Perseus Digital Library (frequently identical with the bilingual Loeb editions). This I did after a great deal of thought, because I realized that it would facilitate the work of students who wished to read larger selections of text through internet consultation.

Bonnie MacLachlan
University of Western Ontario
January 2013

Abbreviations for works cited

Bernand, A. and E.	Bernand A. and E. 1960 (eds) *Les Inscriptions grecques et latines du Colosse de Memnon.* Cairo
CIL	*Corpus Inscriptionum Latinarum.* 1863–1959. Berlin
CMG	*Corpus Medicorum Graecorum.* 1927–. Berlin
De Caesaribus	*Sexti Aurelii Victoris Liber de Caesaribus.* 1966 (ed.) F. Pichlmayr. Leipzig
FIRA	*Fontes Iuris Romani Antejustiniani.* 1940 (eds) S. Riccobono *et al.* Florence
Gaius	*Gai Institutiones* or *Institutes of Roman Law.* 1904 (ed.) E. Poste. 1925 (revised and enlarged by) E. A. Whittuck. Oxford
ILLRP	*Inscriptiones Latinae Liberae Rei Publicae.* 1963. vols 1 and 2 (ed.) A. Degrassi. Florence
ILS²	*Inscriptiones Latinae Selectae.* 1962. vol. 2, part 2 (ed.) H. Dessau. Berlin
Kühn	Kühn, C. G. 1964 (ed.) *Claudii Galeni, Opera Omnia.* Hildesheim
Marshall	Marshall, P. K. 1977 (ed.) *Cornelii Nepotis. Vitae cum Fragmentis.* Leipzig
ORF	*Oratorum Romanorum Fragmenta.* 1955 (ed.) H. Malcovati. Turin
Pap. Oxy.	*The Oxyrhynchus Papyri* 1898–. London
PG	*Patrologiae cursus completus. Series graeca posterior.* 1857– (ed.) J. P. Migne. Paris
RTLA	*Receuil de Textes Latins Archaïques* 1957 (ed.) A. Ernout. Paris
Skutsch	Skutsch, O. 1985 (ed.) *The Annals of Q. Ennius.* Oxford
Tab. Vindol.	*Tabulae Vindolandenses* 2003 (eds) A. K. Bowman, J. D. Thomas and J. Pearce. London

PART 1

ROME'S BEGINNINGS

Women and the legendary past

CREUSA

The written record of Rome's earliest historical period is a legendary one. While we cannot be sure of the degree to which these tales were based in historical reality we can be confident that in their retelling they shaped, reflected and reinforced the attitudes of the people telling and hearing them. The cultural patterns that were sustained in this way included those governing the interactions between women and men.

This story of the foundation of Rome reflected an attempt to link the Roman world to Greece's heroic past. Vergil's great Latin epic *The Aeneid*, disseminated at the end of the last century BCE and in the early decades of the first century CE, forged a mythical link between the Roman Empire and the Trojan War. Aeneas, a Trojan prince who escaped the destruction of his city, turned his back on this chapter of his life, driven by destiny to establish a new kingdom on the Italian peninsula. Vergil describes Aeneas' development as a Romanized hero in two emotional vignettes in which he detaches himself from women with whom he has had an intimate relationship but who cannot be part of his Roman destiny.

The first is his Trojan wife Creusa. With the city conquered and in flames Aeneas cries out for her, running through the streets. Startled suddenly, he sees her ghost coming out of the shadows. She explains to him that the gods have decreed that his Roman destiny does not include her.

"What good is there in giving yourself over to such insane grief,
my dear husband? These things have not come to pass without the will of the gods.
Nor is it permitted for you to take your companion Creusa away from here;
not even the ruler of Olympus on high permits it.
There will be a long period of exile for you, and you must plow the vast expanse of sea
before you come to the Hesperian (Western) land, where the Lydian Tiber
flows through the fertile fields of men with a gentle swerve.
There good fortune and a kingdom and a royal wife
have been prepared for you. Banish your tears for your beloved Creusa."
(2.777–84)

Creusa assured him that she would not be led away into slavery by the Greeks, for the gods had willed it that she not leave Trojan soil. After asking him to take care of their young son, she disappeared into the air. Three times Aeneas tried to clasp her, and three times her image disappeared, as Vergil says, like a fleeting dream. Aeneas departed with their son Ascanius, his aged father and a band of Trojan followers.

DIDO

En route to Italy, Aeneas was blown off-course by a storm and stopped at Carthage, a city on the north coast of Africa that had been founded by the Queen Dido of Sidon, who gave him unexpected and exceptional hospitality. The hero's mother, the love-goddess Venus, had arranged a passionate encounter between the two, and the relationship continued for a year until Jupiter sent a divine emissary with the directive that Aeneas depart.

Dido, suspecting that Aeneas had departure in mind, was less compliant than Creusa when he tried to explain why he must leave. After raving in mad distraction she confronted the hero.

"Did you actually hope to keep it a secret, you faithless one –
that you could pull off something so great, so terribly impious, quietly slipping
away from my land?
Did not our love hold you back, or the pledge that you once gave,
or Dido, who will die a cruel death?
Why indeed are you launching your fleet under a wintry star
and rushing to travel over the deep in the midst of northerly winds,
cruel one? What would happen if you were not seeking foreign soil
and an unfamiliar home, but ancient Troy still stood?
Would Troy be the destination of your ships over the billowy sea?
Is it from me that you are fleeing? Oh, by these tears and your pledge,
when in my distress I have left myself nothing else at all,
by our marriage, by our wedding rites initiated,
if I deserved anything good from you or if there was anything
endearing you got from me, take pity on my household in tatters, and I beg you –
if there is any place for prayers to this point – cast off this intention of yours!"
(4.306–19)

Dido then appealed to Aeneas on the grounds that she needed his protection from local chiefs who wished to marry her. She considered theirs a marriage relationship, and lamented the fact that they had not at least produced a son (and male heir) whose face would keep alive his memory.

"If only before your flight there had been a child from you taken up into my arms,
a tiny Aeneas to play in my hall,
such as to bring you back to me by his looks.
In that case I would not seem to be so entirely forsaken and deserted."
(4.327–30)

Aeneas kept his mind focused on the dictates of the gods, but answered her appeal.

"Finally he answered her briefly. 'I will never deny, Queen,
that you are deservedly right about the many things you listed as you spoke to me.
It will not displease me to recall Elissa (another name for Dido)
as long as my memory holds, as long as breath governs these limbs.
I will now speak briefly about the issue. I did not hope to cover up this flight from you in secret –
don't imagine this – nor did I ever carry wedding torches
nor did I come to the point of taking this marriage vow.
If the fates had permitted me to live out my life under my own direction,
and to arrange my concerns in accordance with my own will,
I would be looking after the city of Troy first, and the cherished remains of my kin –
if the lofty towers of King Priam had remained
and if I could have rebuilt Pergamon for her defeated people by my own hands.'"
(4.333–44)

Aeneas assured Dido that it was not of his own free will that he was now drawn to the shores of Italy, but because of the directives of the gods and the future that lay in store for his son. Like Dido, he was subject to Fate, and he asked her to calm down.

"Now even the interpreter of the gods, sent by Jupiter himself –
I swear this by your head and mine – has brought down his message through the swift air.
I saw the god himself entering the walls openly in broad daylight,
and I drank in his voice with my ears.
Leave off inflaming me and you both with your complaints;
it is not of my own free will that I go in search of Italy."
(4.356–61)

But Dido answered with renewed fury, accusing him of being a savage brute and of ingratitude for the shelter she had provided the Trojans.

"Traitor, no goddess was your parent; no Dardanus was the forefather of your race,
but the brutal Caucasus gave birth to you on its harsh peaks,

and Hyrcanian tigresses gave you suck at their teats.
Why should I feign it, or for what more critical moment am I keeping myself?
Did he feel sorrow in the face of my weeping? Did he soften his look?
Was he overcome and did he shed a tear? Did he feel pity for the one who loves him?
What could I anticipate from this? At this very moment neither great Juno nor the father,
the son of Saturn, looks upon this with eyes of equanimity.
Nowhere is trust safe. A castaway on the shore, in dire need,
I took him in, and – fool that I was – I gave him a place with a share in the kingdom.
His lost fleet and his companions I brought back from death's door.
Oh, how I am set awhirl by fires of rage!"
(4.365–76)

Dido dismissed him with threats that when she died her ghost would torment him. Aeneas later encountered her ghost when he descended to the Underworld (while alive) to consult with his father, who had died before they could reach Italy. Dido had committed suicide when Aeneas left Carthage, and was wandering in the Fields of Mourning with others who had suffered from the cruel pangs of love.

"Among them through the deep forest wandered Phoenician Dido,
newly dead from her fatal wound. The Trojan hero,
as soon as he saw her, stood still and recognized her shadowy form
in the dark, just as one sees, or thinks he has seen,
the new moon appearing through the clouds at the beginning of the month.
He shed tears and spoke to her with tender love,
'Unhappy Dido, the news that came to me then was true,
that the light of your life was extinguished and you pursued your own destruction with the blade.
Oh! was I the cause of your death? I swear by the stars,
by the gods above and by whatever pledge of truth there can be deep beneath the earth
that it was against my will, Queen, that I departed from your shore.
But the commands of the gods, which now compel me to go through this shadowy realm,
through places rough with neglect and through the depths of night –
they compelled me to carry out their orders. I could not believe
that you were carrying such great pain because of my departure.
Halt your steps and don't pull yourself away from my sight.
From whom are you fleeing? This is the last word that I can address to you with fate's consent.'

With these words Aeneas tried to soften the soul that was burning
and looking fiercely at him, and he shed tears.
But she was turning away, with her eyes fixed on the ground,
nor was her look changed when he had begun his speech, any more
than if she were hard flint or stood there as a rocky marble cliff on Paros.
At length she detached herself and fled, still hostile,
into the shadowy grove."
(6.450–73)

When Aeneas finally landed on the Italian shore it was not long before war erupted with the local inhabitants. Eventually the Trojans were victorious, and a new alliance was forged with the local king Latinus, cemented by the marriage of Aeneas with Latinus' daughter Lavinia. In Vergil's version his Trojan son Ascanius was renamed "Iulus" (= "Julus"), and he became the founder of the Julian clan of Romans to which the poet's patron Augustus belonged.

ILIA

Ennius, a poet who preceded Vergil by about 200 years and also composed an epic poem about the early history of Rome, referred to a daughter of Aeneas named Ilia. In a fragment of his poem preserved by Cicero, Ennius described Ilia's being awakened by a disturbing dream in which an unknown man abducted her. Ilia cried aloud, which summoned her aged nurse, and the young woman recounted the dream to her sister (or half-sister). In the legendary history of Rome, the stranger is the god Mars, and his rape of Ilia (more frequently called Rhea Silvia) would result in the births of the twins Romulus and Remus.

"The old woman with feeble limbs brought the light in a hurry.
Then tearfully [Ilia] recounted the following, frightened out of her sleep:
'Child of Eurydice, whom our father loved,
now strength and life have abandoned my whole body.
For a handsome man seemed to carry me off through a pleasant willow grove
by the banks of the river – places unfamiliar to me.
And so, after this, true sister of mine, I seemed to wander all alone,
to search after you with halting steps and ask for you,
but could not reach you with my heart.
No pathway steadied my feet.
Then my father seemed to call to me with his voice,
using these words: "Oh, child, first you must endure hardship,
but afterwards your fortune will rise again, out of the river."

Once he said this, Sister, our father suddenly left.
He didn't present himself to my sight, although wishing it in his heart,
even though again and again I held up my hands to the azure vault of the sky
weeping, calling to him with the voice of persuasion.
But then sleep abandoned me, leaving my heart in turmoil.' "
(Ennius, *Annals* 1.29 Skutsch = Cicero, *On Divination* 1.40–1)

RHEA SILVIA

In the better known version of Rome's early history a line of kings succeeded
Ascanius/Iulus, who moved the settlement to the Alban hills. The best known
of these early kings is Romulus. The story with its legendary frame is picked up
by the Roman prose historian Livy, a contemporary of Vergil's who compiled
a history of Rome from its earliest foundation until the first century CE. The
historian describes the foundation of the city of Rome as beginning with the
rape of Rhea Silvia, daughter of King Numitor. The king's brother had taken
the throne by force, killing Numitor's sons and making his daughter Rhea Silvia
a Vestal Virgin, committing her to celibacy (see below) in order to secure his
position. Raped by the war god Mars, however, Rhea Silvia gave birth to twin
boys, Romulus and Remus.

"The Vestal was raped, and when she had given birth to twins – whether she
believed it or felt she was made more respectable by a claim that a god was
the cause of her sin – she declared that Mars was the father of her offspring in
question. But neither gods or men freed her or her babies from the king's cruelty.
The priestess was bound and placed in custody; he ordered the boys to be thrown
in a running river." (1.4.1–3)

A familiar tale in the narrative of early Rome is that of the rescue of Romulus
and Remus, and the suckling of the infants by a she-wolf. Romulus eventually
became king, and established the city that took his name on a place situated on
the River Tiber surrounded by hills. The traditional date for the foundation of
Rome is 753 BCE.

2

Women and the early kings

THE SABINE WOMEN I

Romulus extended the population of his new city by inviting refugees from the surrounding population to settle in Rome. Soon, however, he realized that he was facing a shortage of women. Confronting difficulties when trying to arrange intermarriage with neighbouring communities, he came up with a strategem. He sent messengers throughout the region announcing a lavish celebration of the festival Consuelia, in honour of Neptune as patron of horses. Out of curiosity to see the new town, Livy tells us, crowds of men, women and children convened in Rome, including a large number of Sabines who were neighbours in Latium. The guests were offered generous hospitality while they admired the extensive fortifications and buildings. But when the formal part of the festival began, a signal was given and all the strong Roman men dashed about seizing the young Sabine women.

"When the show had turned to disarray because of the panic then the distraught parents of the young girls escaped, with accusations against the compact of hospitality that had been violated and calling upon the god to whose festival they had come, having been deceived in their religious duty and trust. The outrage of the seized women was not less than this, nor was their hope for their future any greater.

But Romulus himself went about and pointed out that this had been done because of the arrogance of their parents, who had refused intermarriage with their neighbours. Nonetheless, the girls were now married women sharing all the fortunes of Rome, all the privileges of the community. There would be children, too, than which nothing is dearer to human nature. Let them only relent in their wrath and to those whom chance had given their bodies let them give their hearts. Often (he said) out of a wrong there arises later a feeling of affection, and to that degree they would be treated by their husbands more kindly because each one would strive on his own behalf so that when his part of the obligation was discharged he would also compensate them for what they were missing from their parents and their homes. Added to this were the sweet words spoken by the husbands, that the action was done from a desire to make amends and out of love – words that are most effective as appeals to touch a woman's heart." (1.9.13–16)

The loyalty of the Sabine wives was divided as time passed, between their Roman husbands and families and the Sabine families they had lost. The latter did not weaken in their remorse and their resolve to take revenge for the abduction of their young women.

"The minds of the abducted women were completely softened. But the parents of the seized girls then stirred up the cities by wearing mourning vestments and pouring out their tears and lamentations. Not only was their indignation confined to their hometowns but they also assembled from all parts at the home of Titus Tatius, king of the Sabines. Delegations assembled there because Tatius was the greatest name in that part of the country." (1.10.1)

Tatius and the Sabines were slower to act than other neighbouring people who went ahead and invaded Roman territory. Romulus and the Romans easily defeated these two incursions. While King Romulus vaunted in his success, his wife Hersilia appealed to him to offer a conciliatory gesture to the Sabines.

"While Romulus was exulting in his double victory, Hersilia his wife, harassed by the appeals of the abducted women, pleaded with him to pardon their relatives and invite them into the state. In this way the situation could be consolidated with a friendly alliance. Her appeal succeeded with ease." (1.11.2–3)
(Livy, *History of Rome*)

TARPEIA

A certain amount of amicable trust was achieved in the region, with Roman settlers moving into neighbouring territory and a number of the relatives of the captured women moving to Rome. A significant body of the Sabines remained hostile, however, and under King Tatius they mounted a carefully planned attack on the city of Romulus. A Roman girl named Tarpeia, the daughter of the commander of the Roman garrison, was tricked by the Sabine king into opening the gates to the invaders.

"The last battle was instigated by the Sabines, and that was the greatest by far, for nothing was undertaken out of anger or greed, nor did they give notice of war before they launched it. Furthermore, treachery was added to their design. Spurius Tarpeius was in charge of the Roman citadel. Tatius bribed the virgin daughter of this man with gold, so that she would admit the armed men into the citadel. It happened at the time that she had gone outside the fortifications to seek water for sacrifices. Once they were inside they covered her with their weapons and killed her, either so that the citadel could seem to have been taken by force or so that, by making a public case of it there would never be any trust placed in a traitor. There is also the tale that the Sabines were widely known to wear heavy gold bracelets on their left arms and conspicuous jewelled rings, and that the girl had demanded what they held in their left hands. The outcome was that their shields were piled on her, standing in for gifts of gold. There are those who say that she, when the agreement was arranged to hand over what was in their left hands, demanded their shields, and when she was seen to be acting with treachery she herself was dispatched by means of the price she had set." (1.11.5–11)

Today one can see the "Tarpeian Rock", a cliff face of the Capitoline Hill from which traitors and criminals were thrown for many centuries.

THE SABINE WOMEN II

With the Sabines in possession of the fortified Capitol, a fierce battle was waged below in the area of what became the Roman Forum. Eventually the issue was decided by the very women who had been the reason for the fighting.

"At this moment the Sabine women, from whose unjust treatment the battle had begun, with loosened hair and torn vestments, their womanly fear overcome by the evils at hand, dared to thrust themselves into the midst of the flying weapons. Making it through the crossfire they parted the hostile ranks, dissolving the men's fury, pleading on the one hand with their fathers, on the other with their husbands, not to spatter themselves with the accursed blood of their sons-in-law and fathers-in-law, lest they stain with parricide their offspring, who were grandsons of men on one side, free-born sons of men on the other side. 'If there is a grievance over the relationship between you, if our intermarriage is provoking you, turn your anger against us. We are the cause of the war; we are the cause of the wounds and slaughter of our husbands and fathers. We would rather perish than live as widows or orphans, without either of you.'

Their appeal moved both the throng of men and their leaders. Suddenly there was silence and suddenly nothing stirred. Then the leaders came forward to conclude a treaty. And they produced not only peace but one state out of two. They shared the kingdom, conveying the entire rule to Rome." (1.13.1–5)
(Livy, *History of Rome*)

EGERIA

The city prospered under Romulus. The next king, Numa Pompilius, was a Sabine. According to Livy, the military expansion that had established the city of Rome under his predecessor was replaced by Numa's devotion to setting up a legal and religious framework that would ensure its stability. He put in place a lunar calendar and established priesthoods, which included the Vestal Virgins (pp. 39–40 below). Numa drew his inspiration from a divine figure, according to Livy, the wood-nymph Egeria.

"There was a grove in the midst of which was a spring that came out of a dark grotto and watered it all year long. Because Numa often took himself there on his own without witnesses, for 'an encounter' with the goddess, as it were, he declared this grove sacred to the Camenae (Nymphs of sacred springs who were identified with Muses), the place where they would hold conversations with his wife Egeria."
(1.21.3–4)
(Livy, *History of Rome*)

Later ancient sources are more skeptical about the role played by Egeria.

"And to be sure it is generally agreed that wondrous good fortune guided the long-lasting kingship of Numa. But that a certain Egeria, one of the wood-nymphs and a wise divinity, a sexual partner of the man, guided and shaped the constitution, is something of a fable."
(Plutarch, *Moralia* 321B [first/second century CE])

Framed as a conversation between a certain Paris and Nepotianus, the following comments of Valerius Maximus (first century CE) are in the same vein, taken from his collection of anecdotes compiled for use in rhetorical schools. The spelling of the names varies slightly from other accounts.

(Paris) "Numa Pompilius, so that he might bind the Roman populace with rituals, wanted it to seem that there were nightly meetings with the goddess Egeria, and that with her counsel he instituted rituals that would be most acceptable to the immortal gods."
(Nepotianus) "Numa Pompilius, when he noticed that the Romans had become fierce through continual warfare, taught them how to worship the gods. And to the same end, so that they might more easily be tamed, he concocted a story that he was accustomed to having the nymph Egeria as his advisor, so that he would have greater authority among his fierce subjects."
(Valerius Maximus, *Nine Books of Memorable Deeds and Sayings* 1.2)

LAWS OF THE KINGS

Various ancient sources supply us with laws that were attributed to Romulus and Numa. Documentary accounts such as that of Dionysius of Halicarnassus (first century BCE) were composed as many as 900 years after the traditional dating of these kings, and may well represent a popular but inaccurate record of restrictive measures the kings put in place. From Dionysius we get the following report of regulations connected with marriage attributed to Romulus. The first presents some limitations placed upon women of a certain type of marriage.

"Romulus, by not giving to the husband the right to bring a charge against his wife for adultery or for leaving the house without justification, nor to the wife to bring a suit against her husband for wrong-doing or for leaving her without justification or for not making legal arrangements for the return or recovery of her dowry by the enactment of a single law – by not regulating any other of the affairs for these people – with a single law which held sway over all such cases, as the effects themselves have shown, he brought women to exercise moderation and self-control. This was the law: a woman who was married in a 'sacred marriage' joined with her husband and there was a common sharing of possessions and sacred rites." (2.25.1–2)

The sacred marriage is commonly understood to refer to marriage with *confarreatio*, in a ritual marked by the sharing of bread before the chief priests and ten witnesses.

Joining with her husband in a "sacred marriage" placed the bride *in manu*, "in the hand" of her husband, giving him complete control over her. If she behaved well, however, according to Dionysius she would share the household management in equal measure with him and stood to inherit property. If she misbehaved, however, the penalty was severe.

"This law compelled the married women, inasmuch as they had no other place to turn, to live their life in accordance with the manner of the man they had married, and the men to rule over their wives as necessary and inalienable property. A wife who was prudent and obedient to her husband in all matters was mistress of the household in the same way her husband was its master. If her husband died she became heir to the property, as a daughter would become heir of her father's estate. If he had no children and were to die without a will she was mistress of all that he had left, but if he had offspring she had a share equal to that of the children. If she had committed some wrongdoing she was subject to the injured party as judge and he was in charge of the severity of her punishment. But in the following cases

her kinsmen passed judgement together with her husband. Among the offences was adultery and – something the Greeks would think of as ranking least of all faults – if a wife had been found drinking wine. For both these [crimes] Romulus allowed the death penalty, as being the most shameful offences committed by women. He thought of adultery as the first sign of a loss of judgement, and drunkenness as the first step to adultery." (2.25.4–7)
(Dionysius of Halicarnassus, *Roman Antiquities*)

An example of a husband killing his wife for drinking wine is also recorded by Valerius Maximus in the chapter on "Severity" found in his collection of deeds and sayings.

"Severity in these men was stirred to exacting punishment for a serious crime, but that action of Egnatius Mecennius for a much lesser cause. Because his wife had drunk wine he killed her by beating her with a cudgel. Not only did the deed fail to find a prosecutor but even a critic, and there was unanimous agreement that through an excellent example she had paid the penalty for violating the laws of sobriety. And clearly every female who seeks the use of wine beyond moderation closes the door to all virtues and opens it to vices."
(Valerius Maximus, *Nine Books of Memorable Deeds and Sayings* 6.3.9)

Pliny, in his *Natural History* (14.89), mentions that this took place during the reign of Romulus and that Mecennius was tried and acquitted.

A further law attributed to Romulus by Dionysius awarded the father complete control over his son, to whip him, sell him, put him in prison or even kill him (2.26.4–27.1).

Plutarch, in his parallel biographies of ancient Greeks and Romans, describes a law of Romulus giving the terms for divorce.

"[Romulus] put in place some laws among which is a severe one. 'A wife is not permitted to divorce her husband, but he is allowed to divorce his wife for poisoning children or for substituting the keys or for adultery. If a man should divorce his wife for another reason [the law] ordered that part of his estate should go to his wife and part be dedicated to Demeter (Ceres for the Romans). Anyone who sold his wife would be sacrificed to the Underworld gods.'"
(*FIRA*, "Romulus" 9, cf Plutarch, "Romulus" 22.3)

Other laws were attributed to Numa, such as the following.

"From the laws of Numa who ruled after Romulus, in which this also was written: 'if a father allows his son to take a wife there will be a common sharing in religious

rituals and property, in accordance with the laws. It is no longer permissible for a father to sell his son.' "
(Dionysius of Halicarnassus, *Roman Antiquities* 2.27.4 = FIRA "Numa" 3)

"A law of the kings forbids that a woman who has died while pregnant be buried before the fetus has been cut out. Whoever acts contrary to this is seen to have destroyed a living being together with the mother."
(Marcellus 1.28 = FIRA "Numa" 12)

The following law attributed to Numa indicates that concubines were a feature of early Rome.

"Moreover, a woman was called a concubine and considered shameful who was habitually intimate with a man in whose control and possession was another woman in a state of matrimony. This is demonstrated by a very ancient law that we understand as originating with King Numa: 'A concubine is not permitted to touch the altar of Juno. If she does touch it she must slaughter a female lamb to Juno with her hair loosened.' "
(Aulus Gellius, *Attic Nights* 4.3.3 = FIRA "Numa" 13)

HORATIA

A warrior-king named Tullus Hostilius succeeded Numa and war was set to break out with the Albans, who inhabited territory that had been settled originally from the Trojan settlement at Lavinium. Instead of a full-scale battle, however, both sides agreed to abide by the outcome of a combat between two sets of triplets, one Alban (three Curiatii) and one Roman (three Horatii). After a deadly encounter, a single Roman remained alive, and he marched with the Roman army back to the city with the spoils of the three vanquished Albans. As Livy tells the story, the victory was not sweet for a young Roman woman, the sister of the victorious Horatius.

"His virgin sister met him outside the Capena gate, a young woman who had been betrothed to one of the Curiatii. She recognized on her brother's shoulders the soldier's cloak that she herself had made for her betrothed. She unbound her hair and in tears called out the name of her dead fiancé. The lamenting of his sister, in the midst of his victory and such great public celebration, shook the spirit of the fierce young man. Drawing his sword, therefore, he drew his weapon and plunged it into the girl, shouting at the same time 'Get away from here and take your girl-love to your lover. You have forgotten your brothers, dead or alive, you have forgotten your fatherland. So may any Roman woman perish who grieves for an enemy!' " (1.26.2–5)

The spectators were horrified and Horatius was charged with treason. He was about to be hanged when King Tullus intervened. He had been stirred to do so by Horatius' father, who argued that his daughter had deserved her death and that if it had been otherwise he would have exercised his paternal right to kill his son. He embraced the young man and reminded the men of Rome that his son had saved the city from falling under the sway of Alba. The younger Horatius was acquitted, but obliged to undertake ceremonies to expiate his crime. A stone tomb was built for his sister on the spot where she had been killed.

3

The Tarquins

After a succession of various kings the throne passed to an Etruscan. The Etruscans (see below) were people who inhabited modern Tuscany, north of Rome, and maintained close contacts with the Greeks from about the eighth century BCE.

TANAQUIL AND TARQUINIUS PRISCUS

Livy describes a dramatic sequence of events that unfolded in the sixth century when Lucumo, the son of a Greek man who had moved to Etruscan Tarquinia, eventually took over the throne in Rome. Lucumo had married Tanaquil, an ambitious Etruscan woman who felt that Rome would offer them more opportunities for advancement than Tarquinia.

"Lucumo on the other hand, the sole heir of all his father's property, married Tanaquil, who increased the self-confidence that his wealth had already produced. She was born in a position of privilege, and was not one to put up with circumstances in which she had married that were humbler than those into which she had been born. When the Etruscans showed contempt toward Lucumo for being born of an exile newcomer she could not bear the indignity, so ignoring any inborn affection for her homeland as long as she could see her husband respected, she seized upon a plan to move away from Tarquinia. Rome seemed to be the most suitable place for this purpose. Among a recently settled population, where all nobility might be achieved swiftly and be determined by native ability, there would be a place for a strong and vigorous man." (1.34.2–6)

The pair left with their belongings and came to the Janiculum, one of the seven hills amidst which Rome had been built. At this point an eagle swooped down and removed the cap from Lucumo's head. Shortly afterward it flew down again and replaced it as if, in Livy's words, it had been sent by heaven. Tanaquil as an Etruscan was well versed in augury (the interpretation of the gods' will through omens) and embracing her husband she foretold success in their venture.

"'The bird came from that region of the sky and is a messenger from that god. It made the sign around a man's head, the highest point. It removed the crown that

had been placed on a human head and replaced it as a divine sign.' The two entered the city carrying with them these hopes and reflections." (1.34.9–10)
(Livy, *History of Rome*)

The couple settled in Rome, where Lucumo took a Roman name, Lucius Tarquinius Priscus "Tarquin the First". Their wealth and hospitality facilitated their welcome, and this Tarquin quickly became an intimate of King Ancus, even being named in the king's will as the guardian of his sons. At the death of the king an election for his successor was held, and Tarquin sent the king's sons out of town on a hunting expedition, thereby easily winning the election. He proceeded to embark on some successful military campaigns against the Latins and Sabines, and undertook considerable public works projects in the city.

A Roman practice in later periods that tradition associated with Tarquin was the consultation of the Sibylline Books. In times of confusion or peril, this collection of oracular advice provided guidance akin to that given the Greeks by Apollo's priestess at Delphi. Sibyls were consulted in various oracular places by the Greeks, and tradition located one in Cumae, a town near modern Naples that had been settled by Greeks. (It was this Sibyl who guided Aeneas to the Underworld in Vergil's epic.) Dionysius of Halicarnassus preserves the story of the presentation of the Sibylline Books to Tarquin.

"It is said that some other truly wonderful piece of good fortune came to the city of the Romans during the reign of Tarquin, awarded through the favour of some god or a divinity. This was not a gift that lasted a short period, but oftentimes throughout the whole life of the state it has saved her from terrible disasters.

A certain woman, not a native of Rome, came to the king wanting to sell him nine books filled with Sibylline oracles. When the Tarquin didn't think that the books were worth purchasing at the requested price she went away and burned three of them. After a short time, bringing the six remaining books she offered to sell them for the same price. Since she seemed crazy and was laughed at for asking the same price for the reduced number of books that she couldn't get for the greater number, she went away again and burned half of those that were left. Bringing the remaining three she asked for the same amount of money. Tarquin, wondering what could be the intention of the woman, sent for the augurs and when he had described to them what had happened he asked them what he should do. These men, knowing from certain signs that he had turned away a blessing sent from the gods, and explaining that it was a huge misfortune that he had not purchased all the books, ordered him to calculate the money owed the woman, however much she asked, and to get hold of the oracles that remained. The woman then gave him the books and showed him how to take good care of them, and disappeared from the sight of the people. Tarquin selected two distinguished men from among the

citizens and attached to them two public servants, and entrusted them with taking care of the books."
(Dionysius of Halicarnassus, *Roman Antiquities* 4.62.1–4)

Tanaquil's skills as king-maker were engaged again when a little boy in the palace was found sleeping with his head in flames. The queen stopped efforts to quench the fire, which went out when the boy awoke. Taking her husband aside she asserted that the boy would grow up to be their saviour. Livy gives us the story.

"'Don't you see this boy,' she said, 'whom we are raising in such mean circumstances? You should realize that one day this boy will be a beacon for us when our situation is precarious, and he will be a bulwark for our throne when it is in trouble. So let us rear him with all attention, as a source of great glory publicly and privately.'" (1.39.3–4)

This Servius, who may have been the child of a slave, was raised as a royal prince and given in marriage to the daughter of Tanaquil and Tarquin. Trouble began when the two sons of the former King Ancus, having decided that they had been wrongly deprived of the throne, laid plans to kill Tarquin. They chose two rough shepherds to do the deed, who managed an audience with the king and took the opportunity to split his skull with an axe. As Tarquin lay dying, Tanaquil closed the palace gates and then treated his wounds as if he were merely injured. She sent for Servius and made plans for the next stage.

"Holding his right hand she pleaded with him not to leave the death of his father-in-law unavenged, nor to allow his mother-in-law to be an object of ridicule in the eyes of their enemies. 'The kingdom belongs to you, Servius, if you are a man,' she said, 'not to those who have carried out this most despicable crime, using the hands of outsiders. Stand up and follow the leadership of the gods who once foretold, by surrounding this head of yours with divine fire, that it would be famous. Now let that heavenly flame rouse you; now is really the time to bestir yourself. Even as foreigners we ruled. Think again about who you are, not about where you were born. If your plans are paralyzed by this shocking crisis just follow my plans.'" (1.41.2–3)

While they were thus conferring there was a great deal of commotion in the street, as crowds tried to learn what would be the outcome of the attack on Tarquin. Tanaquil bought some time. Livy describes her flinging open an upper window of the palace and addressing the people.

"She urged them to be calm. The king had been knocked out by a sudden blow. The weapon had not penetrated too deeply into his body. He was now returning to his senses. The wound had been examined when the blood had been wiped off. All prospects for health were good. She was confident that they would see him for themselves shortly. In the meantime she urged the people to hearken to the words of Servius Tullius. He would restore justice and would attend to the other duties of the king.

Servius came out wearing the robe of state, preceded by the lictors (individuals bearing the signs of office). Sitting on the royal seat he made judgements in some cases, but in others he pretended that he would refer them to the king. In this way for several days when Tarquin had already died, by concealing his death and through the appearance of administering the affairs of another as a stand-in, Servius strengthened his own position." (1.41.5–6)
(Livy, *History of Rome*)

Livy continues his account with reports of the ways in which Servius consolidated his leadership role in Rome, engaging in a number of military campaigns, undertaking a wide-sweeping socio-political reorganization of the populace and extending the boundaries of the city. But the drama inside the palace continued. The sons of King Ancus, who had arranged the murder of the Etruscan, had gone into voluntary exile, but the two sons (or possibly grandsons) of Tarquin and Tanaquil posed a new threat, questioning Servius' legitimacy as king. Servius married them to his own two daughters, undertook some popular land distribution and then called for an official vote to give him title to the throne. He was successful, but one of the two young Tarquins, later to be known as Tarquinius Superbus "Tarquin the Arrogant" continued to foster distrust and intrigue. Livy likens it to the makings of a Greek tragedy.

TULLIA AND TARQUINIUS SUPERBUS

The two young Tarquins who were married to daughters of Servius Tullius (both called Tullia, following the Roman custom of taking their father's clan or *gens* name) were opposite in disposition to each other and to their wives. The elder Tullia, who was married to the mild-mannered Arruns, was fiercely ambitious, but the younger Tullia who was married to the other (ambitious) Tarquin was not. Livy reads the next development as a consequence of the designs of the strong-minded Tullia.

"The headstrong Tullia was infuriated that there was nothing of substance in her husband, and no ambition or daring. She turned her attention completely to the other Tarquin, admiring him, calling him a true man and born to the throne by his bloodline. She despised her sister because having acquired a husband she was failing to support him with womanly courage. Likeness of character quickly drew them together, as usually happens. Evil is most suited to evil.

But the beginning of the upheaval sprung entirely from the female front. [The elder Tullia] in regular conversations with her sister's husband withheld no words of abuse about her husband to his brother, or about her sister to her sister's husband. And she pressed the point that it would have been more appropriate for her to have been single and he a bachelor than to have been joined in a bad match, to waste away because of someone else's inaction. If the gods had given her as husband a man that she deserved she would soon have seen the royal rule in her house that she was looking at in her father's.

Swiftly she filled the young man with her own recklessness. There were two funerals in quick succession (of Arruns Tarquinius and the younger Tullia). When the pair had made space in their homes for a fresh marriage they were joined in wedlock, with Servius rather not standing in the way than approving. On that day, to be sure, Servius now in his senior years was increasingly under threat, and his royal rule began to be more vulnerable. The wicked woman looked from one crime toward another. She didn't allow her husband to relax by day or night, lest the earlier kin-murders had been for nothing. She wasn't going to go without a man to whom she was said to be married, but not one whom she would serve in silence. She was missing one who thought he deserved the throne, one who recalled that he was the son of Tarquinius Priscus, who preferred to possess the kingship rather than hope for it. 'If you are the one whom I reckon I married, I call you both husband and king, but if you are less than that, then the situation has now changed for the worse, because that crime of yours is bound up with cowardice. Why won't you prepare yourself for action?'" (1.46.6–47.4)

Livy describes Tullia as goaded on by the thought of the successes of Tanaquil.

"By chiding the young man with these and other taunts she stirred him to action. She herself couldn't rest while Tanaquil, a foreign woman, had been able to set her mind in gear such that she had conferred the royal rule on two men in succession, on her husband and then on her son-in-law, but while she herself, being of royal blood, was having no influence on bestowing or removing the crown." (1.47.6)

Tarquin, stirred into action by his wife's baiting, canvassed the populace, currying favour with the senatorial classes and bribing young men to gain their support, all the while vilifying Servius. At an opportune moment he forced his way into the Forum with an armed guard and sat on the king's chair in front of the Senate House, sending heralds to summon the senators to appear before "King Tarquin". When all were assembled he condemned Servius as a slave-usurper of the crown.

When Servius learned of this he rushed to the Forum. Tarquin seized the aged king and threw him down the steps of the Senate House into the street. As he stumbled back to the palace, the king was killed by assassins. Livy returns once more to Tullia as the source of the crime.

"It is believed that the deed was done at the instigation of Tullia, because she was not averse to other crime. There is certainly general agreement that she entered the Forum in a carriage, undaunted by the gathering of men, and called her husband away from the Senate house, being the first to call him 'King'. Ordered by him to leave because of such a great uproar, as she was heading home and had come to the top of Cyprus Street, where the shrine of Diana stood recently, her driver who was steering the team of horses turned the carriage to the right to climb up the Urban hill so that he could drive up the Esquiline. He stopped in terror and checked the reins, then showed to his mistress the body of Servius lying there mutilated. According to tradition, because of the abominable and inhuman crime the location is marked by a memorial; they call it the 'Street of Crime'. This is the street where Tullia, driven crazy by the avenging spirits of her sister and her (first) husband, is said to have driven the carriage over the body of her father. Stained and spattered herself, she carried part of the blood and gore from her father on her bloodied carriage to the household gods of the house she shared with her husband. With their spirits outraged at the bad beginning of the reign, a similar end would soon follow." (1.48.5–7)
(Livy, *History of Rome*)

Today one can walk in this place, known as the *Vicus Sceleratus* (the "Crime District") leading to the University of Rome.

LUCRETIA

Despite expanding Roman territory by military means, and some considerable expansion of public building programmes, the reign of the younger Tarquin was marked by tyranny and brutality. Its end was, as the gods had predicted, marked by violence, and saw the conclusion not only of the Tarquins but of royal rule itself in Rome. The strength necessary to oust the king and his family was mustered by public outrage when a member of the royal family raped a respectable married woman.

A Roman garrison had been posted outside the neighbouring city of Ardea where it had mounted a siege. Among the troops were sons of the king and other Roman officers including a man named Collatinus. One evening they fell to discussing their wives, with rival claims made about the virtue of each man's wife. Collatinus proposed that they make a surprise visit to their homes and ascertain just what their wives were doing during their absence. Livy picks up the story as they left for Rome.

"They were heated with wine. 'Come on, let's go!' they all said. They flew off to Rome on their swift horses. They arrived there just as dusk was spreading, and then proceeded to Collatia, where Lucretia was engaged in ways quite unlike the wives of the royal family, whom they had seen spending their time partying with friends in luxurious surroundings. They found her on the other hand sitting in the middle of the house, given over to her wool-working late at night, together with her maid-servants working by lamplight. The prize for the contest of women was in Lucretia's hands. When her husband and the Tarquins approached her they were welcomed hospitably. The victorious husband graciously invited the royal youth to come in. On that occasion an illicit desire to rape Lucretia seized Sextus Tarquinius; both her beauty and the chastity she had demonstrated inflamed him. Then, however, following their nocturnal youthful exercise, they returned to camp.

A few days later Sextus Tarquinius, without the knowledge of Collatinus, came to Collatia with one companion. There he was received kindly by those ignorant of his design, and after dinner was led to the guest quarters. Burning with desire, after all seemed safe enough around him and everyone seemed to be asleep, he drew his sword and came to the sleeping Lucretia. With his left hand he leaned on her breast and said, 'Be quiet, Lucretia. I am Sextus Tarquinius. I have a weapon in my hand; if you make a sound you will die.' When the terrified woman woke up and saw that there was no help at hand and death was imminent, then the Tarquin confessed his love, pleaded with her, mixed his prayers with threats, bent her womanly heart in every direction. When he saw that she was unyielding and that not even the fear of death would change her mind he added dishonour to her fear. He said that when she was dead he would cut the throat of a slave and place him beside her naked, so that it would be said that she had been killed like one caught in foul adultery. By means of this terror he vanquished her resolute chastity, just as lust (with force) wins out. Then brutal Tarquinius set out from there, once the woman's honour had been completely compromised.

Lucretia, distraught at such a terrible calamity, sent a message to her father in Rome and the same one to her husband at Ardea, asking them to come with a single trustworthy friend. They needed to do this as quickly as possible: a terrible thing had happened. Spurius Lucretius came with Publius Valerius, the son of Volesus. Collatinus came with Lucius Junius Brutus, with whom he had happened to be returning to Rome when he was met by the messenger from his wife. They found Lucretia sitting in misery in her bedroom. With their arrival her tears erupted. When her husband asked, 'Are you well?' she answered 'Hardly, for what is well with a woman when her chastity has been lost?' There is the imprint of another man in your bed, Collatinus. But only my body has been violated; my heart is innocent. Death will be my witness. But give me your pledge and promise that there will be no amnesty for the adulterer. It was Sextus Tarquinius who came last night as an enemy in the guise of a guest, armed with force. He took from here his pleasure, a destructive one for me, and for him too if you are men.

They all gave her their pledge in turn. They offered consolation in her distress, by deflecting the fault from the one who had been forced to the perpetrator of the crime. It is the mind that sins, not the body, and where one's intention is not present so is guilt absent. 'You,' she said, 'will see to what must be done to him. Although I absolve myself of the crime I do not absolve myself from punishment. Let no unchaste woman live in time to come because of the example of Lucretia.' The knife, which she had kept hidden under her robe she drove into her heart and she fell forward, dying from the wound." (1.57.8–58.12)
(Livy, *History of Rome*)

Brutus, the companion who had hastened with Collatinus to Rome in response to Lucretia's summons, vowed to avenge the rape – to pursue the king, his wife and children, and to eradicate royal rule from Rome. Lucretia's body was carried into the Forum, and the people's grief turned to anger at the Tarquinii and support for Brutus. A large armed force marched through the city behind Brutus. He delivered a speech in the Forum condemning the rape, the arrogant and tyrannical rule of the king, and the dreadful murder and mutilation of Servius by the Tarquins. When the king rushed from Ardea to Rome the city was closed against him. Tullia fled and their sons went into exile. The Roman Republic was born, and sole rule was replaced thereafter by a government led by two consuls elected by popular vote.

4

Etruscan Women

Livy's account of the powerful women in the Etruscan dynasty at Rome is complemented by material evidence that has survived from Etruscan centres such as Caere or Tarquinia, including tomb frescoes where women are depicted quite differently from their Greek or Roman counterparts – in positions of prominence. In some of these paintings they are seated with men watching public spectacles; in others they are dining on couches with men who appear to be their husbands. Etruscan sarcophagi depict couples on a couch together, even embracing. Aristotle, in a discussion of Etruscan customs, felt this was worthy of note, according to the antiquarian Athenaeus (third century CE).

"Aristotle, in his *Customs of the Tyrrhenoi* (Etruscans) said 'But the Etruscans dine with their wives, lying at table, reclining under the same cloak.'"
(*Deipnosophistae, Banqueters* 1.23d = Aristotle, fr. 565 Bekker)

Chariots have been found in the tombs of some Etruscan women along with items for personal adornment and wool-working. Some 3000 engraved mirrors have also been recovered from these tombs, many of which contain inscriptions – a sign of the literacy of the women who used them. Not infrequently the scenes depicted on the mirrors are erotically suggestive, and many of the bronze figurines from Etruria that have survived seem to reflect a way of life in which the erotically playful was enjoyed. This fuelled a Greek and Roman disdain for the "otherness" of the Etruscans, and led them to make assumptions about their sexual laxity and the freedom accorded their women, and to draw conclusions from this about their family life. The longest surviving testimony of this is that of the Greek historian Theopompus (fourth century BCE) preserved in Athenaeus, who includes a summary reference to a remark by Timaeus (a Sicilian historian, also fourth century BCE) about female slaves of the Etruscans.

"Timaeus tells us in his first book that among the Etruscans, who most outlandishly live in luxury, that the servant girls wait on men naked.
Theopompus, in the 43rd book of his *Histories*, says that it is also the custom among the Etruscans for women to be common property. These women take exceptional care of their bodies and exercise frequently, even with men, and

sometimes also with each other, for it is not shameful for them to be seen naked. They dine not with their own husbands, but with whoever happens to be present, and they propose toasts to whomever they wish. They are formidably skilled at drinking and extremely beautiful to look at. The Etruscans raise all the children born to them, not knowing from what father each one came. The male offspring live the same lifestyle as those who raised them, having frequent drinking parties and having sex with all the women. Nothing is regarded as disgraceful in the eyes of the Etruscans, not only when they are doing something out in public but also when having something done to them, for this is a local custom among them. They are so far from regarding it as shameful that they even say, whenever the master of the house is the recipient of the sexual act and someone comes looking for him, that he openly describes the affairs that he is engaged in as 'this and that', in disgraceful terms.

When they get together socially with their friends or relatives they behave like this: first, when they have stopped drinking and are about to go to sleep, while the lamps are still lit the servants bring in to them sometimes courtesans and sometimes boys, uncommonly handsome ones, sometimes even their wives. When they have had their enjoyment of these, the servants bring them youths in their prime, who take their turn having sex with them. They engage in sex and have intercourse while watching one another, but most of the time they put screens around their couches woven from branches, having thrown coverlets over top of them.

They really like to have sex with women, but far more do they enjoy being with boys and youths, for the young men among them are extremely handsome to see, inasmuch as they live in luxury and shave their bodies smooth. All the barbarians living in the West remove their hair with pitch and shave their bodies, and among the Etruscans are many shops equipped for this, and there are professionals in this trade just like our barbers."
(Athenaeus, *Deipnosophistae* 12.517d = Timaeus, *FGrH* 566F1B; Athenaeus, *Deipnosophistae* 12.517d–518a = Theopompus *FGrH* 115F204)

FURTHER READING

Bonfante, L. 2003. *Etruscan Dress. Updated Edition.* Baltimore, MD
—1994. "Excursus. Etruscan Women", in E. Fantham et al. (eds) *Women in the Classical World.* New York/Oxford. 243–59
— 1986. (ed.) *Etruscan Life and Afterlife. A Handbook of Etruscan Studies.* Detroit
Brown, R. 1995. "Livy's Sabine Women and the Ideal of Concordia". *Transactions of the American Philological Association* 125, 291–319
Claassen, J. M. 1998. "The Familiar Other: The Pivotal Role of Women in Livy's Narrative of Political Development in Early Rome". *Acta Classica* 41, 71–104
de Grummond, N. 1982 (ed.) *A Guide to Etruscan Mirrors.* Talahassee, FL
Hemker, J. 1985. "Rape and the Founding of Rome". *Helios* 12, 41–7

Joplin, P. K. 1990. "Ritual Work on Human Flesh: Livy's Lucretia and the Rape of the Body Politic". *Helios* 17, 51–70

Joshel, S. 1992. "The Body Female and the Body Politic: Livy's Lucretia and Verginia", in A. Richlin (ed.) *Pornography and Representation in Greece and Rome*. Oxford/Toronto. 112–30

Macnamara, E. 1973. *Everyday Life of the Etruscans*. London

Miles, G. B. 1995. "The First Roman Marriage and the Theft of the Sabine Women", in *Livy: Reconstructing Early Rome*. Ithaca, NY. 179–219

Watson, A. 1979. "The Death of Horatia". *Classical Quarterly* 29, 436–47

PART 2

THE EARLY AND MIDDLE REPUBLIC

5

The early laws and women: the Twelve Tables

The codification of laws for the new Roman Republic was the responsibility of "decemvirs" – ten men who, in 452 BCE according to Livy, were given plenipotentiary powers to govern Rome. This was during a period when there had been vigorous opposition to the consuls, particularly from the lower classes (the plebeians) who felt they had been unfairly treated by the upper classes (patricians) with their arbitrary application of informal laws. The new laws were produced after consulting those in Greece designed by the proto-democratic Athenian lawgiver Solon in the early 6th century BCE. The decemvirs had these laws inscribed on tablets and set up in the Forum. There were ten laws at first, which were supplemented by two more and referred to as the "XII Tables". Livy claimed that these laid the foundations for Roman law for centuries (*History of Rome* 34.6–7). Articles from several of these laws were quoted by various ancient authors and by jurists like Gaius (second century CE). These writers make it clear that the jurisdiction of the XII Tables was both public and private. In family law the power of the male head of the household (the *paterfamilias*) was supreme, and women were to be under the guardianship (*tutela*) of their father, husband or nearest male relative. Although from this early period a woman could avoid being under the complete control of her husband (*in manu*), she would be subject to some guardianship by the nearest male relative in her birth family.

Tablet 4
1 "A child showing signs of deformity is to be killed immediately, in keeping with the XII Tables." (Cicero, *Laws* 3.19.13–15)
2 a. "The law awards to the father the power of life or death over his son." (*FIRA*, "XII Tabulae" 4.2a)
3 "From the XII Tables [the husband divorcing] his wife orders her to keep her property with her; he takes the keys and expels her." (Cicero, *Philippics* 2.69 = *FIRA*, "XII Tabulae" 4.3)
4 "I learned that a woman with a good and upright character, whose chastity was not in question, had given birth in the 11th month after the death of her husband. Because of the calculation of time that had passed the inheritance arrangement was made as if her husband had died and she had conceived afterward, since the decemvirs had written that a legitimate child is produced

in the tenth month but not in the eleventh." (Aulus Gellius, *Attic Nights* 3.16.12, cf. Ulpian, *Digest* 38.16.3.9 = FIRA "*XII Tabulae*" 4.4)

Tablet 5

1 "The men of old, even if their wives were of the age of seniority, wanted them to be under guardianship because of the unpredictability of their mind ... This was not the case for the Vestal Virgins, whom even the men of old wanted to be independent in the duty of priesthood. And so this was decreed even by the law of the XII Tables." (Gaius, *Institutiones* 1.144–5 = FIRA, "*XII Tabulae*" 5.1)

2 "The property of a woman who is under the guardianship of her male relatives cannot be seized by the right of appropriation, unless it has been handed over by her with the endorsement of her guardian. It was so decreed in the law of the XII Tables." (Gaius, *Institutiones* 2.47 = FIRA, "*XII Tabulae*" 5.2)

4 "If someone dies intestate (without a will) who has no heirs the nearest male heir will have the family property." (FIRA, "*XII Tabulae*" 5.4)

5 "If there is no male heir the males of the same clan will have the family property." (FIRA, "*XII Tabulae*" 5.5)

6 "For those to whom a guardian is not given by a will the male relatives are the guardians, according to the law of the XII Tables." (Gaius, *Institutiones* 1.155 = FIRA, "*XII Tabulae*" 5.6)

Tablet 6

5 "According to the law of the XII Tables it is decreed that if any woman does not wish to marry in this way – *in manu* with her husband – she should absent herself for three consecutive nights and in this way shall interrupt his legal control for each year." (Gaius, *Institutiones* 1.111 = FIRA, "*XII Tabulae*" 6.5)

Tablet 10

4 "Women are not to tear their cheeks nor wail in lament because of a funeral." (Cicero, *Laws* 2.64.7–8 = FIRA, "*XII Tabulae*" 10.4)

6

Courageous women of the Early Republic

CLOELIA

The expulsion of the Tarquins did not bring peace to Rome. Livy reports that the Tarquin sons who had taken refuge with Lars Porsena, king of the powerful Etruscan city of Clusium, had been urging the king to amass a large force and seek redress both for the dissolution of the monarchy in Rome and for the loss of Etruscan prestige that had come with the expulsion of the kings. Porsena quickly saw the advantage of this for himself and his people and mounted a siege of the city. An act of heroism by a Roman named Mucius Scaevola led to terms being negotiated for the lifting of the siege. These included the taking of hostages, among whom were a number of women. One of those kept in the Etruscan camp was Cloelia, who undertook a remarkable act of bravery. For this she was rewarded not only by the Romans but by Lars Porsena himself.

"In consequence of [Mucius'] courage being so honoured the women were also roused to earn public recognition. Cloelia, an unmarried girl, was also one of the hostages. Since the camp of the Etruscans was located not far from the bank of the Tiber, she eluded the guard and swam across the Tiber amid a shower of the enemies' weapons as leader of a troop of girls, and restored them safe and sound to their families.

When this was reported to the king at first he was fired up with rage and sent emissaries to Rome to demand the hostage Cloelia. (He considered returning the others of no great consequence.) Then his mind gave way to admiration. He said that her deed exceeded those of [Horatius] Cocles and Mucius; on the other hand he made it clear that if the hostage were not returned the treaty would be considered broken, but if they surrendered her he would relinquish her and send her back untouched and unharmed to her friends. Both sides acted in good faith. The Romans restored the pledge of peace in accordance with the treaty and, as for the Etruscan king, her courage was not only protected but even honoured. He said that he was giving the girl he admired a number of the hostages; she could choose those whom she wished. When they were all led out she is said to have chosen the young boys; this was because of her maiden modesty and by the common consent of the hostages themselves that probably the age that was most at risk of harm by

the enemy was to be preferred for liberation from the enemy. With peace restored the Romans rewarded this act of courage – unprecedented in a woman – with a new type of honour, an equestrian statue. At the top of the Sacred Way a statue was placed of a young girl on horseback."
(Livy, *History of Rome* 2.13.6–11)

Plutarch wrote an essay entitled *"The Bravery of Women"*, in which he gave a livelier and more embellished account of the escape of Cloelia and the other girls. In his account the hostages consisted of ten youths and ten girls, and he adds the detail that the Romans had an underlying admiration for Lars Porsena, seeing in him a person with a reputation for fairness.

"The girls went down to the river, a short distance from the camp, as if they were going to bathe. When one of them named Cloelia urged them on they fastened their tunics around their heads, dove into the swift current and the deep-whirling eddies and by swimming together they made it across, but not without having an enormous struggle. There are those who say that Cloelia found herself a horse and mounted it, steered it across gradually and acted as a guide for the others, encouraging the swimmers and coming to their rescue. What they use as evidence for this I will mention shortly." (250C-D)

In Plutarch's account the reaction of the Romans to the feat accomplished by the girls was surprisingly harsh. One of the Tarquins who had gone into exile with Porsena tried to foil the king's attempt to be seen as acting in good faith. Another one of the girls taken as hostage demonstrated bravery.

"When the Romans saw that they were safe they admired their courage and bravery, but did not like their recovery nor were they content with proving themselves of less worth than that one man when it came to keeping faith. They ordered the girls to go back again, therefore, and sent men to lead them. When they had crossed the river a Tarquin set an ambush for them, and came close to getting the girls under his control. But the daughter of the consul Publicola, Valeria, escaped to the camp of Porsena with three of her servants. The son of Porsena, Arruns, quickly went to the aid of the others and rescued them from the enemy. When they were brought to him Porsena looked at them and ordered them to say which was the one who had instigated and launched the plan. The others out of fear kept quiet about Cloelia. But when Cloelia herself said it had been she, Porsena, in admiration of her, ordered a horse to be brought and outfitted with fine tackle. He gave it to Cloelia and sent them all back with kindness and benevolence.
    Many see this as evidence that Cloelia rode across the river on a horse. Others deny this but say that he admired her strength and daring as being mightier than

that of a woman, and decided upon a gift that was appropriate for a male warrior. In any case the statue of a woman on horseback was set up on the so-called 'Sacred Way', a statue which some say is that of Cloelia and others of Valeria." (250D-F) (Plutarch, *Moralia*)

CORIOLANUS AND HIS MOTHER

Etruscan influence would be felt in Rome for some time during the early phase of the Republic. With the threat of war reduced on this front, however, and a treaty made with the Latin communities in the region, the Romans turned their attention to expanding the territory under their control. The Volsci, neighbours to the south of Latium, fought back. Marcius Coriolanus, a Roman general, had succeeded in mounting a successful attack against one of the principal Volscian cities, but in Rome he was losing support because of harsh measures he had proposed to curtail plebeian access to grain during a food shortage. Angry at his rejection by the Romans, he defected to the side of the Volsci to punish his countrymen.

Coriolanus led the Volsci on a campaign to liberate some of their towns that had come under Roman control, and then he turned to march on Rome. The plebeian faction there did not support a military clash and persuaded the Senate to send envoys to the defector Coriolanus. They were refused a hearing. Then, Livy tells us, the women took matters into their own hands.

"At this point the Roman matrons gathered as a group at the house of the mother of Coriolanus, Veturia, and his wife Volumnia. Whether this had been an official decision or was the result of womanly fear I can't determine. They certainly succeeded to the point where both Veturia – a woman of senior years – and Volumnia, bringing with her the two young sons she had with Marcius [Coriolanus], went to the enemy camp. Since men were not able to defend the city with weapons, the women would defend it with prayers and tears. When they came to the camp it was reported to Coriolanus that a large contingent of women had arrived. At first, as expected of someone who would not be moved by the public magnificence of a state delegation or the enormity of religious awe spread before his eyes and spirit with the presence of priests, he was much more obstinate in the face of women's tears.

Then one of his friends recognized Veturia standing between her daughter-in-law and her two boys. She was conspicuous among the other women because of her distress. 'Unless my eyes are deceiving me,' he said [to Coriolanus], 'your mother, your wife and your children are here.' Coriolanus, startled and almost beside himself, rushed from his seat. When he went to embrace his mother the woman resorted to anger instead of pleading. 'Permit me to know, before I accept your embrace, whether I have come to an enemy or to a son, whether as your mother I am in your camp as a captive. Has my long life and my unhappy old age brought me to the point where I look upon you first as an exile then as an enemy? Have you been able to despoil this land that bore you and raised you? When you set foot upon its borders did your anger not fall aside, albeit that you had acquired a disposition that is both hostile and threatening? When you were within sight of Rome did this thought not occur to you: "Inside those fortifications are my home, my household gods, my mother, my wife and children?"

'So then, if I had not given birth Rome would not be under attack. If I had no son I would die a free woman in a free country. But now I cannot endure anything more wretched to me, nor in any way more shameful to you – I as one who am the most unfortunate woman of all, but it will not be for long. When it comes to these others, if you keep on this path, you will see that either premature death or a long life of slavery awaits them.'

Then his wife and children embraced him; weeping broke out among the whole crowd of women, and the loud lamentation on behalf of themselves and their state at length broke the spirit of the man. He embraced his family and sent them home. He himself moved his troops back away from the city."
(Livy, *History of Rome* 2.40.1–10)

Livy mentions that his best historical source indicated that Coriolanus remained an exile with the Volsci, experiencing increasing sadness in his old age (2.40.11). Both Livy and Dionysius of Halicarnassus (8.55.3–5) describe the Senate as wishing to give public recognition to the women for their efforts, although rejecting their proposal to erect at their own expense a temple to the divinity "Women's Fortune" (*Fortuna Muliebris*). Instead, the women were permitted to pay for a statue that would be set up in the goddess' temple, in addition to the one that was funded by the state. Dionysius of Halicarnassus describes the women's statue as speaking aloud on the day that the temple was dedicated, commending the women's gift as being legitimate. The words of the statue were interpreted as follows.

"Married women, you have made this dedication in keeping with the sacred law of the city."
(Dionysius of Halicarnassus, *Roman Antiquities* 8.56.2–3)

Dionysius describes the women as well as the others present as finding it difficult to believe that the statue had actually spoken, but on a later religious occasion at the temple the statue repeated its words even more loudly, and the audience was convinced. A priestess of the cult advised the women that only those who had been married once (*univirae*) should be permitted to crown the statue with garlands or to touch it (8.56.4). Annual rituals for the goddess were presided over by a woman elected by the matrons who had participated in the embassy to Coriolanus. Valeria, who had first proposed the embassy, was chosen as the first to officiate (8.55.4).

Valerius Maximus, describing acts "Of the Grateful", in his *Memorable Deeds and Sayings*, includes this and other actions of the Senate in response to the women's actions that led to Coriolanus' change of heart.

"In their honour the Senate glorified the rank of matrons with the most beneficent of decrees. They ordained that men would give way to women on the street, admitting that there had been more saving of the state by matrons' robes than by weapons. To the age-old decorations on women's ears they added the new distinction of a chaplet for their heads. They also permitted them to wear purple clothing and gold trimming. Beyond this they saw to the construction of a temple and altar to *Fortuna Muliebris* on the spot where Coriolanus had been won over by their entreaty, with a carefully considered religious cult that demonstrated that their minds were mindful of the benefaction."
(Valerius Maximus, *Nine Books of Memorable Deeds and Sayings* 5.2.1)

7

Women and religious life

THE CULTS OF PATRICIAN AND PLEBEIAN CHASTITY

In the year 295 BCE the "struggle between the orders" – tensions between patricians and plebeians that dominated political life in Rome as the Republic developed – was also dividing women. Livy's record of the founding of the women's cult of Plebeian Chastity is one example of this.

"In that year there were many prodigies. To avert them the Senate decreed two days of supplications (public petitions to the gods). Wine and incense were publicly supplied, and both men and women went in great numbers to offer prayers. Strife broke out between the matrons in the chapel of Patrician Chastity that stands in the Cattle Market near the round temple of Hercules, making the supplication memorable. The matrons barred from the ceremonies Verginia, daughter of Aulus, on the grounds that she had married outside the patrician class. Born a patrician she had married the plebeian consul Lucius Volumnius. A brief argument was kindled into a blaze of controversy between minds, owing to the passionate nature of women. Verginia boasted, justifiably, that she had entered the temple of Patrician Chastity as a patrician and a chaste woman, had been married to the one man to whom she had been brought as a virgin bride, and that she was not ashamed of her husband nor of his honours and his accomplishments. Then she augmented her fine words with an outstanding deed: on the Vicus Longus, where she lived, she closed off part of her house that would be enough space for a chapel of modest proportions, placed an altar there and called together the plebeian matrons. She complained of the insult she had received from the patrician women. 'I dedicate this altar to Plebeian Chastity,' she said, 'and I urge you that, just as competition for valour grips men in this state, so let there be competition for chastity among the matrons, and may you devote your energies so that this altar may be said to be nurtured with more reverence and by women more chaste than that [altar] of theirs, if it is possible.'

This altar was tended with almost the same strict rituals as the one of greater antiquity, so that no matron, unless one of proven chastity and someone who had been married to only one man, would have the right to sacrifice. Later the cult was

degraded by polluted women, not only from the rank of matrons but from every class, and finally it passed into oblivion."
(Livy, *History of Rome* 10.23.1–10)

Marriage was one of the many sites of tension between the orders. Cicero refers to a very early law, possibly going back as far as the XII Tables, which prohibited intermarriage between the classes, a law that was revoked in 442 BCE after a plebiscite (*On the Republic* 2.37.62). That Verginia had ignored this law may have been overlooked because of the fact that her plebeian husband had been consul.

THE VESTALS

According to Livy, the important cult of the Vestal Virgins was first instituted by King Numa.

"He chose the virgins for Vesta, a priesthood originating in Alba and by no means unsuitable to the race of the founder. So that they might be constant overseers of the temple he established for them a stipend from the public treasury. He saw to it that they were treated with reverence and sanctity because of their virginity and because of their other ritual observances."
(Livy, *History of Rome* 1.20.3–4)

There was a circular temple of Vesta in the Forum in Rome, the remains of which can be seen today. It contained the hearth-fire for the city, and the Vestal Virgins were charged with keeping it burning and purifying it once a year. Ovid (late first century BCE/early first century CE) in his *Fasti* describes the traditional circular temple.

"They recall that Rome had celebrated the Parilia forty times
    when the goddess, guardian of the flame, was received into her temple.
It was the accomplishment of the peaceful king, and the Sabine land
    raised no one of a more god-fearing nature than he was.
What you now see roofed with bronze you would have seen then covered with thatch
    and the walls were woven with tough willow branches.
This little place, which now supports the Hall of Vesta
    at that time was the great royal house of unshaven King Numa.
The shape of the temple, however, which stands today, is said to have been the same then,
    and the cause of its shape is subject to investigation.

Vesta is the same as the earth; underneath both of them is perpetual fire;
    the earth and the hearth signify one's home-base."
(Ovid, *Fasti* 6.257–68)

(The Parilia was the festival celebrating the founding of Rome. Forty years after this event would give a traditional date for the dedication of the temple as 713 BCE.)

Ovid continues his speculation about the Vestals, asking why their virginity was essential. He identifies Vesta with her flame, and connects her purity with that of fire. He comments that there were no statues of Vesta. Today one can see the remains of statues of her priestesses near the ruins of her temple, however.

Plutarch, in his biography of Numa, also raises the subject of the need for the Vestals to remain virgins during their term of office, and also concludes that that this is related to the nature of fire.

"To Numa is attributed the dedication of the Vestal Virgins and he entrusted to them the complete responsibility for tending and worshipping the eternal fire, which these women watch over; either because the nature of the fire is pure and undefiled he entrusted it to undefiled and uncorrupted bodies or because he associated virginity with something that is barren and sterile."
(Plutarch, "Numa" 9.5)

Aulus Gellius (second century CE) describes the process by which young girls were chosen (lit. "taken") as Vestals.

"Those who have written about the taking of a Vestal Virgin, of whom the most thorough writer was Antistius Labeo (a jurist of the late first century BCE), have said that it was unlawful for one to be chosen who was younger than six, or older than ten, years of age. Likewise, she must have both father and mother living, not be disabled in speech or someone with limited hearing ability, or be marked by any other bodily defect. In like manner, she must not have been liberated from her father's control, even if her father is still living and she is under the control of her grandfather. Similarly, neither one or both her parents could be in service as slaves or engaged in lower-class occupations."
(1.12.1–5)

A father's control (the *patria potestas*) was obligatory for children unless the father had died or lost his civic rights or had voluntarily released them from his control. Once her credentials had been established and she became a Vestal, the girl immediately began to acquire certain privileges.

"Now as soon as a Vestal Virgin is chosen and taken to the Hall of Vesta and given into the hands of the Pontiffs, from that moment she leaves the control of her father without the ceremony of release from *patria potestas* or a lessening of civic rights, and she acquires the right to make a will.

But about the customary ritual for choosing a Virgin there are no extant ancient records, except that the first to be captured was taken by King Numa. But we have found a Papian Law by which it is stipulated that twenty Virgins are to be picked out from the populace in accordance with the decision of the chief Pontiff and that a selection by lot be conducted from that number in the Assembly. The lot of a virgin will be drawn, then the chief Pontiff is to 'take' her and she is to become Vesta's. But that selection by lot following the Papian Law is not routinely seen to be necessary now. For if someone born of a respectable class were to go to the chief Pontiff and offer his daughter for the priesthood, provided that deliberation on her behalf can be carried out while preserving the requirements of religion, exemption from the Papian Law is given through the Senate.

The Vestal is said to be 'taken' on this account, it seems, because she is grasped by the hand of the chief Pontiff, and led away from the parent under whose control she was, just as if she were a prisoner of war. In the first book of Fabius Pictor (a historian of the third century BCE) the formula that the chief Pontiff must use when he takes a Vestal is written: 'I take as a Vestal priestess one who is to perform the rites that are lawful for a Vestal Priestess to perform on behalf of the Roman people, for her citizens. I take you, Amata (lit. "Beloved"), as [one who has been selected as] the best in accordance with the law.'" (1.12.10–14)
(Aulus Gellius, *Attic Nights*)

The Chief Pontiff (the *Pontifex Maximus*) was the senior religious official in Rome, and head of the college (i.e. association) of pontiffs.

The Vestals were to remain virgins for the period of their service. They were awarded honours not available to other women, but were subject to an extreme form of punishment should they be found guilty of violating their vow of chastity, as we learn from Dionysius of Halicarnassus.

"In the beginning the virgins serving the goddess were four in number, with the kings choosing them in accordance with the rules Numa laid down. Later, because of the large number of sacred tasks which they carry out they became six, and this has remained the case up until our own time. They continue living in the sanctuary of the goddess during the period they serve, the place where no one who wishes is prevented from entering during the day, but at night it is unlawful for any man to remain.

For thirty years they must remain chaste and unmarried, carrying out sacrifices and other religious observances in accordance with the law. In this time-period they must learn the rituals for ten years, then for ten years discharge these religious duties, and for the remaining ten teach the other young women. When the thirty years have been completed nothing prevents those who wish from removing their headbands and the other token signs of their priesthood and marrying. Some – very few – have done this. For them the remaining years of their lives were unenviable and not at all happy, so that the rest, reading the misfortunes of those women as inauspicious, remain virgins in the sanctuary of the goddess until their death. At that time, to fill the number of those who have left, another is chosen again by the chief priests.

Honours are awarded them by the state, many fine ones, on account of which they do not feel the desire for children or marriage.

Severe penalties are imposed upon those who fail in their duties. The chief priests are those charged with investigating and punishing them, according to the law. Those who have committed one of the other lesser offences they whip with rods, but those who have been sexually unchaste they sentence to a death that is most shameful and pitiable. While they are still living they carry them in procession on a bier, conducting the formal funeral display used for corpses. With their friends and families mourning them and joining the procession, they are brought as far as the Colline Gate and placed in an underground tomb prepared inside the walls, dressed in funeral garb. They do not get a tomb marker or funerary offerings or any other customary rites.

There are many other indications, it seems, of a Vestal's not performing her sacred duties in a state of purity, but the principal one is the extinction of the fire, which the Romans fear above all dreadful occurrences, taking it as a sign of the destruction of the city – whatever might be the cause. They bring [the fire] back again to the temple with many propitiatory rituals."
(Dionysius of Halicarnassus, *Roman Antiquities* 2.67.1–5)

Plutarch gives us a fuller picture of the Vestals' privileges and more details about their punishments, including the manner in which they were put to death for unchastity.

"[Numa] bestowed great privileges upon them, among which was the right to make a will while their father was alive, and to conduct other affairs without living under the control of a guardian, like mothers of three children (a privilege available to women in Plutarch's time). When they go out they are preceded by the lictors, and if they accidentally come across someone being led to execution he is not killed. But the virgin must swear an oath that the meeting was not deliberate and was by chance, not design. One who passes under the litter on which they are carried is put to death.

The Virgins' punishment for other offences is being beaten. The Chief Priest administers the punishment when the offender is naked, in a dark room with a curtain hung across it. But the one who has violated her vow of chastity is buried alive by the so-called Colline Gate. In this place there is a ridge of earth inside the city that extends some distance. It is called a *choma* ("mound") in the Latin dialect. There they construct an underground room, not large, having a way to get down from above. In it is placed a couch with coverings laid over it, a burning lamp and some small tokens of the necessities of life, such as bread, water in a bowl, milk, olive-oil. This is as if they would acquit themselves of the charge of destroying by hunger a body that had been consecrated to the greatest of holy rites.

Then they place the one being punished on a litter, and covering her over from above they fasten her down with cords so that not even a cry would be heard from underneath, and they carry her through the Forum. They all stand in silence and escort it without uttering a word, with a terrible downcast look. There is no other spectacle more horrifying, nor does the city endure any day gloomier than this. When the litter is brought to the place the attendants untie the cords while the Pontifex Maximus makes some secret prayers and, lifting his hands to the gods before the necessary act, leads her out veiled and places her on the ladder leading down into the chamber. Then he himself turns away, along with the other priests. When she has gone down, the ladder is lifted out and the chamber is covered over with much earth piled over it from above, so that the place is level with the rest of the mound. This is the way in which those who disregard their sacred virginity are punished." (Plutarch, "Numa" 10.3–7)

Oppia

In the early decades of the Republic, battles were fought with neighbouring towns and tribes as the Romans sought to expand throughout the Italian peninsula. These frictions were combined with internal hostilities between the patricians and plebeians, producing great anxiety inside Rome. This seemed to coincide with the appearance of unusual events that were read as signs of the gods' displeasure (*prodigia*). These prodigies caused widespread unease, and some act of expiation was felt to be required to restore peaceful relations with the gods (the *pax deorum*). The explanation for a prodigy was not infrequently named as a Vestal's breaking her vow of chastity, and her being buried alive was the ritual that would restore the gods' pleasure. One such case occurred in 483 BCE, according to Livy.

"Next war broke out with Veii, and the Volsci resumed hostilities. The military resources were pretty well sufficient to handle the external wars, but were being entirely used up by the infighting among the Romans themselves. Prodigies from heaven now were adding to the troubled minds of everyone, occurring almost daily in the city and the countryside, indicating foreboding. The prophets, consulting first the entrails then the flights of birds, announced that in both the public and

private realm there was no other cause of the divine signals than that the sacred rituals were being carried out in an improper manner. These terrors eventually reached the point where the Vestal Oppia was condemned for unchastity and was executed."
(Livy, *History of Rome* 2.42.8–11)

THE SUPPRESSION OF BACCHIC RITUALS

In the year 186 BCE the consuls were charged with investigating "secret conspiracies", and attention was focused on a cult in honour of Bacchus, the god of wine. Because it involved secret rituals and the initiation of the participants into a group that was independent of state control, and because towns in some regions where it enjoyed great popularity had earlier allied themselves with Hannibal, the cult aroused considerable suspicion in Rome. Livy speaks of the cult's founder as a dangerous Greek instigator who had spent time with the Etruscans.

"To both consuls the investigation of secret conspiracies was decreed. An obscure Greek came first to Etruria, with none of the many arts that the [Greek] people – the most learned of all – introduced to us for the cultivation of our minds and bodies. This fellow was a religious charlatan and a fortune-teller; he was not one who by being candid about his religion and openly declaring both its benefits and its teachings tainted people's minds with error, but he was a priest of secret rites held at night.

These initiatory rites were at first administered to a few, then they began to be spread among men and women. To the religious element were added the pleasures of wine and feasting, so that they might entice the minds of more people. When wine had inflamed their minds, and nighttime – together with the mingling of males and females and of youthfulness with age – had extinguished every mark of modesty, corruption of every kind began to be practised. This was because each person had pleasure ready-to-hand, lust to which his own nature was more inclined. There was not only one type of vice: there was promiscuous sex between freeborn men and women and perjured witnesses, forged seals and wills and allegations by informers, all coming out of this same outfit. Poisons too, and domestic murders, of the sort where at times not even the bodies existed for burial. Much was ventured through guile, more through violence. The violence was concealed because amid the debauchery and murders no cries of the victims could be heard above the shrieking and the din of drums and cymbals.

The destructive force of this evil spread through Rome from Etruria like the contagion of a plague. At first the size of the city, with lots of space and its being more tolerant of such evils, concealed them." (39.8.3–9.1)

Livy's account describes the means by which information about the cult was brought to one of the consuls from a courtesan, a freedwoman named Hispala Faecenia. The consul summoned his mother-in-law and together they extracted details from the woman who, while still a slave, had been initiated with her mistress into the Bacchic mysteries. When freed she had abandoned the cult.

"Then Hispala disclosed the origin of the rites. At first it had been a sanctuary for women, and it was not the custom to admit any man. There had been three days appointed each year on which initiations were held into the Bacchic rites during the day. Married women were customarily appointed in turn as priestesses. Paculla Annia from Campania, when she was priestess, changed everything, acting as if it were on the advice of the gods. For she was the first to have also initiated men, her sons Minius and Herennius Cerrinius. She had conducted the rites by night instead of during the day, and instead of three days a year established five days each month for initiations.

From the time when the rites were conducted indiscriminately and men mingled with women with the free rein afforded by the darkness, no type of crime, no kind of disgraceful conduct was overlooked. More debauchery occurred among the men with each other than among the women. If someone was less tolerant of disgraceful acts and more reluctant to participate in crime he was sacrificed as a victim. To think of nothing as unholy, this was the height of piety among them. Men, as if their minds were possessed, prophesied with a fanatic contortion of their body. The married women, in Bacchic costume with their hair disheveled and carrying burning torches, ran all the way to the Tiber. They plunged their torches into the water and, because there was non-composite sulphur mixed with calcium, they brought them out again with the flame intact. Men were said to have been carried off by the gods, those men who had been bound to a machine and snatched out of sight into hidden caves. These were the ones who had refused to join the conspiracy or to join in the crimes, or to put up with debauchery. A huge crowd it was, almost making up a separate state. Among them were certain nobles, men and women. Within the last two years it had been decided not to initiate anyone older than twenty years; these young people were nabbed because they put up with vice and debauchery." (39.13.8–14)

The consul then presented to the Senate the information he had gathered. Livy highlights the fear that the secret rituals were part of a larger subversive movement.

"Enormous panic seized the Fathers lest in consideration for the state these conspiracies and nocturnal meetings might be introducing some sort of hidden treachery or danger and also, considering each person individually, lest some relative be implicated in the trouble.

The Senate, moreover, decreed that thanks be awarded to the consul because he had investigated the affair with particular attentiveness and without creating a disturbance. Next, they ordered an investigation into the nocturnal Bacchanalian rituals – an investigation beyond the normal duties of the consuls." (39.14.4–6)

The consuls were empowered to procure more informers about the cult's activities by offering rewards. They were to search out its priests and priestesses throughout the city and villages and communities where it operated. Through a Senatorial decree, a proclamation went out in Rome and edicts were sent elsewhere that placed the following severe restrictions on Bacchic gatherings.

" 'No one who had been initiated into the Bacchic cult was to agree to gather or assemble for the sake of celebrating these rituals, or to agree to carry out any divine activity of this sort. Above all, an investigation was to be conducted into those people who had assembled or engaged in a conspiracy through which debauchery or shameful activities might be introduced.'

This was the decree of the Senate. The consuls gave orders to the curule aediles to search out all the priests of this cult, arrest them and keep them in free custody available for the investigation. The aediles of the plebs were to see that no rituals were to be celebrated clandestinely. Orders were given to the three urban triumvirs to place guards throughout the city, to ensure that no nocturnal gatherings took place, and to be on the watch for arson." (39.14.8–10)

(The curule aediles were responsible for regulating public festivals and maintaining public order; the urban triumvirs dealt with serious offences and were in charge of executions.)

The consul then called an open meeting of the people, and began with a prayer to the gods who were officially accepted by the city; these he distinguished from those "foreign" deities worshiped with lust-filled rites.

"On no occasion of an open meeting has this traditional prayer to the gods been not only more appropriate but also so necessary, a prayer that would remind you that these are the gods that your forefathers appointed to be worshipped and venerated and to receive your prayers. They were not those gods who would seize and govern our minds with depraved and alien rituals, as if goaded by Furies to every type of crime and every sort of wantonness." (39.15.2–3)

The consul then hinted that if he informed the crowd of the extent of the cult practices there would be widespread terror. His Roman audience, he knew, was aware of the noise the worshippers made in the city during the night, but were not informed about the type of activity in which they were engaged, and the degree to which the fact that it began as a women's ritual had led to this debased behaviour. The consul continued to link it with a conspiracy whose activities had been provoked by women.

"First of all, then, the majority of them are women, and this was the cause of all this evil. Then there are men very like women, debauched and debauchers, fanatics, smitten because of a lack of sleep, wine, the clamour and the noise during the night. As a conspiracy it has no strength to date, but has an enormous reserve of other resources because it grows in numbers day by day." (39.15.9–10)
(Livy, *History of Rome*)

Emphasizing that the crimes were still of a private nature but that the overall objective was maintaining control of the state, the consul announced that the participants would be rounded up, executed or imprisoned, and the Bacchic shrines throughout Italy destroyed. Livy reports that more than 7000 men and women were named as participants. Several of them committed suicide. Official permission could be sought for a (purified) Bacchic sacrifice ordained by the gods, but no more than five people could participate. There would be no common fund, and no priest appointed to conduct sacrifices (*History of Rome*, 39.18).

The decree of the Senate was passed in 186 BCE, with copies inscribed and posted throughout Italy. One of these copies has been found in the south Italian town of Bruttium, and is now located in the Kunsthistorisches Museum in Vienna. It contains the same restrictions as reported by Livy, including the destruction of Bacchic shrines unless there was a successful appeal to the Senate. No men, whatever their citizenship, could be present among female worshippers unless given permission by the Senate. Activities that would encourage allegiance to a group independent from the State were forbidden.

"No man shall be priest; no man or woman shall be an official of the cult. No organization shall permit there to be a common fund, nor choose to appoint a man or woman as official or acting official. From this point there will be no taking of oaths or vows among them nor mutual promises nor joint agreements. None of them shall give or take a pledge of protection. No one shall perform the rituals in secret, in public or private, nor outside the city, unless he has come before the urban praetor and, in the opinion of the Senate, he (the praetor) has authorized it when there are no fewer than 100 senators present when the matter was broached."
(*Senatus Consultum de Bacchanalibus, ILLRP* 2.511.10 = *RTLA* 126)

(An urban praetor was a senior magistrate with powers second only to consuls.) The inscription makes it clear that should the Senate grant permission to perform the rites, these had to be conducted openly in the presence of no more than five persons. There would be capital punishment for offenders.

8

Gender tensions

VERGINIA

In a case parallel to that of Lucretia the illicit sexual lust of a powerful man resulted in the death of a chaste young woman and launched major political change in Rome. In 451 BCE the culprit was Appius Claudius, a patrician and the senior member of the decemvirs. He developed a passion for the beautiful young daughter of Verginius, a highly respected centurion of the plebeian class. Verginia was betrothed to Lucius Icilius, a champion of the plebeian cause, and the crisis began as the decemvirs were continuing to exercise their political and judicial power beyond the period allotted to them and refusing to call elections.

Tensions that were building between the plebeians and patricians during this period erupted in full when Appius Claudius arranged for Verginia to be seized on her way to school while her father was away from Rome with the army. The decemvir had the young woman brought before the court over which he was presiding. One of his "clients" (individuals who offered support to influential Roman men in return for protection and other types of sustenance) presented Verginia to the court on a trumped-up charge, alleging that she was not the true daughter of Verginius but a slave. The man claimed that Verginia's mother (who had died) had not in fact given birth to the girl but, being unable to produce children, had taken her from a slave-woman belonging to his household and he was now reclaiming her as his own. Appius Claudius ruled in favour of the claim and attempted to take the girl into custody. The girl's maternal uncle and her betrothed, Icilius, both spoke loudly in opposition to this, and were backed by a large number of supporters.

Livy gives an account of the passionate appeal of Icilius to the assembled crowd. The young man who as tribune had acted in an official capacity as an advocate for the plebeians was shoved aside by one of the lictors (individuals selected to carry the emblems of state power and maintain order). Icilius fought back with words, linking the outrage of the seizure of Verginia to others perpetrated by the patrician decemvirs against the plebeians.

"'Appius, it is with an iron blade that you will have to remove me from here,' he said, 'so that you can carry out in silence what you want to hide. I am going to marry this girl and I intend to have a bride that is chaste. So summon all the lictors of the [priestly] colleges as well. Order them to get out their rods and axes. The betrothed of Icilius will not stay outside the house of her father. Even if you take away the protection and right of appeal of the tribunes that belong to the common people of Rome – these two bulwarks for the preservation of freedom – this does not award you the tyranny of your lust to use against our children and our wives. Vent your savage passion on our backs and necks; let our chastity be safe, at least. If you want it to be under siege I will call upon the allegiance of every citizen present on behalf of my bride; Verginius will call upon the allegiance of the soldiers on behalf of his only daughter. We will all invoke the loyalty of the gods and men, and you will never repeat that infamous verdict without slaughtering us. I enjoin you, Appius, to think again and again where you are going. Verginius will see what to do about his daughter when he comes. Let him know this alone: if he gives in to the claims of this man he will have to look around for a marriage agreement for his daughter. As I defend the liberty of my bride my life will sooner abandon me than my trustworthiness.'" (3.45.6–11)

The lictors surrounded Icilius but took no action. Appius accused him of being a disorderly demagogue, the natural disposition of a tribune of the plebs. He permitted Verginia to be free for a day, pending the return of her father. Failing this, he said, he would impose the verdict he had given on the case. The supporters of Verginia and Icilius dispatched messengers with all haste to the military camp to inform Verginius. Appius in turn sent a message to the officers in charge of Verginius demanding that they retain him, but this arrived too late and the next morning Verginius entered the Forum leading his daughter by the hand. He wore mourning garb and Verginia was in rags. There was a large crowd of supporters, including a number of women. Verginius circulated among them, pointing out that as a soldier he fought daily on their behalf, but that loyalty to Rome was meaningless if their children were as much at risk within the city walls as if the city had been captured. Livy comments that the subsequent weeping of the women present had an even greater effect on the crowd. Appius mounted the tribunal (the judge's platform) and repeated his verdict: Verginia was a slave. As his client moved to seize the girl the women burst into tears and there was general commotion. Appius decried the seditious activities of the populace and called for order, warning that he had come with an armed escort.

As Appius ordered one of the lictors to clear the way for taking possession of Verginia, her father, seeing that the crowd shrunk back in fear, asked Appius for permission to speak with her, then grasped her hand and headed to a nearby butcher shop. Livy's narrative captures the climactic moment and its result.

"With permission granted he led his daughter and her nurse down to the shops near the shrine of Cloacina, the place now called the 'New Shops'. And there, grabbing a knife from a butcher he said, 'This is the only way, my daughter, that I can set you free.' He then stabbed the girl in her breast. Looking at the tribunal he said, 'Appius, with this blood I doom you and your head to destruction!'

Appius, shaken by the uproar that arose at such a horrible deed, ordered the arrest of Verginius. With knife in hand the man made his way by whatever means he could until, with the protection of the crowd that was still following him, he reached the city gate. Icilius and Nimitor lifted up the lifeless body and displayed it to the people. They deplored the crime of Appius, and bewailed the tragic beauty of the girl and the necessity that constrained her father. The Roman matrons followed them, shouting, 'Was this the condition under which they were to beget children? Were these the rewards for chastity?'

The other things to which a woman's grief in such a situation is subject are all the more pitiable because with their weak minds it makes them all the more disposed to give in to lamentation. From the men and particularly from Icilius a unified cry went up over the theft of the power of the tribunate and the right of appeal for the populace, together with indignation over the affairs of state." (3.48.5–9) (Livy, *History of Rome*)

The decemvirs eventually went into exile and Appius committed suicide, while the tribunate and the right of appeal were restored to the people. Dionysius of Halicarnassus gives a lengthier and more emotional account of the episode in his *Roman Antiquities* (11.28.1–37.5).

WOMEN CHARGED WITH POISONING

On several occasions women were suspected of using poisons to accomplish their ends. Fears of this were augmented when other events were shaking public confidence. In 331 BCE the weather had been severe and several prominent citizens fell gravely ill. Livy indicates that some of his sources attributed the sickness and deaths that ensued not to a plague but to poisoning.

In the following instance a serving-woman apparently told a curule aedile that certain matrons were to blame.

"She then divulged the fact that the state was being overwhelmed by crimes committed by women and that it was matrons concocting those poisons, and if they wished to follow her right away they could discover the fact in plain view. They followed the informer and found certain women mixing up drugs and they found others hidden away. These preparations were brought into the Forum and some twenty matrons, in whose houses they had been seized, were summoned by an official. Two of these women, Cornelia and Sergia, both of the patrician class, when they argued that the drugs were therapeutic were challenged by the informer and ordered to drink them, so that they could denounce her accusation as false in the sight of everyone. They took some time in discussion, and when the people had been cleared away they referred the decision to the other women. When they too were not at all reluctant to drink them they drank down the liquid and they all perished by their own criminal means.

Their attendants were immediately seized and informed against a considerable number of matrons. Out of these upwards of about 170 were found guilty."
(Livy, *History of Rome* 8.18.6–10)

Other references to the prohibitions against women using drugs included the law attributed to Romulus (p. 14 above) where it occurred in connection with children, likely referring to contraception or infanticide, and an incident in 180 BCE, another year in which leading men in the city had died, including a praetor and the consul Gaius Calpurnius. On that occasion the Sibylline Books (p. 18 above) were consulted, and the recommended rituals were conducted throughout the city and the surrounding region. Livy's report suggests that men harboured a suspicion, however, that poisoning had taken place particularly in the case of the consul, and his wife Hostilia came under suspicion. When Flaccus, her son from a previous marriage, was proclaimed consul to succeed the deceased Gaius Calpurnius, rumours increased and witnesses came forward to accuse her of taking extreme measures to ensure the succession.

"Now when her son Quintus Fulvius Flaccus was declared consul in place of his stepfather, the death of Piso began to be seen as all the more suspicious. There were witnesses who said that Albinus and Piso, after they had been declared consuls at an election in which Flaccus had suffered defeat, [Flaccus] had been reproached by his mother because it was now the third time that he had sought the consulship and been rejected. She added that he should prepare himself to campaign again; in less than two months' time she would bring it about that he would become consul. Among much other testimony pertaining to the case this one report prevailed as well in explaining why Hostilia was convicted, all too truthfully borne out by the result."
(Livy, *History of Rome* 40.37.6–7)

DIVORCING A WOMAN FOR INFERTILITY

Roman wives were expected to be both chaste and fertile. Aulus Gellius reports on a divorce initiated in the early third century BCE by a husband whose wife was infertile.

"It has been passed down through the record that for almost 500 years after the founding of Rome there were no lawsuits nor pledges taken as securities for a wife's dowry (i.e., with the obligation to repay) in the city of Rome or in Latium, since actually nothing was wanted because no marriages were dissolved during that period. In addition, Servius Sulpicius (a Roman orator and jurist of the first century BCE), in the book he assembled called *On Dowries*, wrote that the first pledges for a wife's dowry were seen to be necessary when Spurius Carvilius, whose cognomen was Ruga – a man of noble rank – introduced the divorce from his wife because no children were born from her, owing to some defect in her body. This happened in the 523rd year after the founding of the city (231 BCE) in the consulship of Marcus Atilius and Publius Valerius. And this Carvilius, as the story goes, loved his wife intensely – the one whom he divorced – and valued her very highly because of her character, but he gave preference to the sanctity of his oath over his inclination and his love, because he had been compelled by the censors to swear that he would look for a wife for the purpose of begetting citizen children."
(Aulus Gellius, *Attic Nights* 4.3.1–2)

(The Roman censors were responsible for public morality, while also keeping the state finances and the record of its citizens.)

9

The Punic Wars

For more than 120 years (264–146 BCE), during what is generally referred to as the Middle Republic, the Romans were at war with an enemy from beyond the Italian peninsula, the Carthaginians from the north coast of Africa who were competing with them for trade and influence in the western Mediterranean. The "Punic" Wars, so named because of the Phoenician origins of the Carthaginians, had three phases, with the second (218–201 BCE) the best known as it included the famous invasion of Italy by the Carthaginian general Hannibal. Anxiety over the war frequently coincided with the appearance of prodigies, which the Roman magistrates sought to expiate in the hope of getting divine support.

THE VESTALS FLORONIA AND OPIMIA

By the year 216 BCE the Romans found themselves suffering some serious defeats on Italian soil at the hands of Hannibal and his troops, including a particularly disastrous one at the town of Cannae. Prodigies appeared, and with fear mounting in Rome the people sought direction from the Sibylline Books (also referred to by Livy as the "Books of Fate") as well as from Apollo's oracle at Delphi. Attention turned to the Vestals, and extreme measures were taken.

"They were repeatedly terrified by events beyond these enormous disasters – by the appearance of other prodigies and because two Vestals, Opimia and Floronia, had been found to be guilty of unchastity that year. One had been killed by being buried alive near the Colline Gate, as is customary. The other made the decision to kill herself. Lucius Cantilius, the pontifical scribe, one of those who are now called minor pontifices, who had had sex with Floronia, was beaten with rods by the Pontifex Maximus in the Comitium to the point where he died from the blows.

Since this sacrilegious act took place as it did among so many others, the military disaster was read as a prodigy, and the decemvirs were instructed to consult the Sibylline Books. In addition, Quintus Fabius Pictor was sent to the Delphic oracle, to ascertain by which prayers and supplications they might please the gods, and what end there might be to such great calamities in the future.

In the meantime, several extraordinary sacrifices were carried out, as ordained by the Books of Fate. Among these a man and woman from Gaul and a man and woman from Greece were sent to their death underground in the Cattle Market, in a place enclosed by stone."
(Livy, *History of Rome* 22.57.2–6)

COLLECTIVE OFFERINGS BY WOMEN TO JUNO AND FERONIA

Livy's record of the Punic Wars includes the description of a particular concentration of prodigies occurring when Hannibal first invaded Italy in 218 BCE. To expiate these, in order to both placate the gods and assure the populace, married women were called upon to make offerings to the state. Livy's report of a decision taken by the consuls after consultation with the decemvirs indicates that freedwomen (liberated slaves) as well as citizen wives had a role to play in this.

"The matrons, having taken up a collection of money, should donate as much as each one could afford, and bring a gift to Juno Regina (Royal Juno) on the Aventine and a *lectisternum* should be held. (A *lectisternum* is a ritual in which couches, likely with statues, are set up for gods to have a communal meal.) Even the freedwomen themselves should contribute funds in keeping with their means, from which they would give a gift to Feronia." (Feronia was a goddess particularly important to freed slaves.)
(Livy, *History of Rome* 22.1.17–18)

VIRGIN CHORUSES AND ANOTHER COLLECTIVE OFFERING FROM THE MATRONS

A decade later the war continued and prodigies abounded. According to Livy, after a rain of stones and the birth of an enormous hermaphroditic child the priests decreed that 27 virgins should form a procession through the city singing a hymn. While they were rehearsing yet another prodigy occurred, and the matrons were summoned once again to take up a collection for a gift for Juno.

"The pontiffs decreed that three times nine virgins should go through the city singing a hymn. When they were in the temple of Jupiter Stator, learning the song composed by the poet Livy, the temple of Juno Regina on the Aventine was struck by lightning. When the soothsayers had responded that this prodigy concerned the matrons and that the goddess should be appeased by a gift, the matrons whose houses were in the city of Rome or inside the tenth milestone of the city were summoned to the Capitol by an edict of the curule aediles. They themselves chose twenty-five from their number to whom they would bring a contribution from their dowries. From this a golden bowl was made as a gift and carried to the Aventine. A sacrifice was made, without defilement or blemish." (27.37.7–10)

The decemvirs called for another procession and sacrifice to Juno Regina. Along with the sacrificial animals paraded through the city they carried cyprus-wood statues of the goddess. These were followed by the 27 virgins singing their hymn. Livy comments that the virgins' contribution was central, although he is sceptical about the quality of their song.

"Then the twenty-seven virgins went in procession, wearing long robes and singing their hymn for Juno Regina, a song that might have been praiseworthy in the assessment of the listeners of that time, with their lack of refinement, but if repeated now it would be abhorrent and uncouth. Behind the column of virgins followed the decemvirs, crowned with laurel and wearing their purple-bordered togas. From the gate they came into the Forum along the Vicus Iugarius. The procession halted in the Forum and the virgins advanced, passing a cord hand-over-hand and beating time to the sound of their voices with a stamp of their feet."
(27.37.12–14)
(Livy, *History of Rome*)

CLAUDIA QUINTA

By the end of the third century the Roman people were hopeful that the battleground could be shifted to Africa, but their terror was aroused by several extraordinary prodigies that occurred in the year 204 BCE, according to Livy. Ambassadors, including one Marcus Valerius, were sent to Delphi to consult the oracle of Apollo about appropriate action to take.

The prodigies happened just as the Romans were complying with a prophecy that had recommended that they import a divinity from Mount Ida in Phrygia, the Great Mother Cybele. As Livy tells the story, a man named Publius Scipio was elected by the Senate as the best man to receive her when the Phrygian ship arrived at the mouth of the River Tiber. Scipio met the ship and received the goddess from her priests, but it was the Roman matrons who formed a line to pass her in succession on her way to Rome. Prominent among these was Claudia Quinta, who demonstrated her purity as well as her piety, a quality that had been in question.

"The situation had filled their minds with superstitions, and they were inclined to report and believe that portents had occurred. To that extent many were announced widely: two suns had been seen and had shone forth at intervals during the night; at Setia a comet had been seen shooting from east to west; at Tarracina the city gate and at Anagnia both the gate and the wall had been hit by lightning in many places; in the temple of Juno Sospita at Lanuvium a noise had erupted with a dreadful crash. To address these there had been public supplication for one day and, because there had been a shower of stones, a nine-day period of religious rites had been performed. Added to this there had been deliberation over the reception of the Idaean Mother whom Marcus Valerius, one of the ambassadors arriving beforehand, had announced would be arriving in Italy anytime soon. There had been a recent report that she was already at Tarracina." (29.14.2–7)

"The foremost maidens of the state, among whom the name of Claudia Quinta was prominent, received her. As someone whose reputation was in question before – as tradition has it – by such a religious service she made her chastity the more distinct for posterity. The matrons passed the goddess hand over hand to one another, while the whole city poured out to meet her. Censers had been placed in front of the doors where she was being carried. By lighting incense, and with prayers that she might enter Rome willingly and with kind intention, they carried the goddess to the sanctuary of Victory that is on the Palatine. This was on the day before the Ides of April, a festal day. People thronged to the Palatine, bearing gifts for the goddess. There was a banquet of the gods and games were held, called the Megalensia." (29.14.12–14)
(Livy, *History of Rome*)

Ovid, in his *Fasti*, where he cites stories associated with Roman religious festivals, offers more details about the actions of Claudia Quinta. Her singular success silenced rumours that had been circulating about her lack of purity, for in his account she resolves the crisis when the ship bearing the goddess up the Tiber went aground in the shallows and the men of Rome failed to free it.

"Every man who participated in the effort put in more than his share of the labour
    and offered encouragement to strong hands with the sound of his voice.
But the ship stayed unmoving, like an island in the middle of the sea.
    Astonished at the portent, the men stood and trembled.
Claudia Quinta went back in her family lineage to Clausus of long ago
    and her beauty was in no way inferior to her nobility.
A chaste woman she was, to be sure, but she was not believed to be. An unfair rumour
    had caused her pain, and she was being accused by a false charge.
It was wrongly alleged that she had gone forth decked out, with her hair finely arranged,
    that her tongue was swift in insulting the stern old men.

Her mind was aware of her innocence; she laughed at the untruths of the report
    but we of the mob are ready to believe in people's faults.
When she stepped out from the line of the chaste matrons,
    she drew up the pure water of the river in her hands,
sprinkled her head three times and three times raised her palms to the sky.
    (Whoever watched her thought she had lost her mind.)
With knee bent she fixed her gaze on the image of the goddess,
    and with her hair unbound she uttered these words:
'Propitious one, fruitful Mother of the Gods, accept the prayers of your suppliant
    on one condition:
I am said to be unchaste; if you condemn me I will confess that I have deserved this,
    and as one convicted by divine judgement I will pay the penalty by my death;
but if there is not a guilty verdict do you give by some act a pledge of my right to
live,
    and, chaste as you are, follow my chaste hands.'
She spoke, and drew the rope with slight effort.
    (I may be saying something strange, but it is also attested on stage.)
The goddess was moved and followed this leader, and by following demonstrated
her praise.
    A sound, an indication of joy, was carried to the stars."
(Ovid, *Fasti* 4.301–28)

The reference to an enactment on stage is evidence that the event became part of
a dramatic performance during the festival of the Great Mother, the Megalensia.

THE OPPIAN LAW

In 215 BCE, following the disastrous defeat at Cannae and several losses at sea
against the Carthaginians, the Romans were desperately short of resources to
rebuild their military. The Senate passed the Oppian Law, by which the male
citizens were obliged to contribute gold and silver to the treasury. This would
be drawn from their wives' jewellery, household items, their decorative horse
trappings and their bronze coins. Severe restrictions were now placed on the
amount of gold a woman could own, and any display of opulence on their part
was forbidden. Twenty years later, in 195 BCE, the critical phase of the war had
passed, and the women engaged in a massive public protest to repeal the law.
Livy offers his own version of a vehement speech given by the stern consul
Marcus Porcius Cato and the reply to this given by the tribune. (Cato's account
may be significantly influenced by views about women and wealth that were
circulating in Livy's own day.)

"Amid the anxiety over the enormous battles that were barely completed or soon to come there intervened something that is trifling to relate but which, because of the zealous passions aroused, boiled over into a major conflict. Marcus Fundanius and Lucius Valerius, tribunes of the plebs, brought forward to the Plebeian Assembly a motion to repeal the Oppian Law. Gaius Oppius, tribune of the plebs, had carried the law during the consulship of Quintus Fabius and Tiberius Sempronius in the heat of the Punic War. The law specified that no woman could possess more than half an ounce of gold, nor wear multi-coloured garments, nor ride in a carriage through the city or in a town closer than a mile from Rome, unless she was riding because of a public festival. The tribunes of the plebs, Marcus and Publius Iunius Brutus, supported the Oppian Law and said that they would not pass its repeal.

Many men of the noble class came forward, attempting to persuade or dissuade them. A crowd of men, supporters and opponents of the law, filled the Capitoline Hill. Matrons, who could not be kept inside, either by official authority or shame, or by order of their husbands, blocked all the streets of the city and the entrance to the Forum. As the men came down to the Forum they stood in their way, pleading that the luxuries women had enjoyed before be permitted to be restored to them, given that the state was prospering and the private fortunes of everyone were increasing daily. The crowd of women increased with each passing day, for now they were even assembling from the towns and market districts. Soon they even dared to go up and appeal to the consuls, the praetors and the other magistrates.

They found one of the consuls, Marcus Porcius Cato, impossible to move or convince. He held forth with these words about the law that was up for repeal. 'If each of us, Citizens, had resolved to uphold the rights and dignity that belong to a husband with respect to his own wife we would be having less trouble with women in general. Now our liberty at home has been overcome by the ungovernable nature of women. Here too, in the Forum, it is being crushed and trampled underfoot, and because we could not keep them under control individually we live in fear of all of them.'" (34.1.1–2.2)

Cato cites as a mythical precedent the case of the women of Lemnos who killed their husbands, then continues his diatribe.

"'From every group is there not the greatest danger if you permit there to be gatherings and meetings and secret consultations? I can scarcely decide in my own mind if this affair itself is worse than the precedent it sets. The situation concerns us consuls and the rest of the magistrates; the precedent concerns you more, Citizens. Whether it is in the interest of the state or not, what is being brought before you is your decision, you who are about to take a vote. This disturbance by the women, whether it arose from their own volition or your instigation, Marcus Fundanus and Lucius Valerius, the fact is that without a doubt it reflects badly on the magistracy. I don't know, tribunes, whether it is more disgraceful for you or the consuls – for you, if you have brought these women here to stir up sedition by the tribunes, and for us if laws are to be accepted now through a secession of the women, as once happened with the plebs.

Indeed, I was embarrassed when a short while ago I came into the Forum right through a column of women. If respect for the dignity and modesty of some individuals restrained me more than my feelings about them all – so they would not be seen to be rebuked by a consul – I would have said, "What is this practice of running around in public, blocking the streets and calling out to the husbands of other women? Could you not each have asked this of your own husbands at home? Are you more winsome in public than in private, and with the husbands of others rather than your own? Although not even at home, if modesty were to restrain married women within the confines of their own rights, does it become you to concern yourselves with laws that are passed or repealed here?" Our forefathers did not want women to conduct any affair, not even a personal one, without the authority of a guardian. They wanted them to be under the control of their parents, their brothers, their husbands. We – gods help us! – now allow them even to lay their hands on the affairs of state, to meddle with our meetings and assemblies in the Forum! What else are they doing now on the streets and at the crossroads, other than pushing the proposal of the tribunes, the law that they think ought to be repealed? Give reins to their uncontrollable nature, to this untamed creature, and expect that they will themselves set limits on their licence? If you don't do something, this is the least of the things imposed upon a woman by custom or by the law to which they will submit with a sense of injustice. They want liberty – actually licence – in everything, if we want to speak truthfully.

If they win now with their assault what won't they attempt? Think back on all the laws pertaining to women with which your forefathers reined in their licence and made them subject to their husbands; even with all these restraints you can hardly control them. What then? If you put up with them grabbing these controls one by one and wrenching themselves clear and in the end placing themselves on the same level as their husbands, do you think you will find them bearable? As soon as they begin to be your equals they will be your superiors. By Hercules, they object when any new law is passed against them; they complain not of the law but, on the contrary, of the way it has wronged them. A law that you have passed and ratified with your votes, which in its trial and application over so many years you have accepted – this they are demanding that you repeal. By getting rid of one law you weaken the others. No law is convenient enough for everyone. It only need be asked whether it is, on the whole, beneficial to the majority. If a law is detrimental to each one personally, that law is repealed and abolished. What will be the conse-quence of introducing laws for everyone that are immediately annulled for those to whom they apply? I want to hear, nonetheless, what it is on account of which the matrons have rushed into the public space in a state of alarm, and barely keep themselves from the Forum and meeting of the Assembly!'" (34.2.4–3.6)

(On several occasions during the early phase of the Republic, the common people had felt they were being badly treated by the patricians, and "seceded". This amounted to a general strike, and because these people were the producers of food and other goods for the Romans, their complaints were heard. The institution of a "tribune of the plebs" gave them a voice in state decision-making.)

Livy continues his version of Cato's objections by having him compare the women's actions unfavorably with their helpful public display of concern when the situation with Hannibal had been dire – when they appealed to the officials to ransom their fathers, husbands and brothers who were captives of the Carthaginians, or when they came out to receive the Magna Mater from Phrygia. Instead of these noble causes, he says, their current pretext was to preserve their ability to flaunt their luxury.

"What excuse is being put forward, honorable at least to speak about, for this insurrection of women? 'So that we might be conspicuous in our gold and purple,' one says, 'and so that we ride in our carriages through the city on festal and working days as though triumphant over the law that was defeated and repealed, and over your votes that we have seized and snatched from you. All this, so that there would be no limit to our expenses or our luxury.'" (34.3.8–9)

Cato then was said by Livy to have held forth on the ways in which greed, wealth and excess luxury had had a detrimental effect on Romans, and how men and women of the earlier period of the Republic had been content with simplicity. At that time there was no need for an Oppian Law to curb women's extravagance. With an influx of wealth had come a division between rich and poor women, and the motivation for competing with one another for conspicuous display. He concluded his speech with a vehement appeal to retain the law.

Tribunes who opposed the repeal endorsed the speech but Lucius Valerius, the tribune who had introduced the motion to repeal the law, spoke in the women's defence as follows, in Livy's record.

"Cato, however, used up more words in chastising the matrons than in dissuading us from our proposal, and in fact he left in some doubt whether what he was reproving in the matrons was inspired by their own free will or by our instigation. I will defend the proposal rather than ourselves, against whom this consul has levelled his accusations, which were more for the sake of airing his words than for addressing the issue. He called the gathering of the women 'an act of sedition' and at times 'secession', because the matrons had asked you in public that you revoke a law when the state is at peace and prosperous and happy, a law that was passed against them during the harsh conditions of war." (34.5.3–5)

Lucius Valerius continued by pointing out the power of Cato's oratory to sway his listeners, but also his personality that could be severe. As precedents where women had benefited the state by their public actions he cited the actions of the Sabine women who had stopped the war between their Sabine fathers and brothers and their Roman husbands, and the initiative of Coriolanus' mother and wife in preventing the general from leading the Volsci against Rome. When the Gauls took over Rome in 399 BCE and demanded a specified sum before they would release control of the city, the women agreed by unanimous consent to contribute their gold. During the war with Hannibal the women had once again contributed their wealth, and at the height of the terrors associated with this phase of the war it was the matrons who went down to the mouth of the Tiber to receive the Great Mother.

Valerius continued by making a clear distinction between laws that had been passed with the understanding that they would be fundamental to the ongoing health of the state, and those that were temporary – emergency measures passed to deal with a specific situation. The former were rarely, if ever, repealed; the latter were invoked and repealed as circumstances demanded. The Oppian Law had been passed when Hannibal held much of the surrounding area and was poised to march on Rome. Soldiers and supplies had been diminishing, and senators and commoners alike, men and women, contributed to the state treasury. The law was not passed in order to restrain women's greed for luxury. In peacetime men and boys were permitted to wear purple; why not women? Gold jewellery was a way of safeguarding wealth. Women among the Latin allies were permitted to wear purple and gold and to ride, not walk, through the city; how would Roman men feel if they were prohibited the privileges enjoyed by their Latin counterparts? Valerius used this and other arguments in his defence of women's right to these luxuries.

" 'What do you make of mere women, whom even trifling things affect? No magistracies, nor priesthoods nor triumphs nor marks of distinction, no gifts or spoils of war can be extended to them. Finery, adornments and elegant attire, these are the badges of honour for women; in these they take delight and pride. Our forefathers called them the 'women's world'. What else do they put aside in times of mourning, apart from purple and gold? What do they put on when they go public again? What do they add except their finer ornaments in times of public thanksgiving and supplications?

Of course, if you repeal the Oppian Law, it will not be in your power if you want to ban anything that the law forbids at the moment. Daughters, wives, even sisters of some will be less under control. Never, while their men are in good health, is the slavery of women cast off. But even they detest the freedom which widowhood and the loss of fathers affords. They prefer that their finery be under your control than subject to the laws. You too ought to keep them in control and under guardianship, not in slavery, and prefer to be called fathers or husbands rather than masters. The consul just now used hostile language in calling this the 'sedition' or 'secession' of women. For the danger is, he implies, that they will seize the Sacred Hill, just as the angered plebs did at one time, or the Aventine Hill. Their frail nature must put up with whatever you decree. The more you have power the more moderately must you exercise your authority.'

After these things had been spoken in opposition to and in favour of the law a substantially greater crowd of women poured into the public space the next day. As a single group they all blockaded the doors of the Brutuses, who were opposing the proposal of their colleagues. They did not relent until the veto was rescinded by the tribunes. Then there was no doubt but that all the tribes would repeal the law. Twenty years after it was passed the law was repealed." (34.7.7–8.3)
(Livy, The History of Rome)

Women and property

THE VOCONIAN LAW

By the end of the third century BCE women could be named as heirs or designated beneficiaries in a will, and could own property. A woman's right of inheritance was derived from her husband and his family if she had married *in manu*, and from her birth family if not. In either case she was subject to the authority of her guardian (*tutor*), and she could not dispose of property such as land, agricultural implements, and so on (*res mancipi*) without his permission. She was free to control "movable" property such as jewellery, money etc., however. During the course of the second century BCE, considerable wealth was accumulating in the hands of some Romans, and the bequests from large estates became a subject of some concern. The *Lex Voconia*, passed in 169 BCE, placed restrictions on inheritance in the case of wealthy families: those who had been assessed as belonging to the wealthiest class (calculated in a census) could not name beneficiaries who stood to inherit more than the officially designated heirs and they could not name women as beneficiaries (Gaius 2.274). We have no complete citation of the law, and there is no consistent view about the reasoning behind it. Some argue that there was a felt need to curb the amount of wealth that had been coming into the hands of women, enabling them to became creditors and loaning money even to their husbands. Others prefer to see the law as aiming to distribute wealth more broadly so that a greater number of men would have the means to sustain an active social and political role in the activities of the growing state.

Not surprisingly, Cato supported this law, proposed by the tribune Voconius Saxa. Some of Cato's remarks are preserved in a summary of Livy's Book 41 that was made in the fourth century CE.

"In the first place a woman brings you a large dowry. Then she retains a large sum of money that she does not hand over to the control of her husband, but she gives him on loan. Lastly, when she becomes angry at him she orders a slave under her control to follow him and beat him down (to get it back)."
(*ORF* 158 p. 60)

The law was still in place in the first century BCE, and was decried by Cicero as perpetrating an injustice toward women. His comment makes it clear that Vestals were not subject to the Voconian restrictions.

"This law itself was proposed because of its usefulness for men, and is full of injustice toward women. For what reason, I ask, would a woman not have the right to possess money? Why could she inherit from a Vestal Virgin, and not be able to inherit from her own mother?"
(Cicero, *Republic* 3.17)

Saint Augustine, a North African Christian bishop who lived in the fourth and fifth centuries CE, looked back on the Voconian Law in the same critical vein as Cicero.

"That Voconian Law was passed, forbidding a man from designating his daughter as heir even if she were his only daughter. If there is a law that could be stated or conceived that is more unjust than this law, I don't know of it."
(St Augustine, *City of God* 3.21)

AEMILIA TERTIA

One woman who clearly sidestepped the constraints imposed by the Voconian Law was the wealthy Aemilia Tertia. She was married to Scipio Africanus, the brilliant Roman general who was responsible for the defeat of Hannibal in Africa in 202 BCE that ended the Second Punic War (his cognomen earned by this victory) but he was less than heroic as a husband, according to Valerius Maximus.

"So that we might also take up the subject of wifely fidelity, Aemilia Tertia, wife of the elder Africanus and mother of Cornelia of the Gracchi, was so understanding and patient that when she found out that one of her slave girls was a favourite of her husband's, she feigned ignorance of the matter, lest she as a woman bring a charge of wanton behaviour against a great man, Africanus, conqueror of the world. Her thoughts were so far from taking revenge that after the death of Africanus she freed the servant-girl and gave her in marriage to one of her freedmen."
(Valerius Maximus, *Nine Books of Memorable Doings and Sayings* 6.7.1)

The eldest son of Scipio Africanus was Publius Cornelius Scipio, who adopted the nephew of Aemilia Tertia, a man who was then called Scipio Aemilianus. This young man would be the general who concluded the Third Punic War (the last) in a decisive defeat of the Carthaginians in 146 BCE. Scipio Aemilianus inherited a considerable fortune from Aemilia, his aunt (by birth) who was also his adoptive grandmother. Polybius, a Greek historian who had been brought to Rome as tutor to Scipio Aemilianus when he was a boy, described the wealth enjoyed by Aemilia when she was alive. When she died, Scipio passed on his inheritance to his (birth) mother.

"[Aemilia] possessed a splendid cortège during the religious outings for ladies, inasmuch as she shared in the good fortune of Scipio when he was at the peak of his life and his good fortune. For apart from the clothing around her body and the decoration of her carriage, the baskets and cups and the rest of the equipment for the sacrifice, was sometimes silver and sometimes gold, and all of it accompanied her continuously along the major streets. The number of maidservants and household servants that followed was of comparable size to these.

Immediately after the burial of Aemilia the whole selection of goods was given by Aemilianus to his mother, who had been separated from Lucius many years earlier, and who had fewer resources for her upkeep than would support the appearance of noble birth." (31.26.3–7)

Scipio Aemilianus also took over the care of Aemilia's daughters (his aunts by adoption).

"After this Scipio was obliged to pay half their dowries on behalf of the daughters of the Great Scipio, who were the sisters of his adoptive father. For their father had agreed to pay 50 talents for each of his daughters. Their mother had paid half of this to their husbands right at the time of their marriage, but when she died she left the other half still owing. So Scipio had to liquidate the debt on behalf of his father's sisters. According to the laws of the Romans the money from the dowry that was still owing had to be paid to the women within three years, with the portable assets being first handed over within ten months, as is customary among them." (31.27.1–5)
(Polybius, The Histories)

11

Women of the upper and lower classes

CORNELIA GRACCHUS: THE IDEAL *MATRONA*

Scipio Africanus had betrothed one of his daughters, Cornelia, to Tiberius Gracchus. As the mother of 12 children, three of whom survived, she became a symbol of the virtuous Roman wife and mother. When her husband died she remained loyal to his memory, refusing subsequent marriage proposals, including one from Egypt's Ptolemy VIII. This earned her the title *univira* ("with one husband"), an attribute that would be cited as an admirable ideal but in conflict with efforts to encourage widows to remarry and produce more children. It also deprived widows of protection by a husband. Cornelia was well educated, familiar with Greek and Latin texts, and facilitated the bringing of Greek scholars to Rome.

Although a patrician herself, she supported the political efforts of her two sons, Tiberius and Gaius, to strengthen the plebeian cause. Her pride in her children is reflected in this story found in Valerius Maximus.

"Cornelia, mother of the Gracchi, when a Campanian woman – a guest in her house – held up her jewellery as the most beautiful of the century, drew her out in conversation until her children came back from school. 'These,' she said, 'are my jewels.'"
(Valerius Maximus, *Nine Books of Memorable Deeds and Sayings* 4.4 *praef.*)

Quintilian taught and wrote about rhetoric in Rome in the first century CE. His *Institutio Oratoria*, a treatise on oratory, begins with a discussion of the important elements in education, and he pays special tribute to the instruction given to her sons by Cornelia.

"In the case of parents, in truth I would like to see them as highly educated as possible, and I am not speaking only about fathers. For we have learned that their mother Cornelia contributed greatly to the eloquence of the Gracchi. She was a woman whose very learned manner of speaking has been handed down to posterity as well through her letters."
(Quintilian, *Institutio Oratoria* 1.1.6)

The following is drawn from a letter apparently composed by Cornelia to her son Gaius when he was canvassing for the office of tribune of the plebs. This was occurring at a particularly turbulent time during the clash between patricians and plebeians in the mid-Republic, one heightened by the actions of Gaius' brother Tiberius, who was eventually murdered in 133 BCE after engineering the passage of a land reform bill that angered members of the Senate. When Gaius sought the tribunate two years later, Cornelia urged him to reconsider. The text is found as a fragment of Cornelius Nepos, a historian and biographer of the first century BCE.

"You will say that it is a fine thing to take revenge on one's enemies. To no one does this seem a greater or finer thing than it does to me, but on condition that one pursues this path while keeping the state secure. But, inasmuch as that cannot happen, our enemies will not perish for a long time and only after much factional fighting, and they will be as they are now rather than having the state brought to ruin and perish.

... I would dare to take an oath, with words carefully considered, that with the exception of those who killed Tiberius Gracchus, no foe has given me so much trouble and so much distress as you have because of these activities. [You], the one who – of all those children whom I have had up to now – ought to have been supportive and concerned on their behalf in seeing that I had the least amount of anxiety in my old age. In whatever you undertake you ought to want to give me as much pleasure as possible, and you should consider it wrong to do anything with a serious impact that opposes my point of view, particularly in my case since there remains a small portion of life left to me.

Is it not even possible to be supportive for a brief period, rather than both to oppose me and to bring ruin upon the state? In short, what end will there be to this? When ever will our family leave off its insanity? When ever can a limit be placed on that business? When ever will we cease both nursing and serving out grievances? When ever will one be ashamed to meddle in and muddle up the affairs of state?

But if all this cannot come about, seek the tribunate when I am dead. Do what you want when I won't be aware of it. When I am dead you will offer me parental sacrifices and invoke the god of your parent. At that time will you not be ashamed to request petitions from those gods whom you abandoned and deserted when they were present and alive? May that god Jupiter not allow you to persist in these matters, nor let such great lunacy enter your mind! Even if you do persist, I fear lest you will take on so much trouble throughout your whole life, through your own fault, that you will never be able to find pleasure while free from danger."
(Cornelius Nepos, Fragment 59 Marshall)

(The phrase "god of your parent" reflects a Roman tradition of awarding divine honours to one's ancestors after their death.)

Gaius Gracchus was murdered 12 years after his brother and a year after he was elected tribune in 122 BCE. According to one ancient source (Appian, in *Civil War*, 1.20) Cornelia, with her daughter Sempronia, engineered the death of Scipio Aemilianus, Sempronia's husband, who had opposed the populist activities of Tiberius and was implicated in his death.

THE HOUSEKEEPER OF THE VILLA

In antiquity, Cato's reputation for sternness was compensated somewhat by broad admiration for his encyclopedic learning, reflected in his speeches (written out and published by himself) and his writings on philosophy, history, jurisprudence and agriculture. In his treatise *On Agriculture* he presented a handbook for Romans who could afford a country estate *(villa)*. His views above about the need to keep women confined for the most part to the house are also found in his advice about how the owner should deal with the house-keeper *(vilica)* of the country estate, although he recommends that her husband (the *vilicus*) also be instructed to be hard-working and not socialize away from the farm. In what follows he addresses the *vilicus*.

"See that the duties of the *vilica* are taken seriously. If the master has given her to you as wife, see that you remain satisfied with her alone. Make sure that she is intimidated by you. Let her not indulge in too much luxury. Let her keep to a minimum her visits to neighbouring and other women, and not receive them in the house or in her quarters. She must not go out for dinner or circulate socially. She must not perform religious rituals or arrange for them to be done on her behalf without the orders of the master or his wife. Let her know that the master conducts religious rites for the whole household.

See that she is tidy, that she keeps the estate swept and tidy. She should keep the hearth clean and swept every day before she goes to bed. On the Kalends, Ides and Nones when there is a festival day let her place a wreath on the hearth, and on those same days let her petition the household gods for a good supply of produce. She should see that there is cooked food for you and for the household. She should see that there are many hens and eggs available for use. She should have dried pears, sorb-apples, figs, pressed grapes, sorb-apples in wine-must and pears and grapes preserved in jars and sparrow-apples, grapes preserved in grape-pulp and crushed in jars in the ground, along with fresh Praenestine nuts in a jar buried in the ground. Scantian apples in jars and other fruits that are usually stored along with wild fruits – see that she stores all these away carefully each year for use. She should also know how to make good flour and spelt ground fine."
(Cato, *On Agriculture* 143)

(The Kalends occurred on the first day of the month; the Ides occurred on the 13th or 15th, the latter in March, May, July, October; the Nones occurred on the 9th day before the Ides, i.e. the 5th or 7th day of the month, reckoning inclusively.)

WOMEN IN THE INSCRIPTIONAL RECORD

Another source of evidence about the lives of Roman women during the mid-Republic appears in inscriptions. Although the following are undated, the form of some of the Latin words suggests that the text was probably inscribed sometime during the second century BCE.

This one accompanied a dedication to the goddess Diana in her sanctuary at Nemi, south of Rome.

"Poublilia Turpilia wife of Gnaeus gave this statue as a gift to Diana in honour of her son Gnaeus." (*ILLRP* 1.82)

Despite the fact that literary evidence suggests that women's participation in the cult of Hercules was restricted, inscriptions attest to the fact that some women were active benefactors for the cult. The following records a substantial dedication made to this god in Rome, one that included a temple that may have replaced an open-air sanctuary.

"Publicia, daughter of Lucius, wife of Gnaeus Cornelius son of Aulus, arranged for the construction of the temple and its doors for Hercules, and saw to the finishing touches of these, and restored the altar sacred to Hercules. All this she did on her own behalf and that of her husband; she took care that it should be done." (*ILLRP* 1.126)

On the face of a large Roman tomb monument in the shape of a bread oven was found an inscription for a baker named Marcus Vergilius Eurysaces. Nearby was a chest-shaped breadbox, the monument for his wife who predeceased him, with the following text.

"Atistia was my wife. She was an excellent wife while she lived. The remains of her body that are left are in this breadbox." (*ILLRP* 2.805a)
(The breadbox coffin is now in the National Museum in Rome.)

In Capua, just north of Naples, was found an upright tombstone depicting a couple holding hands, and containing the following words.

"Dexsonia Solemio, for himself and for his Philema – a woman most beloved."
(*ILLRP* 2.920)

In northern Italy, near the cathedral in Cremona, was found a limestone base likely for an altar (now missing) inscribed with the following poignant text.

"His mother had this monument made, grieving for her son, from whom there was never any grief, except when he was no longer alive." (*ILLRP* 2.966)

Another tomb inscription survives as testimony of a mother's feelings of loss, in this case of a daughter.

"POSILLA SENENIA DAUGHTER OF QUARTUS, QUARTA SENENIA FREEDWOMAN OF GAIUS
Visitor, stop and read this too, what is written.
It was not permitted for her mother to enjoy her only daughter
whom I think some god or other was loath to let live.
Since it was not allowed that she be dressed up [as a bride] by her mother while she lived
after her death her mother had this made as a substitution.
In her final hour she adorned her with a monument, the girl whom she adored."
(*ILLRP* 2.971)

In this succinct tomb inscription a widower invites the passer-by to reflect upon the virtues of his deceased wife. The epitaph (now lost) had been dated to the time of the Gracchi (*RTLA* pp. 77–8).

"Stranger, what I say is modest: stand here and read it through.
Here is the scarcely beautiful burial place of a beautiful woman.
Her parents gave her the name 'Claudia'.
She loved her husband with her heart.
She produced two children. Of these one she left behind
on the earth; the other has been placed under the earth.
She was eloquent of speech, moreover proper in her deportment too.
She looked after the home, she worked the wool. I have spoken. Be on your way."
(*ILLRP* 2.973)

This brief tribute to a young woman, a former slave, was found in Rome.

"Carfinia, freedwoman of Marcus M ... (the stone is fragmented), lived for 20 years.

She was agreeable to her kinfolk, very pleasant to her friends,
dutiful to everyone." (*ILLRP* 2.980)

An inscription found in Cartagena (i.e. New Carthage, a Roman settlement
in Spain) addresses passers-by and honours a maidservant (probably a slave)
who was buried with her mistress, a freedwoman. The tribute was composed
in iambic verse.

"PLOTIA FREEDWOMAN OF LUCIUS AND FUFIA
This maidservant was called Phryne and lies here.
What kind of person she was toward her patron, her patron's wife, her parent, her
husband,
the tomb monument makes clear. Farewell, be well." (*ILLRP* 2.981)

The following "curse tablet" was inscribed on lead and buried outside one of the
gates of Rome's city walls. It reflects a less amicable relationship between mistress
and servant-woman than the above. The former first addresses an underworld
power in the hopes of punishing the latter, then explains to her intended victim
the reason.

"This new maidservant of Capito, Danae. May you take and accept this as an
offering,
and may you destroy Danae. You have cursed Eutychia, the wife of Soterichus."
(*ILLRP* 2.1145)

The following is a verse inscription for a freedwoman who had done well for
herself, entitling her to have a number of clients.

"[She has died] MANLIA GNOME FREEDWOMAN OF TITUS
This is a woman who always lived with an excellent disposition.
I had many clients. I obtained this one place for myself,
And so in this spot I wanted to live out my life.
I never was in debt to anyone. I lived in good faith.
I gave my bones to the earth, I gave my body to the fires of Vulcan,
so it was I who carried out the last injunction, that of death." (*ILLRP* 2.982)

This verse inscription in the voice of Helvia Prima addresses a spectator,
lamenting that she left behind a harmonious marriage.

"You, traveller, who walk about with an untroubled mind,
    and direct your gaze at my Underworld shade:

if you are asking who I am, well I am ashes and burnt embers;
    before my unhappy death I was Helvia Prima.
I took delight in my husband Cadmus Scrateius,
    and we lived in harmony, being of one mind.
Now I have been given to the Underworld god, to stay for a long time,
    a bridal procession with the fires of death and the waters of the Styx."
(*ILLRP* 2.985)

12

Women in Roman Comedy

There were other types of dramatic performances at the Megalensia, including the comedies of Plautus. This remarkable playwright, born in the middle of the third century BCE and active during the Second Punic War (during the invasion of Hannibal), worked as a labourer while studying the work of Greek comic playwrights. He adapted some of the works of Greek New Comedy for a Roman audience. Greek "New Comedy" was distinguished from the earlier "Old Comedy" in being situational, with stock characters rather than actors whose theatrical humour supplied etc. theatrical humour that supplied a pointed commentary on life in Athens. Because of the Greek source, it is often difficult to know how much his female characters reflect characteristics of women familiar to his Roman audience, but Plautus' popularity attests to the fact that these features were not felt to be entirely foreign.

In *Casina*, for example, a citizen wife confounds the schemes of her older husband to arrange for a servant girl to be conveniently married to another house servant so as to be available for his sexual access to her. In one scene, Cleostrata foils her husband's arrangement with his neighbour to have his house vacated so that a liaison with the girl would be possible. With her husband temporarily absent, Cleostrata celebrates her having outwitted both old men.

"Well now, with fine sporting this man has been fooled! How the poor old fellows are in a tizzy!
Now I would like that withered and good-for nothing old soul, my husband, to come so that I might have some fun with him in turn, now that I have fooled this other one.
How I want to pull off some quarrelling between the two of them!"
(Plautus, *Casina* 558–61)

In *The Merchant*, another citizen wife is under the mistaken belief that a young woman being temporarily hidden in her house is in fact the mistress of her husband. Dorippa laments her situation.

"There would never be, nor has there been, a woman more pitiable than I,
to be married to such a man. Oh, woe is me!

Alas, to what a husband you have entrusted yourself and the property you have!
Alas, to what a husband I brought ten talents in dowry!
All so that I might see this, so that I might suffer such affronts!" (700–4)

Dorippa's maid sympathizes, commenting on the miserable lot of women who live under the double standard that permits men to engage in extramarital sex.

"Good heavens! Women do live under a harsh law,
on terms that are much less reasonable for a woman than for her husband.
For if her husband brings home a mistress, kept secret from his wife,
and his wife finds out, the husband gets away with it.
But if a wife steps out secretly away from the house without her husband knowing it
a charge is laid by the husband and she is divorced.
Would that there were the same law for the wife as for the husband!
For a wife who is a good one is content with one husband.
Why should a husband be any less content with just one wife?
By the gods, I would make the case that if men were punished in the same way,
when some fellow brought home a mistress and kept it secret from his wife,
just as those women are divorced who are guilty of a wrong move
there would be more men on their own than there are now!" (817–29)
(Plautus, *The Merchant*)

In another play, *The Two Menaechmi*, a wife's father suggests that there might be limits to what a woman needs to put up with in a philandering husband, although he believes that an overly-possessive wife can drive her husband to other beds. The wife in question has mistaken the identity of a young man who has been visiting a courtesan, thinking he is her husband. The mistake occurs because the two men are twins separated at birth and have not yet met. The wife has summoned her father because he is the one who can release her from her marriage and resume responsibility for her. Her father guesses at why she has sent him an urgent summons.

"This is the thing that is worrying me in my chest and my heart –
what could be the trouble here,
why my daughter has suddenly sought me out in this way, to come to her.
What it might be nothing makes me the wiser, what she wants, why she called me.
To tell the truth, I more or less know already what the issue might be.
I have a notion that some quarrel with her husband has arisen.
That's the way it usually is with women who demand that their husbands toe the line.

Formidable they are, with their dowry in hand.
But those husbands are often scarcely immune from blame.
Nonetheless it's true that there ought to be a limit on how much a wife should tolerate;
By the gods, a daughter never summons her father to come to her
unless either some wrong has been done or there is some just cause for laying blame.
But whatever it is I shall soon know."
(Plautus, *The Two Menaechmi* 761–72)

In Plautus' *Curculio* the slave of a young man reminds his master of the legitimate sexual opportunities available to men, cautioning him against an involvement that would get him into trouble. Access to the sex trade is available to all; not so available are individuals under the control of other men.

"No one prohibits a person from walking on the public road.
As long as you don't make your way through a fenced-in enclosure,
as long as you keep your distance from a married woman, a widow, a virgin,
a youth or freeborn children, love whatever you want."
(Plautus, *Curculio* 35–8)

In Plautus' *The Pot of Gold*, two older men named Megadorus and Euclio converse about the virtues of marrying a poor woman or even a rich one without a dowry, in order to obtain peace and avoid the constant demands for luxurious goods or the power that women could wield when they were wealthier than their husbands.

(Megadorus) "Then no woman would say, 'Well, as I see it, I brought you a dowry larger by far than the supply of money you had;
for it's only fair that purple and gold jewellry be given to me,
slave-women, mules, mule-drivers, footmen,
page-boys, carriages in which to be carried about.'"
(Euclio) "How excellent a grasp this man has of what women do!
I could wish that he be made the supervisor of women's conduct!"
(Megadorus) "Nowadays wherever you go you can see more wagons in front of large houses
than in the country when you come to a farmstead.
But even this is a fine sight compared with [tradesmen] coming to collect their expenses:
there stands the cloth-fuller, with the embroiderer, the jeweller, the wool-worker;
the dealer in dress-decorations, the manufacturer of undies,

veil-makers, dyers of violet, dyers of yellow;
there stand the sleeve-makers, there stand the perfume-mongerers,
linen-salesmen, shoemakers,
cobblers squatting, slipper-makers;
the sandal-makers stand by, so do the dealers in mallow-dye;
the makers of breast-bands are at hand, with the belt-makers alongside.
Now you might think these have been bought off. They move on, and in come
three hundred more with their hands out,
then these collection agents stand right in your halls,
weavers, fringe-makers, toilet-kit makers.
They are brought in and the money is paid up. Now you think they have settled up
when saffron-dyers show up,
or some other cursed fellow is inevitably there who wants something."
(Plautus, *The Pot of Gold* 498–522)

Terence, another Roman comic playwright, was born around the time of the
death of Plautus, in the early second century BCE. A slave from North Africa, he
was brought to Rome by his master, educated and freed. Like Plautus he adapted
Greek originals for a Roman audience.

In *The Self-Tormentor*, Chremes berates his wife Sostrata for not following his
orders when he was away and she was pregnant. She was to do away with the
child if it should be born a girl but had instead given her daughter to another
woman to raise. When he returned she pleaded with her husband – to no avail –
to understand a mother's instinct to preserve a child born to her.

(Chremes) "That at least I know for sure, even if you deny it,
that everything you say and do is done out of ignorance and folly;
in this one act you demonstrate so many faults. Now first of all,
if you had wanted to follow my orders you should have gotten rid of the child,
not made a pretense of its death with your words when in fact you gave it hope
of living.
But I leave that aside: tender-heartedness, a mother's affection, I grant you this.
But think how well in fact you gave forethought to what you wanted,
for your daughter was surrendered by you to that old woman – that is undisputable,
either that through you she might make a profit from her or that she might be sold
in the market as a slave.
I suppose you reckoned it this way: 'anything is enough if only she might live'.
What do you do with those people who know nothing of justice, goodness,
fairness?
Better or worse, whether it's helpful or a hindrance, do they see nothing except
what they like?" (632–43)

Sostrata continued her appeal.

(Sostrata) "My dear Chremes, I was wrong. I admit it. I am convinced. Now I entreat you,
inasmuch as your mind carries more weight be all the more forgiving,
so that in your justice may reside some protection for my simplicity of mind."
(Chremes) "Of course I pardon what you have done. But it's true, Sostrata,
my soft temperament is a bad teacher for you in many ways. But whatever this is about,
for the sake of which this was started, carry on with telling it."
(Sostrata) "As we women are all foolish and miserably superstitious,
when I gave the baby to that woman to be exposed I took a ring off my finger
and told her to expose it together with the little girl.
If she died she would not be without a share of our possessions." (644–52)

Sostrata's gift to her daughter Antiphila was proof of her legitimacy, and the girl was able to marry her beloved.

Earlier in the play the courtesan Bacchis spoke to Antiphila, a beautiful and respectable woman with many admirers, about the difference in their social circumstances.

(Bacchis) "My goodness, dear Antiphila, I commend you and think you fortunate,
in that you have endeavoured to see that your conduct matches your beauty;
and – may the gods bless me – I don't wonder at all that every man wants you for himself.
For your conversation has been proof to me of the kind of character you possess,
and when I now reflect in my mind about the life you lead
and that of all those of your kind who keep the common horde at a distance from yourselves,
it is no wonder that you are of that sort and we are not at all.
For it is beneficial to you to be virtuous; those men with whom we do business won't let us.
For our lovers certainly court us because they are attracted by our beauty.
When this has faded they take their attentions elsewhere.
Meanwhile, unless we have made some provisions beforehand, we live abandoned.
For you women, when once it has been determined that you live out your life with one man
whose character is most similar to yours, those husbands attach themselves to you.
By this kindly feeling you are both truly bound one to each other,
so that no calamity can ever be able to put an end to your love." (381–95)
(Terence, The Self-Tormentor)

FURTHER READING

Beard, M. 1995. "(Re)Reading Vestal Virginity", in R. Hawley and B. Levick, *Women in Antiquity. New Assessments*. London/New York. 166–77

—1980. "The Sexual Status of the Vestal Virgins". *Journal of Roman Studies* 70, 12–27

Bradley, K. 1991. *Discovering the Roman Family. Studies in Roman Social History*. New York/Oxford

—1994. *Slavery and Society at Rome*. Cambridge

Culham, P. 1982. "The *Lex Oppia*". *Latomus* 41.4, 786–93

Dixon, S. 2007. *Cornelia, Mother of the Gracchi*. London/New York

Gardner, J. 1986. *Women in Law and Society*. Bloomington, IN

—and Wiedemann, T. 1991. *The Roman Household*. Oxford

Hallett, J. P. 1984. *Fathers and Daughters in Roman Society: Women and the Elite Family*. Princeton, NJ

Hemelrijk, E. 1987. "Women's Demonstrations in Republican Rome", in J. Blok and P. Mason (eds) *Sexual Asymmetry: Studies in Ancient Society*. Amsterdam

Miles, G. B. 1995. *Livy: Reconstructing Early Rome*. Ithaca, NY

Parker, H. 2007. "Why Were the Vestals Virgins? Or the Chastity of Women and the Safety of the Roman State", in *Virginity Revisited. Configurations of the Unpossessed Body*. Toronto. 66–99 (revised from publication in 2004, *American Journal of Philology* 125, 563–601)

Pomeroy, S. 1976. "The Relationship of the Married Woman to her Blood Relatives at Rome". *Ancient Society* 7, 215–27

Rei, A. 1998. "Villains, Wives and Slaves in the Comedies of Plautus", in S. R. Joshel and S. Murnaghan (eds) *Women and Slaves in Greco-Roman Culture. Differential Equations*. London/New York. 92–108

Saller, R. 1984. "*Familia, Domus* and the Roman Conception of the Family". *Phoenix* 38, 336–55

Staples, A. 1998. *From Good Goddess to Vestal Virgins: Sex and Category in Roman Religion*. London/New York

Walsh, P. G. 1996. "Making a Drama Out of a Crisis: Livy on the Bacchanalia". *Greece and Rome* 43, 188–203

PART 3

THE LATE REPUBLIC

With the close of the second century BCE, new tensions in Rome were surfacing that affected the lives of everyone. Now it was not external but civil wars that erupted, as strong men with military experience and backing jostled for power in a city that was building an enormous empire. The internal violence that eventually led to the deaths of leading figures like Pompey, Julius Caesar and Cicero would only end with the defeat of Mark Antony and Cleopatra after the Battle of Actium in 31 BCE. The victor was Octavian, the great-nephew and adopted son of Julius Caesar, who took the name Augustus and launched what is now referred to as the "Principate".

13

Women and powerful men

A discussion of the women of the turbulent period that immediately preceded the Principate cannot be detached from the portraits of the strong men in whose hands the fate of Rome rested. The pattern of marrying and divorcing daughters and wives for political advantage or revenge became a strategic move.

WOMEN AND SULLA

In the first two decades of the first century BCE two individuals, Gaius Marius and Lucius Cornelius Sulla, backed by private armies, fought for control of Rome amid much bloodshed. Finally, in 82 BCE, Sulla, after the massacre of thousands of his opponents, took control of the city and had himself declared dictator. Plutarch describes his confiscating estates on a whim, and bestowing on his favourites women who were already married or obliging men to divorce their wives in order to marry a woman of Sulla's choice. Aemilia, the daughter of his fourth wife Metella he gave to Pompey, wanting to secure a useful political bond with him. This obliged Pompey to divorce his own wife. (Plutarch, "Sulla" 6.11, 33.2–3)

As Sulla celebrated his dictatorship with lavish feasting and drinking, his own wife Metella lay dying. Sulla's callous disregard for the marriage-bond was evident in Plutarch's record of the dictator's life.

"Through the midst of the feasting that carried on for many days Metella was dying from a sickness. When the priests did not allow Sulla to come near her, or to have the house polluted by funeral rites, Sulla composed a writ of divorce and ordered her to be carried while still alive to another house." (35.2)

Despite this dismissal of her, Sulla held a grand funeral for Metella when she died. Plutarch tells us that it was only a few months later that his fancy turned to another woman named Valeria, who had been recently divorced.

"After a few months had passed there was a gladiatorial spectacle, not yet of the sort where people's seats were separated, but the theatre still had mixed seating for men and women. A woman happened to be sitting near Sulla, of remarkable beauty and distinguished lineage. She was the daughter of Messalla, and sister of the orator Hortensius – Valeria by name. It happened that she had recently been divorced from her husband. As she walked along behind Sulla she rested her hand on him and pulling off some wool from his cloak, she passed by him to her own seat. When Sulla looked at her in surprise she said, 'It's nothing of consequence, Dictator, but I too want to take a little sample of your good fortune.' Sulla did not hear this with displeasure, but it was immediately clear that his interest was aroused. Sending her a secret message he asked her name and learned of her family background and life. As a result of this glances were cast from their eyes at one another, and there was a constant turning of their faces and exchanges of smiles. Finally agreements were made and a marriage compact." (35.3–5) (Plutarch, "Sulla")

It seems that this woman did not satisfy the desires of the dictator, for Plutarch continues with the report that Sulla spent the days drinking with actresses, musicians and actors (36.1).

WOMEN AND CATILINE

Twenty years later, in 62 BCE, another Roman surrounded himself with a bodyguard of reprobates and sought by various means to overthrow the government and become consul. A colourful report of the maneuvering of Catiline is provided by Gaius Sallustius Crispus (better known as "Sallust"), who was a provincial governor under Julius Caesar but retired to write history after the assassination of Caesar. His portrait of Catiline is of a reckless and unprincipled individual who as a young man preferred sex with virgins, including a Vestal. He married several women, and when the beautiful Aurelia Orestilla refused him because she feared his stepson from a former marriage he had the young man killed (15.1–3). Sallust reports that Catiline gathered a large number of the dispossessed around him to whom he promised the benefits derived from his proscription (i.e., condemnation with confiscation of the property) of the wealthy, adding to this official offices and priesthoods and general plunder. Catiline lost the consulship in 62 BCE, however, in part because of the betrayal of his designs by a lover of one of his supporters, a Roman woman of the noble class and one with a fearless disposition (21.2, 23.3). The woman's disclosure earned him the abiding hatred of Cicero, who obtained the consulship in his stead. Catiline continued to amass supporters, among whom, in Sallust's colourful account, were women of questionable repute.

"At that time he is said to have admitted to his side all sorts of men of various types, even some women. These had at first covered their enormous expenses by prostitution. Later, when age placed a considerable limit on their means of earning but no limit to their extravagance, they contracted debts on an enormous scale. Through these women Catiline believed he could rouse the support of the urban slaves, set fire to the city and either add their husbands to his ranks or kill them." (24.3–4)

From the foregoing it is clear that some women found the means to become politically involved at this time. Sallust's portrait of Sempronia, in which he balances praise for her education and talent with criticism for her want of moral scruples, is doubtless influenced by her entanglement with Catiline.

"But among these women was Sempronia, who had often committed many crimes of masculine daring. This woman was well blessed in her birth and beauty, and particularly in her husband and children. She was well-schooled in Greek and Latin literature; she played the lyre and danced more gracefully than was necessary for a woman of upright character, and skilled in many other means of serving an excessive way of life. But to her everything was more precious than dignity and chastity. You could hardly discern whether she was less sparing of her money or her reputation. Her lust was so inflamed that she more often sought out men than was sought out by them. Before [her involvement with Catiline] she had often gone back on her word, disowned her debts, been party to murder. Her wantonness and her lack of funds had driven her headlong. To be sure, her talent was far from inconsequential. She could compose verses, tell jokes, use language that was discreet, genteel or wanton. In plain terms she possessed a great deal of wit and charm." (25.1–5)
(Sallust, *The War with Catiline*)

WOMEN AND POMPEY

A near-contemporary of Catiline was the brilliant Roman general Pompey. With him as well as with other powerful figures like Sulla, and later Caesar and Octavian/Augustus, marriage was an important tool in sealing political alliances. As mentioned above (p. 83), Pompey's first marriage was to Antistia. Plutarch tells us that this marriage had come about because her father, in the course of serving as judge in a case where Pompey was defending himself against a charge of theft, admired the young man's acumen, acquitted him and offered him his daughter ("Pompey" 5.1). When Sulla had decided to procure the loyalty of Pompey by awarding him his stepdaughter Aemilia as wife, Pompey was obliged to divorce Antistia and, from Plutarch's account, the consequences for both women were serious.

"Admiring Pompey because of his prowess and thinking he was a strong support for his undertakings he was eager in some way to connect with him through some sort of family bond. His wife Metella agreed with him, and they persuaded Pompey to divorce Antistia and take as wife Aemilia, the stepdaughter of Sulla, born from Metella and Scaurus. But she was already living with a husband and was pregnant at the time.

The arrangement for the marriage was a product of tyranny and suited the opportunism of Sulla rather than the disposition of Pompey, considering that Aemilia was given to him in marriage when she was pregnant by another man, and Antistia was driven out in a dishonorable and pitiable manner, in that she had been recently deprived of a father because of her husband. For Antistius had been killed in the Senate-house for appearing to be a sympathizer of Sulla because of his connection to Pompey. And her mother, conscious of this, had taken her own life voluntarily, by suicide. The result was that this misfortune was also added to the tragic situation of that new marriage, and – what's more – there was the fact that Aemilia died in childbirth soon after moving in with Pompey." (9.1–3)

After Sulla's death in 78 BCE, the jostling for power continued among Romans who were in possession of armies with which they were directing Rome's expansion through the north of Italy into Gaul, in the East and westward to Spain. Pompey prevailed over the ambitions of two of these men, Brutus and Lepidus. When the latter lost his bid to become consul in Rome for a second term, he fled to Sardinia. (Plutarch reports that he died there of a broken heart, not because of his political defeat but because he had discovered some correspondence alleging that his wife was committing adultery [16.6].)

The year 60 BCE saw Pompey joining forces with two other powerful Romans, Julius Caesar and the wealthy Crassus. Caesar became consul in that year, and the political traffic in women continued. Caesar had married Cornelia, the daughter of Cinna who was a close friend of Crassus, and he strengthened his connection with Pompey by presenting him with his daughter Julia. Plutarch describes the marital configuration thus.

"Pompey married Julia, the daughter of Caesar, something that no one expected. She was engaged to Caepio and about to be married in a few days. As appeasement for the anger of Caepio Pompey promised him his own daughter, although she had earlier been betrothed to Faustus, the son of Sulla." (47.6)

Shifting political alliances doubtless influenced the rhetoric that informed later historical accounts such as that of Plutarch. When he reports that the young Julia enjoyed the affection of Pompey he describes this as a distraction with negative consequences for Rome. While Pompey dallied with her, he says, another ambitious Roman named Clodius took advantage of the situation.

"Soon Pompey was yielding to his passion for the young girl and devoted himself for the most part to her and spent his days in the country and in the gardens and neglected the activities in the Forum, with the result that Clodius, a tribune of the people at the time, despised him and touched upon some daring measures." (48.5)

These "daring measures" included the exile of Cicero. The enmity between Cicero and Clodius would figure in a forensic speech of the former (p. 97 below) in which Cicero attacked the tribune's sister. Pompey's devotion to Julia continued, despite public pressure to divorce her in order to distance himself from Caesar, for whom hostility was increasing in Rome. Delegating his military responsibilities to trusted subordinates, Pompey continued to enjoy his private life.

"... [H]e handed over his armies and his provinces to his trusted senior men, taking himself to the pleasure-spots around Italy, going from one to another while spending the time with his wife, either because he loved her or because he could not endure the thought of leaving her because she loved him. For this too is what is reported. The love of the young girl for her husband was much talked about, with her desire for Pompey not in keeping with his age, but the fidelity of the man seems to have been the reason, since he confined himself sexually to his wife alone. His seriousness was not severe, but full of charm when it came to relating to others, and he was particularly attractive to women. If it were called for, not even Flora the courtesan would testify to the contrary. During an election of officials, when some people came to blows and a number of them were killed near him he was covered in blood and changed his clothes. Amid the turbulence and running around that was happening the servants carried the garments to his house. His young wife, who happened to be pregnant, seeing the bloodstained toga, fainted and only with difficulty was revived. As a result of the shock and her distress she miscarried. From this point not even those who were most critical of Pompey for his friendship with Caesar blamed him for his love for his wife. She conceived again, nonetheless, and in giving birth to a daughter she died during labour, and the child did not survive for many days." (53.1–4)
(Plutarch, "Pompey")

The informal political alliance of Julius Caesar, Pompey and the wealthy Crassus came to be known as the "First Triumvirate" (a coalition of three men), an arrangement that helped them achieve their private aspirations when these were being curbed by the Senate. Their agendas were advanced by the election of Caesar as consul in 59 BCE. Their pact had been fortified by their marriages, however, and it began to unravel with the deaths of both Julia and Crassus, and the break between Caesar and Pompey became inevitable.

Pompey was elected sole consul in 53 BCE (an extraordinary move, since by law there were normally two) and he married once again, this time to Cornelia, the daughter of a conservative aristocrat whom he chose to take as his colleague in the consulship.

In an account of the Roman civil war by Lucan (a poet of the Neronian period, who composed what remains of his work between 61 and 65 CE) Pompey's deceased wife Julia visits him in a dream, warning him of the dire consequences of the shifting allegiance marked by this new bride.

"Thereupon a shade full of fearful dread
seemed to raise her gloomy head above the gaping earth
and to stand Fury-like at her flaming tomb.
'Driven out from the Elysian Fields and the plain of the Blessed Ones
I am dragged to the Stygian shadows and among the guilty shades
in the wake of the civil war. I myself saw the Eumenides
grasping torches to shake in keeping with your fighting forces.
The ferryman of scorched Acheron is readying countless boats;
Tartarus is expanding for the punishment of many.
All the Sisters, although their hands are nimble, are scarcely enough for the task;
the Fates are weary from breaking off the threads.
While I was your wife, Great Pompey, you conducted joyful triumphs.
Fortune has changed with the shift in your marriage-bed;
condemned by Fate always to drag down powerful husbands into disaster
Cornelia, bed-partner, married you while my tomb was still warm.' "
(Lucan, *Civil War* 3.9–23)

Like Sempronia (p. 85 above), Cornelia was a woman of culture and education. As in Pompey's earlier marriage there was an age disparity and it was another relationship that Plutarch describes as diverting Pompey from the affairs of state.

"Pompey entered the city and married Cornelia, the daughter of Metellus Scipio. She was not a virgin but had been recently left a widow with the death of Publius, the son of Crassus with whom she had lived as a virgin bride before his death in Parthia. In the young girl there were many alluring qualities apart from her youthful beauty. For she was superbly accomplished in literature, in playing the lyre and in geometry, and had accustomed herself to listen to philosophic discourse, to her advantage. In addition to this she had a disposition that was free from unpleas-antness and officiousness that such a degree of learning imparts to young women. Her father was beyond reproach, owing to his family lineage and reputation. Nevertheless to some it was not acceptable because of the age difference, for Cornelia was of an age more suited to marry his son. Those who were more scrupulous considered that Pompey had been overlooking the needs of the city, which was in difficult straits because of which it had chosen him as healer and entrusted itself to his care alone. He, on the other hand, had been wearing garlands and celebrating his marriage when he ought to have thought of his sole consulship as ill-fated, since it would not have been given to him in such an illegal manner if the city had been enjoying good fortune." (55.1–3)

Nonetheless, Pompey presided successfully over the courts according to Plutarch, but interfered in the trial of Cornelia's father, earning him more opprobrium. When serious skirmishes broke out between Pompey's forces and those of Caesar he sent Cornelia to Lesbos for her safekeeping (66.3). After a decisive rout by Caesar's forces at Pharsalus in northern Greece in 48 BCE, Pompey found a merchant sailor willing to transport him to Lesbos (73.3–4). When he arrived he sent ahead a messenger to his wife, informing her of his arrival but also of his defeat. Plutarch describes her as overcome with emotion as she rushed to meet him at the ship, where she insisted on bearing the blame for his fall.

"When Pompey met her he took her in his arms as she stumbled and fell. 'I see you' she said, 'a husband not the result of your own fortune but mine, thrown into one small boat, you who before your marriage to Cornelia sailed around in this sea with five hundred ships. Why did you come to see me and not abandon me to my heavy fate, the one who has also infected you with such bad luck? How fortunate a wife I would have been had I died before hearing of Publius' lying dead among the Parthians, I his virgin bride! And how prudent I would have been even after his dying, if I had cut short my own life as I was hastening to do! But I was saved and, as you see, only ruin befell Pompey the Great." (74.3)

Pompey tried to reconcile Cornelia to her fate in the hope that his fortunes would rise again, and taking her on board along with their son they made their way to Egypt. There he hoped for support from the young Ptolemy Dionysius, who at 15 was married to and shared the rule with his sister Cleopatra VII. Hostilities had erupted between brother and sister, and because of Ptolemy's youth the decision whether or not to accept Pompey rested with an Egyptian council. Fearful of antagonizing Caesar, who now had the upper hand in Rome, the council voted to kill Pompey. When Caesar arrived in Egypt after the murder he was filled with emotion on learning what had happened, and killed the assassins. Pompey's remains were lifted from the funeral pyre and given to Cornelia to bury at his villa near Rome (75–80).
(Plutarch, "Pompey")

WOMEN AND JULIUS CAESAR

Caesar had married a woman also named Cornelia (daughter of the consul Cinna) in 83 BCE when he was 17, divorcing a girl to whom he had been betrothed as a boy. At this time, Sulla was still exerting power in Rome and creating difficulties for Caesar who had displayed sympathies for the Marian faction (his aunt had married Marius). Upon Sulla's death in 78 BCE, Caesar began his upward trajectory in Rome. Having trained in oratory in Rhodes he delivered a funeral oration from the rostra (the speakers' podium) in the Forum when his aunt Julia died in 69 BCE – one of the earliest public funeral eulogies delivered for a woman. Plutarch reports that Caesar's brilliant speech was accompanied by a display of images of the ancestors of Marius, inflaming both the Marian and Sullan factions ("Caesar" 5.2–3). The biographer Suetonius (late first century CE), in his *The Lives of the Caesars,* reports that Caesar took the opportunity to praise his aunt's lineage, all the while presenting himself in reflected glory.

"In the eulogy for his aunt he spoke thus both about her own lineage and that of his father. 'The maternal family of my aunt Julia takes its origin from kings; on her father's side it is linked to the immortal gods. For from Ancus Marcius came the Marcii Reges ("Marcian Kings"), her mother's family name. The Julii, whose paternal name is that of our family, comes from Venus. So in our family line are both the sanctity of kings, which exerts the greatest power among men, and the divine majesty of the gods, to whom kings themselves are subject.' "
(Suetonius, "The Deified Julius" 6.1)

At almost the same time, Caesar's young wife Cornelia died in childbirth and he set another precedent, according to Plutarch, in delivering a public eulogy for a young woman. The reality that women were acquiring a public presence is reflected by the fact that there was a sympathetic response to his words, earning Caesar some new allies.

"The practice of delivering a funeral oration for older women was traditional for the Romans, but was not the custom for young women. Caesar was the first to deliver this kind of speech, giving a eulogy for his own wife when she died. This too brought him a certain amount of goodwill, and together with his grief it persuaded the ordinary people to attach themselves to him as a man of tenderness and one full of sensitivity."
(Plutarch, "Caesar" 5.2)

Shortly afterwards Caesar took another wife, Pompeia, granddaughter of Sulla. The marriage was short-lived, for soon Pompeia was implicated in a scandal involving Publius Clodius. Clodius' intrusion into the (all-female) rites of the Bona

Dea, which were held in Caesar's house in 62 BCE, led to a Senate investigation and to Caesar's divorcing Pompeia. A lively account of this is given by Plutarch. It is worth noting in this passage that Caesar's mother Aurelia clearly held a position of seniority and authority in the household and the festival it was hosting.

"Publius Clodius was a man of noble birth, brilliant in wealth and eloquence, but for arrogance and recklessness was second to none of those who were notorious for their depravity. This man was in love with Pompeia the wife of Caesar, and she herself was not unresponsive. But the women's quarters were closely guarded, and Caesar's mother Aurelia, a prudent woman, was keeping a constant eye upon his bride, making a meeting between the two a hazardous undertaking.

The Romans have a goddess called the Bona Dea 'Good Goddess'. She is like the Greeks' 'Women's Goddess', and the Phrygians, who claim her as their own, allege that she was the mother of King Midas. The Romans believe she was a dryad, bride of Faunus, while the Greeks think that she was one of the mothers of Dionysus, one who cannot be named. That is why the women holding her festival cover their tents with vine branches, and a sacred snake is seated beside the goddess, as myth has it. It is not right for a man to attend, nor even to be in the house while the rites are being celebrated. The women are on their own, and it is said that they carry out many sacred rituals similar to Orphic ones. So when the time for the festival arrives the master of the house – a consul or praetor – leaves along with all other males; his wife takes over the house and arranges everything. The most important rituals happen after dark, with revelry mixed into the nocturnal celebrations, to the accompaniment of much musical entertainment.

Pompeia was presiding over the festival this time. Clodius was still beardless, and on this account thinking he might not be noticed he came dressed up in the clothing and equipment of a harpist, looking just like a young girl. Finding the doors open he was led in fearlessly by a servant-girl who was aware of the plan and who ran ahead to alert Pompeia. Some time passed, and Clodius, not having the patience to stay where he had been left, was wandering around the big house, trying to stay out of the light. An attendant of Aurelia's came across him and invited him, as woman to woman, to come join the fun. When he refused she dragged him into the middle of the room and asked him who he was and where he had come from. When Clodius said that he was waiting for the favourite ['*habra*'] servant-girl of Pompeia (for she was called 'Habra') he was betrayed by his voice. The maid immediately ran off with a shout into the light and the crowd, crying out that she had detected a man. The women were struck with panic. Aurelia put a stop to the ceremonies for the goddess and covered up the sacred objects. She ordered the doors to be shut and went through the house with torches, looking for Clodius. He was found hiding in the quarters of the young servant-girl through whom he had been let in and was taking shelter. When he had been recognized by the women he was driven out through the doors. That very night the women went home and told their husbands of the affair. The next morning the story spread through the city, how Clodius had committed a sacrilege and not only owed compensation to those he had outraged but also to the city and to the gods.

As a result, one of the tribunes indicted Clodius for impiety, and the most powerful men in the Senate gave the tribune their backing. They provided evidence of other egregiously wanton behaviour of his, even incest with his sister, whose husband was Lucullus. But in the face of these efforts the people registered their opposition and defended Clodius. This helped him greatly with the jurors, who were terrified and frightened by the mob.

Caesar immediately divorced Pompeia, but when called into court as a witness he claimed that he knew nothing of the allegations against Clodius. Since this statement seemed strange, the accuser asked 'Why did you divorce your wife?' 'Because,' he said, 'I thought my wife should be above suspicion.'" (9.1–10.6)

Plutarch concludes this episode with the report that while some people thought Caesar was being sincere, others felt he was playing to the mob in their eagerness to see Clodius acquitted. Most of the jurors spoiled their votes.

Plutarch follows this with mention of Caesar's attempt to cement an alliance with Pompey by betrothing to him Julia, his daughter by Cornelia (p. 86 above). As co-consul in 59 BCE, Caesar himself married once again, this time to Calpurnia, the daughter of Calpurnius Piso. He repaid Piso by designating him consul for the ensuing year (14.7–8). Plutarch quotes Cato the Younger on this marriage-brokering.

"At this point Cato protested vehemently, and shouted that it was unbearable, that the leadership of the state had been bargained away through marriages, and that through women they were distributing to each other provinces, armies and powers." (14.5)

Cato himself was not above trafficking in wives for personal gain, however. In Plutarch's biography of Cato the Younger we read of a remarkable trading off of women. His wife Marcia enjoyed a reputation for beauty and respectability and had given him a daughter, Porcia. In 56 BCE the renowned orator Hortensius at the age of 60 requested Porcia as his bride, despite the fact that she was already married to Bibulus (co-consul with Caesar in 59 BCE), who was very attached to her. Porcia was pregnant at the time, and her fertility was one of her attractive features, along with the advantage of cementing a connection with Cato.

"Desiring to be not only a close friend and companion of Cato, but to unite in some way or other their complete households and bloodlines, he set himself to convince him that he should hand over his daughter Porcia as fertile ground in which to sow a new crop of children. (She was living with Bibulus and had produced two children for him.)

'Such a thing might seem strange to men, but it is by nature an honorable and politically advantageous thing for a woman in the prime of her youth and at the peak of her fertility not to lie fallow, extinguishing her fruitfulness, and there is no need for her to burden and impoverish a home by bearing more children than needed. Successive sharing among worthy men makes for an increase in valour and increases through posterity, and the city itself will have been refreshed in its polity through the marriage alliances.'"

After this rhetorical appeal to Cato, Hortensius conceded that Bibulus might not agree to divorce his wife, and if so he would return her as soon as she had given him a child. Cato answered that, while he was fond of Hortensius and approved of uniting their households, he thought it strange for him to take Porcia when she was already married to someone else. Hortensius did not abandon his petition but changed direction slightly, asking instead for Cato's wife Marcia. Marcia was pregnant and had already produced two children, hence Cato did not need any more. Cato recognized his earnest determination, and agreed to the proposition if Marcia's father concurred. The couple were divorced and Marcia married Hortensius, giving him an heir before he died five years later. Two years after his death, Marcia rejoined Cato's household.

Caesar's military and political successes continued after his acquisition of the consulship in 59 BCE. However, for the next 15 years he was never free of the suspicion of having autocratic ambitions. With the death of his daughter Julia in childbirth the bond with Pompey had been weakened, and in time they became arch-rivals for control of Rome. In 48 BCE both generals were commanding expeditionary forces of Roman citizen allies in Greece, and there was a military showdown at Pharsalus. Pompey was defeated and escaped to Alexandria, only to be killed by the Egyptians (p. 89 above). Caesar rushed to Alexandria in pursuit of Pompey, but was presented with Pompey's head.

When hostilities broke out between Ptolemy XIII and his sister Cleopatra, the queen had been driven into exile in Syria. While in Egypt, Caesar planned to broker a resolution of this dispute, and sent for Cleopatra to come in secret. Plutarch comments that Cleopatra's scheme to leave Syria and arrive in Alexandria secretly, wrapped up in a sack of bedding, was what first captivated Caesar (49.1–2).

The co-regency arranged by Caesar was short-lived, and battle ensued. Ptolemy XIII was defeated, escaped and disappeared. Plutarch concludes this with the report of Caesar's leaving Cleopatra on the throne and her giving birth to his son Caesarion ("Caesar" 49.1–10).

Suetonius adds some further details, claiming that Caesar's conquests led him to have love affairs with other queens as well. With Cleopatra, however, he continued to enjoy all-night revelling, and his desire to stay and travel throughout Egypt with her, Suetonius comments, was foiled only by the refusal of his troops to follow him ("The Deified Julius" 52.1).

Back in Rome in 47 BCE, Caesar was granted the honour of celebrating four triumphs and enjoying the title of dictator. Suspicions increased that he was seeking permanent sole rule, even kingship, and these fears would have been increased by the presence of Cleopatra, whom he had installed with her son in a villa just outside the city walls. On the 15th (Ides) of March he was assassinated as he entered the Senate House. There had been unfavourable omens and prodigies in the days prior, and both Plutarch and Suetonius refer to signs that appeared during the night before his murder, when he lay beside Calpurnia in bed. Here is Suetonius' account.

"In fact, on that very night out of which arose the day of the murder he saw himself in a dream flying above the clouds, and in other visions clasping the right hand of Jupiter. His wife Calpurnia dreamed that the pediment of their house collapsed and that her husband was stabbed in her arms. Suddenly the doors of the bedroom flew open of their own accord."
(Suetonius, "The Deified Julius" 81.3)

WOMEN AND CICERO

An important figure whose life intersected with all major figures of the Late Republic was Marcus Tullius Cicero. He held virtually all major political offices and was deeply affected by the civil wars in Rome. He spoke and acted consistently on behalf of the preservation of Republican values, and for this he suffered exile and was ultimately beheaded under the Second Triumvirate. He left a rich collection of writings, including forensic speeches, philosophy, studies in oratory and letters to his friends. From his speeches and writings we can get a glimpse of his views on some Roman women, including his wife and daughter.

About his wife Terentia we get a negative picture from some of his letters and from the account of Plutarch, who describes her as someone who benefited from his frequent absence to get her hands on his money. The strain on the marriage produced by his frequent absence from Rome eventually led to their divorce after more than 30 years of marriage, and Cicero's disaffected correspondence from this period likely accounts for the hostile tone of most accounts of Terentia, ancient and modern.

This was an elite marriage, one in which Terentia as well as her husband had complex financial accounts. For most of their married life Cicero entrusted to her, together with their freedman steward, the management of their properties and financial resources. Cicero also frequently counted on her to intervene with friends on behalf of his political advancement and safety. In the early years of their marriage this security was not threatened, and from letters such as the following, to his friend and regular correspondent Atticus, we get the picture of a man who, when confidantes like Atticus or his brother were not at hand, consoled himself with the deep attachment he felt to his wife, his daughter and his son.

"… what relaxation I get is the time spent with my wife, my little daughter and my darling son Cicero. My opportunistic and counterfeit friendships make for a fine display in the Forum, but at home they are fruitless. And so when my house is well filled in the morning, when I go down to the Forum with a crowded retinue of friends, I cannot discover a soul out of that huge crowd with whom I can joke freely or breathe a sigh on intimate terms."
(Cicero, *Letters to Atticus* 1.18.1)

By the year 58 BCE, Clodius (the intruder in the Bona Dea ritual, pp. 90–2 above) had become tribune, and to seek revenge for Cicero's ongoing hostility toward him he introduced a law that summarily caused Cicero's exile. (This was based upon the charge that Cicero had violated the constitution in ordering the death of the conspirators with Catiline when he was consul.) As Cicero was leaving Italy for exile he was despondent, knowing this could mean the end of his political life, but a letter to Terentia indicates that what grieved him most was the fracturing of his family life and the fact that his own political choices had led to this.

"From the letters of many people and from everyone's reports I am made aware of your incredible courage and strength, and that you are never worn down by your efforts of mind and body. How miserable I am, with the thought that you, with that courage of yours, your loyalty, your integrity, your generosity, have fallen into such hardship because of me! And that our dear little Tullie, in whom her father took such great delight, now feels such grief because of him."
(Cicero, *Letters to His Friends* [here, to Terentia and his family] 14.1.1)

Terentia, along with their daughter Tullia and Cicero's brother Quintus, worked tirelessly for his reinstatement, and he returned to Rome in a little over a year. While Cicero remained close to his brother for most of his life (until contrary political alliances drove them apart), Quintus' wife Pomponia (the sister of Cicero's friend Atticus) appears to have been a source of tension for all of them. There were strains in the marriage from the beginning, and Pomponia seems to have been reluctant to extend the usual courtesies expected of a Roman matron, as Cicero complains in a letter to Atticus in describing a visit to a farm belonging to Quintus.

"When we arrived there Quintus said in a very kindly way, 'Pomponia, you invite the women in and I will fetch the boys.' Nothing could have been gentler, at least as it seemed to me, than the words with which he spoke, together with his disposition and expression. But she, within our hearing, said, 'I myself am a guest in this place.' That was a consequence, I think, of the fact that Statius (Quintus' freedman) had gone ahead to see about the lunch for us. Then Quintus said, 'So you see,' he said to me, 'this is what I put up with every day.'"
(Cicero, *Letters to Atticus* 5.1.3)

The letter continues with the report that Pomponia left the dinner party and rejected the food that Quintus arranged to have sent to her. She refused to sleep with him that night, although it was the eve of his departure with Cicero for Cilicia, where the two men would spend the next year and a half as proconsul and general respectively.

Cicero was deeply devoted to his daughter Tullia, to whom he affectionately referred as "Tullie" (*Tulliola*). From exile in Thessalonica he wrote to his brother saying that just as he missed him so he missed his daughter deeply, for to her father she was a kindred spirit.

"What of the fact that at the same time I miss my daughter? Such faithfulness, such unassuming conduct, such intelligence! The very likeness of me in her face, in her speech, in her mind!"
(Cicero, *Letters to his Brother Quintus* 1.3.3)

Widowed once and divorced twice, Tullia felt a bond with her father that was stonger than with any other man. Her father was devastated when she died from complications after childbirth at the age of 34. Answering a letter of consolation from his friend Sulpicius, he wrote that even his achievements in public life did not offer the compensation of distraction.

"But for me, however, once those distinctions were lost of which you yourself are reminding me, and which I had acquired by the most extreme efforts, there remained one comfort – which has now been snatched from me. My brooding over this was not checked by the affairs of my friends, nor by responsibilities of state. I took no pleasure in activities in the Forum; I couldn't bear to look at the Senate House. I thought to myself, as was the case, that I had lost all the fruits of my hard work and my success. But when I reflected that these losses were shared with you and certain others and when I tried to break through these thoughts and to force myself to bear this patiently, I had a place of refuge where I could take comfort, someone with whose conversation and sweet disposition I could lay aside all my worries and sorrows. Now, however, with

this deep wound even those wounds that seemed to have healed are opening up afresh."
(Cicero, *Letters to his Friends* 4.6.2)

Tullia died in 45 BCE, and Cicero was killed two years later.

Cicero had words of praise for other women, including the daughter of Gaius Laelius and her own daughters and granddaughters, all of whom seemed to have inherited the oratorical skills that ran in the family.

"Speeches of Laelia, the daughter of Gaius, often reached my ears. I saw that her speaking was coloured with the polished manner of her father's. This was true also of both of her daughters, the Muciae, whose discourse was well-known to me, and indeed that of her granddaughters the Liciniae."
(Cicero, *Brutus* 58.211)

Not all women received kindly treatment by Cicero. One who became the target of Cicero's formidable power as an advocate was Clodia, the sister of Clodius, the man responsible for his exile. Well educated in Greek and philosophy, with a reputation as a competent poet, Clodia also led a life of some notoriety. Her marriage to her first cousin was not a happy one, and she seems to have enjoyed liaisons with a number of men, including one Marcus Caelius Rufus. When the relationship ended in 56 BCE, she accused Caelius of attempting to poison her. That year Caelius was indicted on several serious charges involving disturbances in Rome and even murder. Clodia, his ex-lover, supplied evidence to support the prosecution. Cicero took part in Caelius' defence, discrediting her testimony with an attack on Clodia that was filled with some none-too-subtle innuendo. The speech accused her of living the life of a prostitute and of profligacy that included incest with her brother, the real target of Cicero's vehement attack on his sister.

"But if that woman were removed from the case there would remain neither a case against Marcus Caelius nor the means available to his opponents to attack him. What else should we do as his defence counsel except to refute those who are accusing him? That I would certainly do more vigorously if the hostility between me and this woman's husband – I mean brother – were not interfering. (I always make this mistake.) Now I will conduct my case with moderation and not go further than my responsibility to my client and the case itself obliges me. For I never thought I would have to undertake disputes with women, especially with a woman whom everyone has always considered was everybody's girl-friend rather than anyone's enemy."
(Cicero, *Pro Caelio* 13.32)

Clodia may well be the woman called "Lesbia" by the Roman poet Catullus. He composed several poems chronicling a love affair marked by equal intensity in the rapture of its beginning and the bitterness of its end. Lesbia received this pseudonym because of Catullus' high regard for the quality of her poetry, equal in his estimation to that of the famous Greek poet from the island of Lesbos, Sappho.

"Let us live, my Lesbia, and let us love,
and all the gossip of old men, who are too mean-minded,
let us consider hardly worth a penny.
Suns may set and rise again;
for us, when once the brief light of day is over
there is one night for sleeping, without end.
Give me a thousand kisses, then a hundred!
Then another thousand, then a second hundred,
then as many as another thousand, then a hundred!
Then, when we have made up many thousands
we will mix up the record, so we won't know,
and no one with evil intent can cast an evil eye
when he knows how many kisses there are."
(Catullus, Poem 5)

In the following poem, Lesbia has apparently lost interest in Catullus, who confides in his friend Caelius (perhaps the Caelius of Cicero's speech). With a certain amount of playful exaggeration, Catullus dismisses her in mock-epic terms as a woman of the streets.

"Oh Caelius, my Lesbia, that Lesbia,
that Lesbia, the one woman whom Catullus loved
more than himself and all his close friends,
now she strips the descendants of lordly Remus
in the crossroads and alley-ways."
(Catullus, Poem 58)

CHELIDON AND VERRES

Prostitution was a useful rhetorical tool in targeting enemies. In 70 BCE Cicero took on the prosecution of Verres, who had been a particularly rapacious governor of Sicily. The speeches, later published as the "Verrine Orations", succeeded in bringing about Verres' banishment. Cicero highlighted the man's association with prostitutes, and targeted one by the name of Chelidon ("Swallow"), whom he accuses of influence-peddling with the governor, controlling issues of civil law and private disputes that should have been heard publicly.

"They went, as I said, to Chelidon. Her house was full – judicial decisions, decrees, sentences, were being petitioned, and none of them publicly known: 'See that he gives me possession'; 'See that he doesn't take it away from me'; 'See that he doesn't pronounce judgement against me'; 'See that he awards me the property'. Some were paying her cash, tablets of pledges were sealed. The house was crammed full, not with a courtesan's patrons but with a crowd that attends a praetor's court."
(Cicero, *Verrine Orations* 2.1.52)

VESTALS: CRASSUS AND CLODIUS

The Vestal Licinia had the good and bad fortune to own a villa on the outskirts of Rome. In Plutarch's account of Crassus we read that this powerful man, a member of the First Triumvirate with Caesar and Pompey (p. 87 above), wished to purchase the villa, and his attention to her attracted prosecution for sexual misconduct on her part.

"When he was more advanced in years he was charged with having sex with Licinia, one of the Vestal Virgins. Licinia escaped punishment, being accused by a certain prosecutor named Plotius. She had a lovely house in the suburbs that Crassus wanted to obtain for a low price, and because of this he was always at the woman's side and paying attention to her, until he fell under suspicion for that offence. He was let off the charge of corrupting her because of his general disposition toward avarice, and was acquitted by the jurors. But he did not let Licinia out of his clutches until he had gained control of her property."
(Plutarch, "Crassus" 1.2)

Another Vestal who was accused of consorting with a powerful man of the Late Republic was Fabia, the half-sister of Cicero's wife Terentia. Fabia was accused by the infamous Clodius of having been corrupted by Catiline, but the upright and conscientious senator Cato the Younger exposed the ruse, and Clodius was driven out of town (Plutarch, "Cato the Younger" 19.3).

WOMEN AND MARK ANTONY

In Plutarch's biography of Antony we get the picture of a Roman who was at once a strong military leader and a weak man given to overindulging in the softer pleasures. He seems to have earned a reputation for womanizing from a young age. After Julius Caesar had taken control of the city as dictator, Antony was enjoying particular favour because of the military skill that he had demonstrated in supporting Caesar in the defeat of Pompey at Pharsalus in 48 BCE. Plutarch comments, however, that Mark Antony was incurring the hostility of many Roman men for having affairs with their wives (6.6). His first wife, Antonia, a cousin, he divorced because he suspected her of having sex with a popular tribune, Dolabella. He then gave himself over to drinking and debauchery, travelling to other cities with the popular mime actress Cytheris (9.2–7).

Cicero referred to Cytheris in a letter to his philosopher-friend Paetus as a symposiastic courtesan and mistress of one Volumnius Eutrapelus (*Letters to his Friends* 9.26). In one of his *Philippics* (public orations aimed at discrediting Antony) Cicero described a procession in which Antony appeared as tribune together with Cytheris who seemed to be enjoying the status of his wife, a role Cicero likened to her relationship with her earlier lover Volumnius.

"As tribune of the plebs he was being driven in a war-chariot; lictors with laurel-crowns preceded him, among whom a female mime was being carried in an open litter. She was a woman whom respectable men from the towns, coming out expressly to meet her, greeted not by that well-known professional name of hers but as Volumnia. There followed a travelling-carriage with pimps, nefarious companions. His mother in the rear attended the girl-friend of her vile son as if she were a daughter-in-law."
(Cicero, *Philippics* 2.24.58)

When Caesar returned to the city from campaigning in Africa and elsewhere, he began to curb Antony's excesses. A sign of this new restraint was Antony's marriage to Fulvia, the figure before whom Hortensia would plead the cause of the proscribed (p. 107 below). Fulvia's first husband had died – Clodius, the Roman who achieved notoriety for breaking into the Bona Dea celebrations. Plutarch speculates that Antony's having to reckon with Fulvia was training for the challenges he would later face with another woman who wouldn't submit to control by men.

"Putting aside that way of life he turned his attention to marriage, and wedded Fulvia who had been married to Clodius the demagogue. She was a woman who paid no attention to spinning or housekeeping, nor thought it a good idea to rule over a common man, but wished to rule a ruler and command a commander. As a result, Cleopatra was indebted to Fulvia for the training of Antony in being controlled by women, since she took him over completely subdued and schooled from the beginning to listen to women." (10.3)

When Octavian, Mark Antony and Lepidus sealed over their differences and formed the Second Triumvirate in 43 BCE, they followed the practice of cementing political alliance with marriage. Octavian married Clodia, the daughter of Fulvia and Clodius. An intense and violent series of proscriptions ensued (p. 107 below), including the beheading of Cicero. The brother of Antony's mother, Lucius Caesar, was in line for the same treatment, and fled to the house of his sister. Plutarch describes Antony's mother as a woman who would not back down easily, and who had no difficulty in holding the triumvirs at bay.

"She, when the executioners were standing in front of her and forcing their way into her chamber, stood in the doorway and spread out her arms and shouted over and over, 'Do not kill Lucius Caesar, unless you first kill me, the one who gave birth to your imperator.' Being such a woman, then, she got her brother out of their hands and saved his life." (20.3)

Antony then headed to the eastern provinces to raise funds for rewarding Roman soldiers. In 41 BCE he crossed from Greece to Asia, where we are told by Plutarch that he reverted to his earlier mode of living, as kings presented him with gifts and their wives with their virtue (24.1). In Cilicia he first encountered Cleopatra who readied herself for the conquest of a man she in fact regarded as beneath her.

"She received many letters from him and from his friends that were summoning her, but she held the man in such low esteem and mocked him to such a degree that she sailed up the Cydnus river on a barge with a gilded stern, purple sails unfurled and its rowers gliding it forward with silver-handled oars to the sound of the aulos blending with that of the syrinx and lyres. She herself reclined under a canopy woven with golden threads, adorned like painters depict Aphrodite. Children resembling paintings of Erotes stood on either side, fanning her. Similarly, servant-girls – the most beautiful ones – dressed like Nereids and Graces, were positioned, some at the tillers and others at the ropes. Marvelous scents from the many incense-burners wafted over the riverbanks." (26.1–2)

Plutarch's description continues with the report that Antony, who had been stationed at the tribunal in the agora (the public place of assembly), was abandoned by the inhabitants who rushed to the shore to watch. Cleopatra invited him to dinner, where he was overcome with the display of lights that accompanied a sumptuous feast. The following night he entertained her in much simpler style, and the disparity was not lost on either. The queen displayed her charm and brilliance, not least reflected in her command of many languages and dialects. While his wife Fulvia attempted to negotiate tensions with Octavian back in Rome, and while his military responsibilities should have kept him quelling hostilities between the Parthians and Syria, Antony headed for Alexandria with Cleopatra. There they spent their time in luxurious pursuits, feasting, drinking, gaming and hunting. Plutarch received some of this information from his grandfather: the man had heard tales of the extravagant dinners from a friend who had been in Alexandria attending Antony's son by Fulvia, who was accompanying his father (26.3–28.4).

According to Plutarch, word was then brought to Antony that in Rome his brother and Fulvia were waging war against Octavian, and in the East the Parthians were engaging in major expansion along the Ionian coast. He left Alexandria, intending to combat the Parthians, when he received a letter of distress from Fulvia and redirected his course toward Italy. During the voyage he met some friends from Rome who claimed that it was his wife who had initiated the attacks on Octavian, hoping to lure her husband away from Cleopatra and back to Italy. While sailing to meet Antony, Fulvia fell ill and died. Antony sailed on to Rome and reconciled with Octavian, both of them laying the blame for the aggression on Fulvia. They sealed this renewed alliance, in which they divided up spheres of influence, by another marriage. Antony was given Octavian's sister Octavia, who had been recently left a widow. This marriage buoyed up hopes for peace in the city, although Antony's continuing passion for Cleopatra was no secret (30.1–4, 31.1–2).

"Everyone advocated for the marriage, hoping that Octavia, possessing in addition to her considerable beauty nobility and intelligence, once joined in marriage to Antony and loved by him – as is inevitable for such a woman – would be the saviour of the whole situation and assure harmony between the two men." (31.2)

Octavia produced two daughters with Antony and when pregnant with her third child was called upon to intervene between her husband and brother when hostilities once again threatened to erupt. She met Octavian in the south of Italy, while Antony waited offshore with the 300 ships that he had intended to use to threaten his brother-in-law (35.1). She pleaded with her husband on her own behalf.

"In her meeting with him she implored him with desperation and begged him insistently not to let her become – she who had been the most fortunate – the most wretched of women. For now, she said, the eyes of all men were focused on her in relation to two imperators, as the wife of one and the sister of the other. 'If the worse should prevail,' she said, 'and war should erupt, it is unclear which one of you is fated to win and which to lose, but in my case it is disastrous either way.'" (35.2–3)

The two men reconciled once again, exchanging military resources for each other's advantage, and Antony sailed east to Asia with Octavia and the children (both theirs and the others who had been born earlier to Fulvia and Antony).

Cleopatra surfaced once again when Antony summoned her to Syria, and when they met he conferred upon her the control of a number of eastern kingdoms that had been conquered by Rome, heightening resentment against him from his countrymen. He also acknowledged as his the two children who had been born to the queen (36). When she returned to Egypt, Antony resumed military activity against the Parthians and assembled a large force as he moved further east into Asia. His infatuation with the queen led him to make some precipitous decisions, however, in the interest of returning to Egypt. This led to a major defeat and loss of life at the hands of the Parthians (37.4–50). At his lowest ebb he sent for Cleopatra, who sent clothing and money for his soldiers (51.2).

Octavia, meanwhile, had gone back to Rome. She appealed to her brother to permit her to join Antony and Octavian conceded, in Plutarch's view, not out of personal concern for her but to quell popular resentment for the scornful treatment she was receiving from her husband, which was generating pressure for him to revive plans to make war on Antony (53.1). In 35 BCE, Octavia left for Athens, and the correspondence between husband and wife reflected the pathos of her situation.

"When she came to Athens she received letters from Antony bidding her to wait there and describing what was happening with his expedition. She, although upset and recognizing this as a ploy, nonetheless wrote him asking where he wanted sent the things she was bringing to him. She was conveying a great quantity of military clothing, a large number of pack animals, money and gifts for his officers and friends. Besides these there were two thousand elite soldiers equipped to serve as praetorian cohorts outfitted with splendid armour. A friend of Antony's named Niger was sent by her and announced this, and added words of praise as were fitting and merited." (53.1–2)

Plutarch's sources, playing up the drama of the situation, led him to report this as a showdown looming between the two women that was obliging Antony to make a choice. Octavia returned to Rome, living in Antony's house and caring for his children, urging her brother to ignore her ill-treatment by her husband in the interest of avoiding civil war. She intervened with Octavian to meet the needs of Antony's supporters when they came to Rome. This, writes Plutarch, damaged Antony's reputation even more seriously, as Romans perceived the unwarranted neglect by her husband. Hatred for Antony increased with his actions in Egypt when he made public his gifts of several kingdoms to the queen and established Caesarion, the son of Cleopatra and Julius Caesar, as her co-regent. To the sons that Cleopatra had borne to Antony he awarded other kingdoms (54.1–5).

Antony made unequivocal his preference for Cleopatra by ejecting Octavia (with the children) from his house in Rome, and tensions mounted between the two leaders. Over the next year, military preparations increased on both sides and in 32 BCE the Senate voted to declare war on Antony (58.1–60.1). A sea battle was fought off the coast of Actium, a promontory on the west coast of Greece. Antony's fleet was inferior to Octavian's but Cleopatra supplied 200 vessels and to please her, according to Plutarch, Antony agreed to a naval battle although his land forces were superior (56.1, 62.1). Cleopatra, however, stationed herself and her ships in such a position as to make a ready escape if needed (63.5). When she saw that they were being outmanoeuvred by Octavian, Cleopatra fled, followed by Antony in a small boat pursuing her and abandoning his forces (66.8). (Plutarch, "Antony")

In the *Aeneid*, the great epic poem composed by Vergil between 29 and 19 BCE that celebrated the achievements of Octavian/Augustus, the poet describes the defeat of the pair and Cleopatra's escape, a futuristic scene depicted on the shield that had been forged by the Cyclops for the Trojan hero Aeneas as he prepared for battle in Italy.

"She was portrayed sailing off, having called for fair winds,
with the swollen sails loosened more and more.
The Fire-god had rendered her borne through the waves with the westerly wind
through the carnage, pale with the prospect of her impending death.
Beyond her, however, he portrayed the Nile grieving throughout its entire length,
throwing open the folds and inviting the conquered
into the deep-blue bosom of its whole garment and into the refuge of its streams."
(Vergil, *Aeneid* 8.707–13)

Plutarch describes the two as resuming their life at the palace in Egypt where once again they engaged in extravagant living, but now founded an association called "Dying Together" (71.3). Cleopatra was still in charge of her fate. Testing various drugs for their death-dealing properties, she decided that the bite of the asp would bring on a death that was the least troublesome, akin to falling asleep (71.4–5). She had a tomb and monument erected for herself near the temple of Isis (74.2). Antony gave himself a mortal wound with his sword, but did not die before he was carried to Cleopatra's tomb and lifted through an open window where he died at her side (77.2–4). At the news of Antony's death, Octavian sped to Alexandria, hoping to take the queen alive. Antony's son by Fulvia who had accompanied his father to Alexandria was beheaded and Caesarion was killed later (81.1, 82.1).

Receiving word that Octavian was planning to dispatch her to Rome in a few days, Cleopatra arranged for her death. Plutarch reports that she dressed herself in royal attire, reclined on a golden couch and arranged for a servant to deliver to her a basket of figs in which an asp was concealed, baring her arm for the bite. Other versions of her death circulated, but Octavian publicized this one by carrying in his triumphal procession an image of Cleopatra with an asp clinging to her (Plutarch, "Antony" 85.1–3, 86.3).

Throughout the period when Cleopatra held Rome's leading men in thrall, negative propaganda about the Egyptian queen circulated in the city, fuelling fears lest all the hard-fought Roman conquests fall into her hands. The intense relief with which news of her death was received is reflected in this ode by Horace, a leading poet of Rome who lived through the violent years of the civil wars and celebrated the peace that came after Actium.

"Now is the time for drinking, now is the time for drumming the earth
with feet that are unbound; time to decorate
the couches of the gods
with Salian feasts, my comrades!
Until now bringing out Caecuban wine
from our ancient cellars was forbidden,
as long as the queen was plotting mad destruction
of the Capitol and devastation for the empire as well.
This with her polluted herd of men
foul with disease, delirious enough
to hope for anything and drunk
on sweet good fortune.
But a single ship barely preserved from the flames
lessened her fury, and Caesar redirected
her mind that was deluded by Mareotic wine
toward genuine terror.
He chased her speeding away from Italy,
plying his oars just as a hawk
pursues the gentle doves, or a swift hunter
a rabbit over the snowy fields of Thessaly,
so that he might put in chains
the treacherous monster. She, anxious to die
a nobler death, neither blanched at the sword
with a woman's fear nor made her way
to an out-of-the-way shore with her swift fleet.
She even dared to gaze upon her fallen palace
with a serene countenance, and to handle
deadly asps without fear,
that she might drink deeply of the black poison throughout her body.
She was more fiercely set upon death,

especially scorning being ferried on hostile Liburnian ships
for a proud triumph – no longer a queen.
She was a woman not to be laid low.
(Horace, *Odes* I.37)

14

Some remarkable Roman women of the Late Republic

HORTENSIA

In the year 44 BCE after the assassination of Julius Caesar, the Second Triumvirate had been formed (p. 101 above). Unlike the first unofficial alliance, this one was officially recognized and given powers greater even than those of the consuls or the Senate. Encountering opposition from other leading Romans like Cicero, and eager to increase the holdings in the treasury to cover their expenses, the triumvirs instituted proscriptions, in which certain individuals would be targeted for removal of their citizen rights, confiscation of their property and in many cases death. (Proscription had earlier been practised by Sulla when he became dictator for the same reasons.) Still short of funds for their military ambitions, the triumvirs made demands on the wealthy women of Rome.

Appian, a Greek historian of the second century CE who left a valuable account of the period of the civil wars in Rome, describes the edict and the reaction of the women, who first approached the female relatives of the triumvirs then mounted a public rebuttal through their spokeswoman Hortensia, the daughter of the well-known orator Hortensius.

"Announcing this to the people they posted a list of the 1400 women who were most noted for their wealth. These women had to have their possessions assessed and contribute to the war expenses as much as the triumvirs determined in each case. For those concealing some of their property or underestimating its value penalties were imposed and rewards were offered for those people – both free and slave – who disclosed this. The women decided to appeal for help from the female relatives of the rulers. They did not fail in the case of the sister of either Octavian or Antony's mother. But when Fulvia, the wife of Antony, pushed them away from her door, they did not put up with her insolence and forced their way to the Forum, to the podium of the triumvirs. The people and the praetorian guards stood aside and they spoke through Hortensia, who had been selected for this purpose.

'As was fitting for these women making an appeal to you we sought protection from your womenfolk. But what we suffered at the hands of Fulvia was inappropriate, and we were driven as a group by her to come to the Forum. You have already deprived us of our fathers and sons and husbands and brothers by proscribing them, saying that you have been wronged by them. If you rob us of our property as well you will convert our situation to one that is unseemly – unworthy of our families, our way of life and our female nature. If you allege that you have been wronged by us as you were by our husbands, then proscribe us too as you did them. But if not one of us women has voted that any of you is an enemy of the state and we have not demolished your houses or destroyed your army, nor led another army against you or prevented you from seeking office or obtaining honours, why should we share the punishment when we had no part in the wrongdoing?

Why should we contribute, when we have no share in public office or honours or military commands or public affairs at all, to share in such a degree of terrible conflict that is actually your doing? Because, you say, there is a war? Well, when have there not been wars? And when have women joined in paying war taxes? Our nature grants us exemption among all human societies. Our foremothers paid taxes on one single occasion in the past, beyond the expectation for their sex, when you were in danger of losing all power and the city itself, when the Carthaginians were harassing you. On that occasion they paid the taxes voluntarily, and not from their land or their estates or their dowry or houses, without which life would be unlivable for free women, but from the jewellery they had at home, and not when its value had been assessed, nor under the threat of informers or accusers nor from compulsion or force, but as much as these women wanted to contribute. What fear do you have now for your government or your fatherland? Well now, say there is war with the Gauls or with the Parthians and we will not be less cooperative in obtaining salvation than our foremothers. But when it comes to civil war we would never pay taxes nor participate with you in fighting one another. Not under Caesar or Pompey did we pay tax, nor did Marius or Cinna or Sulla compel us (the one who was a tyrant over this country). You, on the other hand, claim to be reinstating the Republic!'" (4.5.32–3)

The triumvirs were angry at first but under pressure from the crowd modified their demands, ultimately broadening the population base from whom they would require contributions.

"When Hortensia had said this the triumvirs were annoyed that, while men were keeping quiet the women were emboldened and making public speeches, interrogating the actions of the government, and while the men were serving as soldiers the women would not even contribute money. They ordered the attendants to drive them away from the tribunal, until a shout arose from the crowd outside, and the attendants halted what they were doing. The triumvirs said that they were deferring the question until the following day. The next day they posted a notice to the effect that they would assess the property of 400 instead of 1400 women, and of men – anyone having more than 100,000 *denarii*, whether a citizen or foreigner, a freedman or priest, no matter what the nation of origin, with no exceptions, and these people too were subject to the same fear of punishment and the same situation regarding informers. They were to lend them immediately two per cent of their wealth and pay a year's tax for the war." (4.5.34)

(Appian, *The Civil Wars*)

Valerius Maximus applauded the actions and words of Hortensia.

"Now when it comes to Hortensia, the daughter of Quintus Hortensius, when the rank of matrons had been heavily burdened by the triumvirs with a heavy tax and none of the men dared to lend them their defence, she conducted the case for the women before the triumvirs both assiduously and successfully. By reviving the eloquence of her father she brought it about that the greater part of the tax that had been imposed was lifted from them. Quintus Hortensius lived again in his female offspring and breathed through the words of his daughter. If his male offspring had wished to follow the path she took, such a great heritage of Hortensian eloquence would not have been cut short by the single action of a woman."

(Valerius Maximus, *Nine Books of Memorable Deeds and Sayings* 8.3.3)

MAESIA

Valerius Maximus pays tribute to several women besides Hortensia who displayed courage and skill. One woman who received his approval was Maesia of Sentinum who, instead of hiring an advocate, defended herself in court in 77 BCE.

"Maesia of Sentium as a defendant pleaded her own case when Lucius Titius was presiding over the court as praetor. She conducted this before a very large assembly of people, following through all the forms and components of her defence not only meticulously but even boldly, and she was acquitted at the first hearing and by almost a unanimous vote. They called her 'Androgyne', because underneath her womanly form she bore the spirit of a man." (8.3.1)

CARFANIA

Some women who spoke up in front of magistrates Valerius Maximus found less impressive, such as Carfania, the wife of a senator during the consulship of Caesar, whom he regarded as simply litigious.

"Carfania, on the other hand, the wife of the senator Licinius Buccio, was ever on hand to invite lawsuits, and always spoke on her own behalf before the praetor. This was not because she was lacking in advocates but because she was spilling over with impudence. So by constantly plaguing the tribunals with her barking – something unheard of in the Forum – she became the most famous example of a quarrelsome woman, to the degree that the name of 'Carfania' is a term of reproach when there is a charge of shameless behaviour in a woman. She prolonged her life, moreover, until the second consulship of Gaius Caesar with Publius Servilius serving as co-consul. In the case of such a monster the date of its death must be handed down to the record, rather than the one on which it was born." (8.3.2) (Valerius Maximus, *Nine Books of Memorable Deeds and Sayings*)

WIVES OF THE PROSCRIBED

The triumvirs' proscriptions of their opponents had broader consequences for the wives than economic constraints. Dispossessed of their houses and property, which were seized to reward soldiers loyal to the triumvirs as well as to fill the state coffers, many men attempted to escape from Rome and take refuge with exiled leaders and sympathizers. Sometimes their wives were essential to their success in evading the centurions sent to seize or kill them.

One such fortunate individual was Acilius. Appian gives us his story as follows, in his compilation of stories of women whose heroic actions saved their husbands.

"Acilius escaped from the city without being detected, but was exposed to the soldiers by a household slave. He persuaded the soldiers with the expectation of a larger reward to send some of their contingent to his wife with tokens that he gave them. When they came she brought out all her jewellery and said she was giving it to them so that they would give back in return what they promised to do, but that she did not know whether they would in fact return the gift. She was not cheated in her love for her husband, for the soldiers hired a boat for Acilius and sent him to Sicily." (4.6.39)

Another one on the run was Lentulus, who had participated in the conspiracy of Catiline, and had also escaped to Sicily but had been reluctant to involve his wife in his plans.

"Lentulus, when his wife decided to share his exile and kept a close watch on him with this in mind, did not want her to share the danger with him, and escaped secretly to Sicily, where he was accepted as a military commander by Pompey. He signalled to her that he was safe and was serving as a commander. She, when she learned where on the earth her husband was, knowing that her mother was watching her, escaped taking two slaves. She travelled with them with difficulty, roughly, like a fellow-slave, until they sailed into Messena from Rhegium towards evening. She easily learned the location of the general's tent. She found Lentulus not as a commander should be but on a sleeping mat on the ground, with his hair unkempt and living wretchedly because he missed his wife." (4.6.39)

Others were helped in various ways by their wives' clever schemes.

"Apuleius' wife threatened to inform on him if he were to flee alone. Against his will he took her along with him, but the lack of suspicion aided his escape, because of his travelling openly with a wife and manservants and maidservants.

The wife of Antius bound him up in a bedding sack and handed him over to some men who were paid to carry him and took him from his house to the sea, where he escaped to Sicily.

Reginus' wife lowered him during the night into a sewer, for soldiers did not enter it during the day because they could not put up with the smell. On another night she dressed him up as a charcoal-seller and gave him a donkey to drive, carrying charcoal. She herself took the lead, carried a short distance ahead on a litter. When one of the soldiers at the gates became suspicious of the litter and was searching through it Reginus became fearful and ran up to him and, behaving like a passer-by, advised the soldier not to annoy women. The soldier replied in anger, as if he were addressing a charcoal-seller, then recognized him (for he had been on a campaign once with him in Syria) and said, 'Be on your way with good heart, Sir. For now it is appropriate for me to address you with this title.'" (4.6.40)

On one occasion a woman offered her body in exchange for her husband's freedom.

"The wifely partner of Coponius enticed this from Antony, she who was formerly chaste but attempting to cure one misfortune with another." (4.6.40)
(Appian, *The Civil Wars*)

15

Weddings

Catullus composed a poem in honour of the wedding of Manlius Torquatus and his bride Junia Aurunculeia. There are several features in the poem that are found elsewhere in descriptions of Roman weddings, although some familiar elements in the ritual are omitted such as the wedding feast. Hymenaeus, the divine figure who presided over weddings, is invoked throughout the poem and invited to perform various nuptial roles including those for the bride at whose house the activities begin.

"Bind your brows with flowers
of fragrant marjoram,
put on the flame-coloured wedding-veil, come here
with gladness, wearing on your snow-white foot
    the saffron slipper.
And wakening on this joyful day
singing along with a clear-toned voice the nuptial songs,
beat the ground with your feet,
shake the pine torch with your hand." (6–15)

The bride is pictured as having left the women's quarters in readiness for the night-time procession to the groom's house.

"Throw open the bolts of the door:
the bride is at hand. Do you see how the torches
shake their shining tresses?" (76–8)

The singing of ribald verses accompanied the procession to the groom's house, along with the throwing of nuts. The groom is expected to give up his boy-beloved.

"Don't let the licentious Fescennine jesting
be silent for long,
and may the boy-favourite not begrudge
nuts to the slaves when he hears that the love of his master
    has abandoned him." (122–6)

The bride is given her instructions as they reach the door of her new home.

"You, too, Bride, what your husband anticipates
be wary of denying
lest he go elsewhere to seek it.
Io Hymen Hymenaeus, Io,
    Io Hymen Hymenaeus!" (147–51)
"Lift your golden feet across the threshold
with a good omen
and enter the polished door.
Io Hymen Hymenaeus, Io,
    Io Hymen Hymenaeus!" (162–6)
(Catullus, Poem 61)

16

Women in the inscriptional record

THE "LAUDATIO TURIAE"

The following testament to a devoted married couple is taken from a tomb inscription of the first century BCE. Known as the "Laudatio Turiae", its reference to a woman named Turia is not secure, but she is commonly identified with the woman married to Quintus Lucretius Vespillo, a consul in 19 BCE, who had saved the life of her husband during the proscriptions of the triumvirs in 43 BCE. The inscription, about 90 lines in all, was arranged in two columns. It resembles a funerary eulogy such as that given by Julius Caesar for his young wife Cornelia (p. 90 above). The violence of the civil wars was a backdrop to their entire married life, as is clear at the outset of the inscription on the left-hand column.

"You were orphaned suddenly before the day of our wedding, when both your parents were killed at the same time in an isolated place in the countryside. It was mainly through you, when I had left for Macedonia and your sister's husband Cluvius had gone to the Province of Africa, that the death of your parents did not remain unavenged." (I 3)
"With such great effort did you carry out the duty of a daughter's loyalty by insistent demands and by claims to justice that if we had been present we would not have accomplished more. But these you have in common with your sister, a most pious woman." (I 7–9)
"While you were busy with this, having obtained punishment for the guilty, you left your father's house to protect your modesty, and came to my mother's house, where you waited for my return." (I 10–12)

External tensions did not seem to weaken the bond between this husband and wife.

"It is a rare thing for marriages to be so long-lasting, ended by death rather than broken off through divorce. For it happened to us that our marriage lasted without strife for almost 41 years. Would that our long-standing partnership had occurred through a change in my life instead of yours, because of which I as the older partner would more justly have yielded to fate." (I 27–9)

"Why should I recall your domestic virtues of modesty, compliance, sociability, your good nature, your industriousness in wool-working, your religious devotion free of superstition, your inconspicuous style of dress, your attention to a moderate way of life? Why should I speak about your affection for your relatives, your devotion to your family? You looked after my mother just as you had your own parents, and saw to it that there was the same calm existence for her as for your own people. You have had innumerable other virtues in common with all women who cultivate a good reputation. The qualities that I am claiming are yours, and very few women have encountered similar circumstances of a sort so as to make them endure such suffering and earn such distinction – sufferings that Fortune has been careful to make rare for women." (I 30–6)

This column concludes with praise for Turia's sharing with him the property she inherited from her parents, and for ensuring that her female relatives were provided with dowries that would guarantee them respectable marriages (I 37–52).

The right-hand column provides details of her intervention to provide for his needs when he suffered during the dark days of the civil war.

"You provided the most important assistance during my flight. You furnished my life with the trappings of comfort when you transferred to me all the gold and pearls taken from your body, and repeatedly enriched me in my absence with servants, money and food while the guards posted by my enemies were cleverly deceived. You begged for mercy for me when I was absent, something your courage prompted you to do; because of your appeals the clemency of those against whom you prepared your assault offered no resistance. Your words were always delivered with steadfast courage." (II 2a, 6a–8a)

The inscription continues with the husband's testimony of Turia's courageous intervention to protect their property against plundering by their enemies and in securing his recall from exile (II 9a–11a). Octavian, the future Augustus, was away from Rome, but had indicated support for his recall. His co-triumvir Lepidus was in Rome and not so inclined.

"Nevertheless, I must confess that the bitterest event in my life befell me through what in turn happened to you. When I was restored to my country as a citizen again through the generosity and judgement of the absent Caesar Augustus, his colleague Marcus Lepidus, who was present, was confronted about my recall through your request. You lay prostrate on the ground at his feet, and not only were you not raised up but you were dragged off and abused like a slave. You were covered in bruises all over your body, but with a most resolute spirit you kept reminding him of the edict of Caesar with its commendation of my reinstatement. Even though you listened to abusive words and received cruel wounds you pronounced the words of the edict for all to hear, so that it should be publicly noted who was the cause of my vulnerable situation. Soon that fact contributed to his downfall." (II 11–18)

The couple's return to normal life was marred only by the fact that they were not successful in having children. The inscription tells us that when his wife's devotion and generosity extended to offering her husband a divorce because of this and even to search for a replacement wife, he was horrified and refused her offer. The text concludes with reference to his grief at her death, his wish that he had predeceased her, and his fear that he would not be able to match her steadfastness (II 25–69)
(*CIL* VI.1527 = *ILS* 8393).

EUCHARIS, ENTERTAINER

This laudatory tomb inscription from Rome, dated during the time of Sulla or Caesar, was written in iambic verse for a young emancipated slave who became a singer and mime performer.

"EUCHARIS, FREEDWOMAN OF LICINIA, WELL EDUCATED, A VIRGIN LEARNED IN ALL THE ARTS WHO LIVED FOR 14 YEARS.
'Hail! You whose eye strays to look upon this house of death
slow your step and read through my inscription,
which the love of my father gave to his daughter
in the place where the remains of her body are to be found.
Here, while my youth was flourishing with accomplishments
and with maturing years embarked on a course of fame,
my sad hour of destiny was hastening forward
and refused me an additional breath of life.
Schooled, accomplished almost by the touch of the Muses,
I who just recently embellished the games of the nobles in choral performance
was also first to appear before the people on the stage for Greek drama.
See how now the hostile Fates have deposited
the ashes of my body in this tomb, with a dirge.
Zeal for my patron, attentiveness, love, fame, honour –
they are silent in my charred body and are, with my death, mute.
As his daughter I left to my father tears to shed
and, although born later, I anticipated the day of his death.

Twice seven birthdays are preserved with me here in the dark,
held fast in the everlasting house of the Infernal God.
I ask that as you depart you invoke the earth to rest lightly over me.'"
(*CIL* I².1214 = *ILLRP* 2.803)

WOMEN MAKING DEDICATIONS

The next five inscriptions accompanied dedications made by women. In the first a woman named Octavia prepared a site for the celebration of the Bona Dea festival in Ostia, the port city of Rome.

"Octavia daughter of Marcus (Octavius), wife of Gamala, undertook having the portico adorned and benches made and the kitchen roofed over in honour of the Bona Dea."
(*CIL* I².3025)

Publicia was clearly a wealthy woman, with the freedom to disburse her own money and that of her husband in order to erect a temple for Hercules.

"Publicia, daughter of Lucius (Publicius), wife of Gnaeus (Cornelius) son of Aulus Cornelius, built this temple for Hercules and the doors and adorned it. She restored the altar sacred to Hercules. She saw to the construction of all this from her own and her husband's [money]."
(*CIL* I².981 = VI.30899 = *ILLRP* 1.126)

Other women record their dedications to divinities in response to a fortunate outcome after some difficulty within the family. The following two inscriptions can likely be explained by the restoration of children's health.

"Publilia Turpilia wife of Gnaeus (Turpilius) gave this statue as a gift to Diana for her son Gnaeus."
(*CIL* I².42 = XIV.4270 = *ILLRP* 1.82)
"Sulpicia daughter of Servius (Sulpicius) gave this gift willingly and with good cause to Juno Lucina for her daughter Paula Cassia."
(*CIL* I².987 = VI.361)

Women sometimes made a collective dedication.

"The matrons of Pisaurum gave this as a gift to Juno Regina."
(*CIL* XI.6300 = *ILLRP* 1.23)

LOWER-CLASS WOMEN

Brief (less costly) funerary inscriptions such as the following give us some evidence for the occupations of non-wealthy women, often former slaves.

"To Matia Prima, freedwoman of Gaia
seamstress from the Six Altars,
lived 46 years,
from her husband Titus Thoranicus
freedman of Titus Salvius"
(*CIL* VI.9884)

This woman appears to have been a dealer in resin, and lived a long life.

"For Julia Agele, resin-worker,
who lived for 80 years.
She constructed [the tomb] for her well-deserving son (or daughter) and herself and her kin
and for their descendants."
(*CIL* VI.9855)

One woman actually owned a business.

"Junia Crocale,
owner of a workshop,
lived thirty years."
(*CIL* VI.9715)

The following inscription was erected for a married couple who produced metal relief-work, possibly gold-leaf:

"Gaius Fulcinius Hermeros, freedman relief metal-worker.
Fulvia Melema
lived 48 years,
a relief metal-worker."
(*CIL* VI.9211)

Another pair, likely a married couple, sold incense. In supplying the measurement of their tomb the inscription suggests that this was a lucrative business.

"Hilaria Tribonia, freedwoman of Sextus
and Sextus Trebonius, freedman of Sextus,
merchants of incense.
In length twenty feet, [in front] twenty-eight feet."
(*CIL* VI.9934 = *ILLRP* 818)

17

Agricultural workers

Marcus Terentius Varro (Varro) was a scholar and prolific writer of the Late Republic. Although active in Rome and on campaigns as a supporter of Pompey, he never abandoned his rural roots. Toward the end of his life he composed *On Agriculture*, a manual for field and animal husbandry, his only extant complete work and intended for his wife who had purchased a farm. The three books are each presented as a conversation. In the following section a man named Cossinius is advising Varro to make use of women on a farm, to benefit from their skills and strength when they are travelling with the herds for winter or summer pasturing (transhumating).

"As concerns the breeding of the herdsmen, for those who stay permanently on the farm the matter is straightforward, because they have a fellow slave in the country villa, and the Venus of herdsmen searches no further than this. Those, however, who pasture their herds in mountain-valleys and woodlands and keep out of the rain not in the villa but in temporary shelters, for them there are many who think it useful to bring along women who follow the herds and bring out food for the herdsmen and make them more attentive to their work. But these women should be strong and not bad-looking.

In many places they are not inferior to men in the work, such as one can see here and there in Illyricum, since they can pasture the herd or carry wood for the fire and cook the food or look after the provisions for the huts. About feeding their young I say this, that they are for the most part both nurses and mothers.' At the same time he looked directly at me and said, 'As I heard you say when you had come to Liburnia, that you had seen mothers carrying at the same time logs and children who were nursing, sometimes one, sometimes two, demonstrating that our new mothers who lie for some days under their canopies, are feeble and worthless.' To which I said, 'Absolutely right, for in Illyricum the contrast is that much greater: often a pregnant woman, when the time comes for her to give birth, moves a little distance from her work, produces the child there and carries it back. You would think she had not given birth to it but found it. And not only this: those whom they call 'virgins' there, those not yet twenty years of age – for them their way of life does not forbid this – can mate before marriage with whomever they wish and wander about on their own and bear children."
(Varro, *On Agriculture* 2.10.6–9)

FURTHER READING

Bradley, K. 1991. *Discovering the Roman Family*. Oxford

Dixon, S. 2001. *Reading Roman Women. Sources, Genres and Real Life*. London

Fantham, E. 1991. "Stuprum: Public Attitudes and Penalties for Sexual Offences in Republican Rome," *Echos du Monde Classique/Classical Views* 35 n.s. 10, 267–91

Gardner, J. F. 1986. *Women in Roman Law and Society*. London/Sydney

Hejduk, J. D. 2008. *Clodia. A Sourcebook*. Norman, OK

Hersch, K. K. 2010. *The Roman Wedding. Ritual and Meaning in Antiquity*. Cambridge

Joshel, S. 1992. *Work, Identity and Legal Status at Rome. A Study of the Occupational Inscriptions*. Norman, OK

Kampen, N. 1981. *Image and Status: Roman Working Women in Ostia*. Berlin

Lattimore R. 1942. *Themes in Greek and Roman Epitaphs*. Urbana, IL

Marshall, A. J. 1989. "Ladies at Law: The Role of Women in the Roman Civil Courts", in C. Deroux (ed.) *Studies in Latin Literature and Roman History*. Brussels. 35–54

McGinn, T. A. J. 2004. *The Economy of Prostitution in the Roman World*. Ann Arbor, MI

Parker, H. 2007. "Why Were the Vestals Virgins? Or the Chastity of Women and the Safety of the Roman State", in *Virginity Revisited. Configurations of the Unpossessed Body*. Toronto. 66–99 (revised from publication in 2004, *American Journal of Philology* 125, 563–601)

Scheidel, W. 1995. "The Most Silent Women of Greece and Rome: Rural Labour and Woman's Life in the Ancient World I". *Greece and Rome* 42.2, 202–17

—1996. "The Most Silent Women of Greece and Rome: Rural Labour and Woman's Life in the Ancient World II". *Greece and Rome* 43.1, 1–10

Schultz, C. E. 2006. *Women's Religious Activity in the Roman Republic*. Chapel Hill, NC

Skinner, M. 1983. "Clodia Metelli". *Transactions of the American Philological Society* 113, 273–87

Treggiari, S. 1969. *Roman Freedmen During the Late Republic*. Oxford

—1979. "Lower Class Women in the Roman Economy". *Florilegium* 1, 65–86

—1991. *Roman Marriage. Iusti Coniuges from the Time of Cicero to the Time of Ulpian*. Oxford

—2007. *Terentia, Tullia and Publilia. The Women of Cicero's Family*. London/NewYork

Walker, S. and Higgs, P. 2001 (eds). *Cleopatra of Egypt: From History to Myth*. Princeton, NJ

Wildfang, R. L. 2006. *Rome's Vestal Virgins. A Study of Rome's Vestal Priestesses in the Late Republic and Early Empire*. London/New York

Wistrand, E. K. H. 1976. *The So-Called* Laudatio Turiae. *Introduction, Text, Translation, Commentary*. Lund

Women of the Julio-Claudian Dynasty

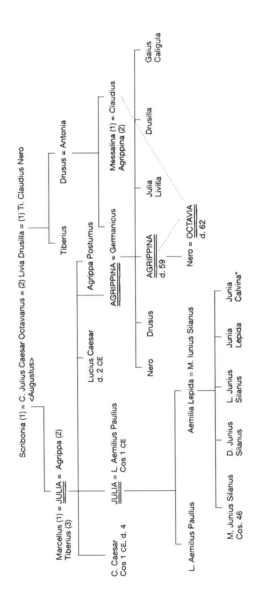

(Genealogical chart courtesy of E. Fantham)

* Junia Calvina, great-great-granddaughter of Augustus and Scribonia, exiled for alleged incest with her brother, the betrothed of Octavia, lived on to 79 CE [Suet. Vesp. 23]

PART 4

THE JULIO-CLAUDIAN PERIOD

With his adoption of the title Augustus ("Venerable", "Consecrated by Ritual") in 27 BCE, Octavian launched the Principate, since he was recognized as the first, or topmost leader (*princeps*) in Rome until his death in 14 CE. He kept the formal structures of the Republic but in effect this amounted to the launch of the Roman Empire, with himself as emperor. As a member of the Julian clan he merged this family line with the Claudians through his second marriage to Livia. The last descendant of the Julians on his mother's side and the Claudians on his (adopted) father's side was Nero, whose death in 68 CE ended the dynastic period known as the Julio-Claudian era.

As Octavian, Augustus had already been married twice, the second time when he was 17 (in 40 BCE) to Scribonia, who was his elder and had also been married previously and borne three children, including a daughter Cornelia Scipio. With Octavian/Augustus, Scribonia produced another daughter, Julia, but with Livia he had no children.

18

Augustan marriage legislation

The civil wars of the final century BCE in Rome had depleted the male population. This, together with a diminishing of paternal control over daughters and an increase in extramarital sexual activity, prompted Augustus to attempt to regain some control through legislation. The surviving record of this is found in later juristic writings: Gaius (*Institutes of Roman Law*, c. 160 CE), the *Epitome*, a work ascribed to Ulpian, a jurist of the second/third century CE, and *The Digest*, a compilation of Roman law assembled under the Emperor Justinian in the 6th century CE. Augustus' law, the *Lex Julia* (issued probably in 18 BCE and taking its title from his family name), employed both rewards and penalties for the purpose of enforcement.

The section in the *Lex Julia* entitled *de maritandis ordinibus* legislation "about marriage between the orders" attempted to regulate marriage between social classes in order to control the legitimacy of children. Senators, together with their children and descendants in the male line, were not to marry women who were freed slaves or other women whose status was suspect.

"Freeborn men are forbidden from marrying a woman who earns her living as a prostitute, a procuress, a woman freed by a procurer or procuress, a woman taken in adultery, one that has been convicted in a public prosecution, or a woman who performs on stage."
(Ulpian, *Epitome* 13.2)

Another section of the *Lex Julia* (*de adulteriis*) dealt with cases of adultery (understood as extramarital sex involving a married woman), and made it a public crime. The following stipulations were recorded by Julius Paulus, a jurist of the second/third century CE whose work was included in *The Digest.*

The father of the woman suspected of adultery was permitted to kill his daughter's lover if caught, or at least to prosecute him; the crime was punishable by exile and confiscation of property.

"In the second chapter of the *Lex Julia* concerning adultery it is permissible for a father, either adoptive or natural, to kill with his own hands an adulterer caught with his daughter in his own house or that of his son-in-law, whatever his rank." (1)

Her husband could kill the lover if he was considered to be of ill repute.

"A husband can only kill those caught in adultery who are 'infamous' and those who make a living by selling their bodies, slaves as well. His wife, however, he is prohibited from having the right to kill." (4)

Although this prohibition was in place, the husband who committed a crime of passion was not treated harshly.

"It has been determined that a husband who kills his wife when she is caught in adultery is to be punished more leniently because he committed this act through a justified intolerance of suffering." (5)

If the wife survived, the husband was obliged to divorce her; otherwise he would be prosecuted as a pimp.

"When the adulterer has been killed the husband must divorce his wife immediately and then within three days declare in public with which adulterer and in which place he had apprehended his wife." (6)
"It has been determined that a man who does not immediately divorce his wife who has been caught in adultery is accused of being guilty of pimping." (8)

The adulterous woman would be sent into exile on an island with limited resources. If her lover survived he would be exiled elsewhere.

"It has been determined that women convicted of adultery are to be restricted to one-half their dowry and one-third of their goods and relegated to an island; for the men convicted of adultery, with comparable exile to an island one-half their property is confiscated. They are relegated to different islands, however." (14)
(Julius Paulus, *Sententiae* 2.26= *FIRA* 2, pp. 351–2)

The poet Horace, celebrating the peace and stability that he associated with the reign of Augustus, included brief praise for the *Lex Julia de adulteriis*.

"The home, chaste, is polluted by no debauchery;
custom and written law have vanquished and driven out defiled wickedness.
Mothers are praised for offspring who resemble their parents.
    Punishment, close at hand, bears down on the crime of unchastity."
(Horace, *Odes* 4.5.21–4)

The focal point in cases of adultery was clearly the woman, while her husband had ready access to a variety of partners, with the exception of other married women.

Several decades later, in 19 CE, a *matrona* named Vistilia attempted to escape prosecution as an adulterer by registering as a prostitute, provoking the Senate to invoke the Julian law.

"In the same year the lust of women was curtailed by strict decrees of the Senate, and precautions were taken lest a woman make a profit from her body if her grand-father, her father or her husband had been a Roman of the equestrian class. For Vistilia, daughter of a praetorian family, had made open profession of prostitution on the aediles' list – the custom preserved among our ancestors, who believed that with the public admission of shame there was sufficient penalty for the unchaste. It was also required of Vistilia's husband, Titidius Labeo, to explain why he had disre-garded the enforcement of the legal penalty in the face of his wife's being exposed as a transgressor. And when he brought forward as an excuse the fact that the sixty days allotted for consultation had not yet elapsed it seemed sufficient to decide about Vistilia, and she was exiled to the island of Seriphos."
(Tacitus, *Annals* 2.85)

There was considerable resistance to the severity of the *Lex Julia* and it was repealed then modified in 9 CE and presented as the *Lex Papia Poppaea* (taking the names of the consuls in office that year). In later juristic sources the laws are frequently referred to jointly, as the *Lex Julia et Papia*.

From the record of Gaius, it is clear that under the revised law, people who did not marry or who did not have children were penalized through a restriction in their access to inherited legacies.

"Further, childless persons by the Papian Law, because they did not have children, lose one-half their inheritances and legacies, those who were formerly thought capable of taking trust-gifts in full."
(Gaius, *Institutiones* 2.286)

Under the new law there were more generous provisions for freed slaves. Cassius Dio, a historian of the third century CE, reported that all freeborn men apart from senators could now marry freedwomen and their children would be legitimate (*Roman History* 54.16.1–2). The reproductive success of both freeborn women and freedwomen who had produced three children was to be rewarded with freedom from guardianship (*tutela*).

"Women of free birth are released from guardianship by right of having three children; freedwomen, if they are under the legal guardianship of their patron or his children may be released from statutory guardianship with four children. Those who have guardians of another type ... are released from legal guardianship with three children." (Gaius, *Institutes* 1.194)

The felt need to increase the birthrate led to further privileges for freedwomen. Under the *Lex Papia Poppaea* freedwomen who produced four children were even permitted to make wills, passing on a portion of their property to their children. An amount was also reserved for their patron, reckoned from the number of their children (Ulpian, *Epitome* 29.3–6). Together with their release from *tutela*, this would have awarded them the same independence that was enjoyed by the Vestal Virgins.

The anxiety around sexual immorality expressed in this legislation was frequently tied to concern over a general decadence that had begun in the Late Republic and continued into the Principate, doubtless in large measure the result of the affluence that came with the growth of Rome as an imperial power. A sign of this social instability, according to Horace, was the sexual laxity of women.

"The Dacian and the Aethiopian almost destroyed the city
that was taken up with internal strife.
One was dreaded because of the fleet;
the other was better at hurling arrows.
Prolific in sin, this age
first defiled marriage-bonds, then the family line and the homes:
springing from this source, devastation
has flooded over the fatherland and the populace.
The girl coming of age delights in Greek dances
and is instructed in accomplishments;
even now she contemplates illicit lovemaking
right down to her dainty finger.
Soon in the midst of the drinking parties of her husband
she seeks younger lovers, and does not choose
the one on whom she would bestow unlawful pleasures
swiftly when the lights are removed,
but openly, when bidden, she rises,
with the full knowledge of her husband, whether it is some peddlar
or the captain of a Spanish ship
who pays dearly the price of shame."
(Horace, *Odes* 3.13–32)

That the sexual laxity of men was not regarded as a threat to the social order is reflected in an essay of Plutarch in which he offers advice to a bride and groom and assumes that the husband will avail himself of the opportunities to have sex with household slaves.

"[In the case of] a man, then, in his private life, who is immoderate in his pleasures and dissolute, if he goes somewhat astray with a mistress or female slave, his wife must not be irritated or angry, but should reason that it is because he respects her that he shares his drunken behaviour, his intemperance and his wantonness with another woman."
(Plutarch, *Moralia* 140B)

19

Women of the imperial households

Women who became wives and mothers within the emperor's extended family functioned as tools of imperial succession, particularly if the emperor had but one child, a daughter. To promote the prospects of a favoured successor, the emperor could arrange the marriage of the man to the imperial princess. In other cases where the emperor wished to withhold such an opportunity, the young woman could be married off to a non-contender for power.

LIVIA

In 39 BCE, after only a year of marriage, Augustus divorced Scribonia, on the same day that she gave birth to their daughter Julia. Suetonius mentions Scribonia's severe temperament, and Augustus' resentment of her jealousy over a rival lover – likely Livia – as factors ("The Deified Augustus" 62.2, 69.1). The *princeps* took Livia as his wife when she was pregnant with her second son (Tiberius) and married to a prominent Roman, Tiberius Claudius Nero. The historian Tacitus (late first, early second centuries CE) describes her attracting Augustus by her beauty, and the pair dismissing convention to begin a life together. But in keeping with Augustus' attempt to restore old-fashioned morality, Livia seems to have earned an exemplary reputation as an ideal *matrona*.

"Then Caesar took her from her husband, overcome by passion aroused by her beauty. It is not clear that she was reluctant, and he was in such haste that he led her to his hearth while she was pregnant, without even allotting the interval of time for her to give birth ... In her upright management of the household she recalled that of an earlier era, although her cordiality went beyond that approved of by women in the past. She was a domineering mother, an agreeable wife and possessed a character suited to the political occupations of her husband."
(Tacitus, *Annals* 5.1.1)

Cassius Dio, a historian of the imperial period, passed on a report of Livia's own comments about her performance as an indulgent wife of the *princeps*.

"When someone asked her how and by what actions she had prevailed over Augustus to such a degree she answered that it was by being perfectly chaste herself and by doing gladly everything that he approved and not meddling in any other of his affairs, and by pretending not to hear about or notice any of his sexual favourites."
(Cassius Dio, *History of Rome* 58.2.5)

The ancient sources are fulsome both in praise for and hostility against Livia, with her detractors going so far as to implicate her in the death of Augustus, by administering poison. There is general agreement, however, that she was an important public figure, a "first lady" as no other Roman *matrona* had been previously. Dio reported that in 35 BCE, four years after Octavian married her, he awarded both Livia and his sister Octavia the same sacrosanctity that protected tribunes. This would save them from the verbal abuse being directed at Octavian and those close to him by supporters of Octavia's husband Mark Antony at a time when Octavia was being badly treated by him, and there was a vigorous propaganda battle between the two factions. The two women were also given the right to administer their estates without supervision by a guardian, and public statues of them were dedicated. All this awarded Livia and Octavia a visible and sanctioned public presence that had not been possible previously for women apart from Vestal Virgins (*Roman History* 49.38.1).

Both women were to suffer a mother's grief at the death of a son. In 23 BCE, Octavia's son Marcellus – Augustus' heir apparent – died from an illness that almost took the life of the *princeps*. In 9 BCE, Livia's younger son Drusus (brother of Tiberius) was killed by a fall from his horse as he was leading a campaign against German tribes on the banks of the Elbe. The reaction of the two mothers was discussed by Seneca, a Stoic who lived a half-century later under the Emperor Nero, in a moral essay of consolation for a woman of his time also bereft of a son. His stance as a Stoic led him to advise against indulging in the excessive grieving he associated with Octavia.

"Through her whole life [Octavia] remained just as she was at the funeral; I don't say that she did not have the courage to get up but she refused to be lifted up, deciding that a loss of tears was a second bereavement. She didn't want to have a single portrait of her beloved son, nor a single mention of him to be uttered in her hearing. She hated all mothers, and was most inflamed at Livia, because it seemed that the happiness promised to her had passed to the son of that woman [Tiberius]. Darkness and solitude were her most frequent companions; not even having a thought for her brother she rejected poems composed to celebrate the memory of Marcellus and other honours conferred by literary works, and closed her ears to all attempts at comforting her. She withdrew from her appointed duties and, detesting the good fortune itself that shone too brightly around her from the greatness of her brother, she buried herself and hid herself away." (2.4)

Livia he described as much more restrained as she was observed accompanying the bier of her son while it made its way back to Rome.

"On the long journey in which she followed behind the remains of her son Drusus, with so many funeral pyres burning throughout the whole of Italy, she was inflamed as if she were losing him again each time a fire burned. But as soon as she laid him in the tomb she put aside at one time both her son and her sorrow, and did not grieve more than was appropriate for Caesar or fair to Tiberius, who was still alive." (3.2)
(Seneca, *Consolatio ad Marciam*)

Despite Augustus' high regard for Livia (and his marriage legislation), he may not have observed strict marital fidelity, according to Suetonius. (The biographer frequently includes salacious personal details that must be read with caution, given the highly charged political atmosphere of the Principate.)

"And not even his friends deny that he indulged in adultery, although they justify this as not committed from lust but from design, so that he more easily might investigate the plotting of his adversaries through their women. Mark Antony upbraided him with – beyond the hasty marriage to Livia – taking the wife of a man of consular rank into the bedroom from her husband's dining room in plain view, and returning her to the dinner-party with her ears blushing in shame and her hair in disarray. [Further,] that Scribonia was divorced because she complained too freely at the influence of his mistress, that liaisons were obtained through his friends who stripped and inspected mothers of families and grown virgins, just as if Toranius the slave-dealer were putting them up for sale."
(Suetonius, "The Deified Augustus" 69.1)

Suetonius adds that in his later life Augustus developed a preference for deflowering virgins, who were delivered to him even by Livia (71.1). He was kissing his wife as he died, however, while uttering the words "Live mindful of our marriage-bond, and farewell!" (99.1).

JULIA

Augustus' daughter Julia was first married to Marcellus, the son of Octavia (her aunt). When Marcellus died from illness in 23 BCE, Julia was only 15.

Augustus quickly arranged a second marriage to a man his own age, his trusted commander-in-chief Marcus Agrippa, who was obliged to divorce his wife, a daughter of Octavia. The following year Julia gave birth to her first son Gaius and two daughters, and a son Lucius Caesar followed. These were succeeded by a son born after his father's death, Agrippa Postumus.

Macrobius, writing four centuries later but using as his source Domitius Marsus, a writer of the Augustan period, describes Julia at 38 as witty, well-read and popular.

"... she took advantage of both fortune and her father. Her love of literature and her extensive learning – which were easily acquired in that household – and particularly her gentle disposition toward others and her even temper, won the woman enormous popularity. Those who were aware of her vices marvelled at such contrasting virtues." (2.5.2)

Macrobius' source attributes to Julia the following reply to one of her companions who was impressed at the resemblance of Julia's children to Agrippa, despite her promiscuity.

"When those people who were aware of her sexual indiscretions marvelled at how her children seemed to resemble Agrippa when she was making the potency of her body so generally available she said, 'I never carry a passenger except when the boat is full.'" (2.5.9)
(Macrobius, *Saturnalia*)

Agrippa died in 12 BCE, and Augustus then arranged for Julia to be married to Livia's son Tiberius, although he was already married to a daughter of Agrippa, with one child and another expected (Suetonius, "The Deified Augustus" 63.1–2, 64.1). Suetonius described Tiberius' distress at his imposed divorce.

"... he was forced to divorce [Vipsania] and marry Julia, daughter of Augustus, in short order. This he did with no small amount of mental anguish, both because he was attached to his relationship with [Vipsania] Agrippina and because he disapproved of the conduct of Julia, since he had observed that she was after him even while her last husband was alive – something that was in fact broadly believed. After the divorce he grieved over the separation from [Vipsania] Agrippina, and on one occasion when he saw her by chance he followed her with a look so happy and so tearful that they took care that she never again came into his sight."
(Suetonius, "Tiberius" 7.2)

Julia's third marriage was an unhappy one. Tiberius abandoned Rome for Rhodes, staying for seven years and leaving Julia alone in the city. In the year

2 CE, Augustus could no longer ignore her sexual laxity. Seneca echoes the report of several others who recorded the difficult decision the princeps felt obliged to make, to punish his daughter in keeping with his own legislation against adultery.

"The deified Augustus sent into exile his daughter, unchaste beyond the curse of unchastity, and made public the scandals of the imperial household: that she had accepted adulterers in swarms, that she had roamed through the city with her nightly revelling; that the Forum itself and the rostra from which her father had carried the law against adultery had suited his daughter for debauchery; that there had been a daily flocking to the statue of Marsyas, when she turned from adultery to prostitution and sought the right to every form of licence with any unknown adulterer. Hardly able to control his rage he had made public these scandals that had to be punished by the princeps but also should have been kept quiet, inasmuch as the disgrace of some misdemeanours also turns on the one who punishes them. Later, when with time passing embarrassment had followed his rage, groaning that he had not suppressed in silence what he had been unaware of for so long until it had been shameful to speak out, he often cried out 'none of this would have happened to me if either Agrippa or Maecenas had been alive!'"
(Seneca, *De Beneficiis* 6.32)

Tacitus provides the details of Julia's punishment and records her death after Tiberius came to power.

"In the same year (14 CE) Julia died; some time before she had been imprisoned by her father for her shameful behaviour on the island of Pandateria and then in the town of the Regini who live by the Sicilian strait. She had been married to Tiberius when her sons Gaius and Lucius were in the prime of their life, but she had despised him as being beneath her. This was, to be sure, the private reason why Tiberius would withdraw to Rhodes. When he obtained imperial power he left her to die, having been banished, destitute through privation and slow decay, disgraced and bereft of all hope after the murder of (her son) Agrippa Postumus. He thought the murder would go unnoticed because of the long duration of her exile."
(Tacitus, *Annals* 1.53)

Tacitus informs us that Julia's daughter (bearing the same name) was also convicted of adultery by Augustus and banished to an island off the Apulian coast. She fared better than her mother in exile: for the 20 years before her death she was supported by Livia who, Tacitus tells us, "secretly undermined her stepdaughters while they were flourishing but openly displayed compassion toward them when they were cast down" (*Annals* 4.71).

AGRIPPINA THE ELDER

Livia also played a role in the life of Julia's daughter, Agrippina (referred to as "Agrippina the Elder" to distinguish her from her daughter of the same name). She was married to Germanicus, the son of Tiberius' brother Drusus (therefore a grandson of Livia). Tacitus' record indicates that there were serious tensions in the imperial household between Tiberius and Germanicus, whom Augustus had obliged Tiberius to adopt as his heir, and between Livia and his wife Agrippina.

"[Germanicus] was perturbed by the secret hatred coming from his uncle and grandmother – the motives of which had a more severe impact because they were undeserved. The truth of the matter was that the memory of Drusus was still alive among the Roman populace, and it was believed that had he been in possession of imperial power he would have restored liberty to the people, whence the same goodwill and hope was placed in Germanicus. The young man possessed the disposition of an ordinary citizen, exceptional affability – in contrast to Tiberius with the arrogance and inscrutability of his speech and expression. Female friction added to this, with the stepmotherly provocations of Livia visited on Agrippina, and Agrippina herself fairly excitable, were it not that through her moral integrity and love for her husband she converted an otherwise ungovernable temper to the good."
(Tacitus, *Annals* 1.33)

In 14 CE, Augustus died and Tiberius assumed imperial power. Agrippina, with her husband and his legions in Gaul, garnered popularity among the soldiers by introducing her sixth child, Gaius, to the army in a military outfit that included small versions of the legionaires' hobnailed boots (*caligae*). These soldier-booties would earn him the name "Caligula", and sympathy for the mother and child among the soldiers would serve to quell a serious mutiny in the field (Tacitus, *Annals* 1.40–4).

The following year, Germanicus found himself and his soldiers in danger of being trapped in Germany while a smaller contingent of the army was in Gaul on the other side of the River Rhine with Agrippina. As Germanicus and his troops, pursued by the Germans, made a dash to cross the river, Agrippina quelled a panic-driven rush to combat the onslaught by tearing down the bridge, which would have meant certain destruction for her husband and his army. According to Tacitus, when the report of this reached Tiberius it served to further inflame the new emperor's antagonism toward Germanicus and his wife.

"Meanwhile a rumour circulated that the army had been surrounded and that a hostile column of Germans was marching against the Gauls. If Agrippina had not

prevented the bridge over the Rhine from being destroyed there were those who would have dared that outrage out of panic. But it was a woman with prodigious courage who assumed the duties of a leader during those days, who, if some soldier was in need or was wounded, supplied equipment and dressings. Gaius Pliny, who gave an account of the German wars, reported that she stood at the approach to the bridge, bestowing praises and thanks to the returning legions. This penetrated the soul of Tiberius all the more deeply: not only was that attention without an ulterior motive, but her enthusiasm for the soldiers was not directed against a foreign enemy. There was nothing left for commanders to do when a woman visited the maniples, approached the standards, lay her hand to the bestowing of bonuses – as if she did not court them enough by daring to parade the son of the general dressed in the regalia of a common soldier, and to request that he be called 'Caesar Caligula'!"
(Tacitus, *Annals* 1.69)

Two years later, Tiberius recalled Germanicus from Germany and sent him to supervise the Eastern provinces. A friend of the emperor's, Gnaeus Piso, was sent as governor of Syria with instructions to keep an eye on the activities of Germanicus. Piso, however, soon incurred the displeasure of the emperor and the Senate by acting independently and with cruelty, and tensions grew into open hostility between Piso and Germanicus. Germanicus fell ill, raising the suspicion that he had been poisoned by the governor.

As he lay dying, Germanicus denounced Piso (Tacitus, *Annals* 71.1) and gave final instructions to his wife.

"Then turning to his wife he begged her, on behalf of the memory of himself and for the children they had in common, to strip off her fierceness of spirit, to bend her will in the face of furious fortune, and when she returned to Rome not to irritate those stronger than she by rivalling them for power."
(Tacitus, *Annals* 2.72)

After Germanicus died, Agrippina sailed for Rome with her six children, carrying the ashes of her husband. In the city the announcement of the death of such a popular leader inflamed passions to such a degree that all civic life was suspended. An enormous contingent of mourners met her boat as she disembarked at Brundisium, and funeral tributes were held in the Italian colonies as Germanicus' remains were carried in procession to Rome. Tiberius and Livia did not appear in public.

Tacitus describes the consternation of Tiberius on the day when the ashes were placed in the Mausoleum of Augustus, when the streets were full of mourners lamenting the loss of a city saviour and praising Agrippina.

"Nothing, however, struck more deeply into Tiberius' heart than the feverish devotion of people for Agrippina, when they called her an ornament to her country, the last of Augustus' blood-line, a peerless model of old-fashioned virtue. Turning to the heavens and the gods they prayed for the preservation of her offspring and that they might outlive those who had done them wrong."
(Tacitus, *Annals* 3.4)

An important document came to light at the end of the twentieth century, when several copies of a *Senatus Consultum* (a Senatorial Decree) were found in Spain, attesting to the fact that Tiberius had requested an investigation into Piso's behaviour toward Germanicus and the imperial household. A public trial was held in which Piso was accused of savagery and sedition. The former governor then committed suicide, and there was some suspicion that Tiberius played a role in his death. A significant detail in the Senatorial Decree, which would have been disseminated throughout the Empire, is its singling out for commendation the imperial women who were relatives of Germanicus. Of Livia (his grandmother), it stated:

"That the Senate praised greatly the moderation of Julia Augusta and Drusus Caesar (father of Germanicus), imitating the justice shown by our *princeps,* and that this Order observed that these individuals had not demonstrated a greater devotion to Germanicus than fairness in holding back their full judgements until the case of the elder Cn. Piso was heard."

Of Agrippina, Germanicus' wife, Antonia (his mother) and Livia his sister, it stated

"That also of those others connected to Germanicus Caesar by a close relationship [the Senate] had strong approval – for Agrippina, whom [in the view of the Senate] the memory of the deified Augustus by whom she had been greatly esteemed and of her husband Germanicus, with whom she had lived in unique harmony, and so many children born by a birth most auspicious for those who survived, [the Senate] render their esteem.
Likewise of Antonia, mother of Germanicus Caesar who, having experienced a single marriage – to Drusus, father of Germanicus – has displayed through the integrity of her character that she was worthy of such closeness to the deified Augustus, and of Livia, sister of Germanicus Caesar, about whom both her grandmother and her father-in-law and at the same time paternal uncle, our *princeps,* declared to be excellent – persons in whose judgement, even if she did not belong to the house, she might deservedly take pride, and much more so as a woman bound by such close personal ties.

That of these women the Senate commended equally both their most steadfast
grief and in their grief their moderation."
(*Senatus Consultum de Cn Pisone Patre* 137–47)

As the result of tensions in the imperial household, fomented by Tiberius' prefect
(equivalent to his Chief of Police) and not eased by Agrippina's headstrong nature,
Tiberius left Rome for Capri. He sent letters to the city banishing Agrippina and
her eldest son. Agrippina the Elder starved herself and died in exile.

AGRIPPINA THE YOUNGER

Upon the death of Tiberius in 37 CE, Agrippina's son Gaius became emperor. He
is better known in the records as Caligula, the nickname he received during his
childhood among the Roman cohorts. His rule was marked by violence, accusations of treason and plots against his life. His two sisters Livilla and Agrippina
were caught up in the web of suspicion of plotting against him, and were exiled.

Four years after his accession, Caligula was assassinated. Claudius, brother
of Germanicus, succeeded him, and recalled the younger Agrippina and Livilla
(his nieces) from exile. Livilla would be exiled once again, as a consequence of
the sexual jealousy of Claudius' third wife Messalina, and this time she died of
starvation. Agrippina married again, to a wealthy man of consular rank but not
a contender for imperial power. Considerably older than she, he died not many
years after their marriage. Messalina, as lusty as she was vindictive according to
the sources, took her own life when hunted down on orders from Claudius after
she had celebrated publicly a "marriage" with another man during Claudius'
absence (Tacitus, *Annals* 11.31–7). At the age of 32 in 41 CE, Agrippina the
Younger married for the third time and became the fourth wife of Claudius (her
uncle). To optimize the chances of her son Nero becoming Claudius' successor,
she saw that he was betrothed to Claudius' daughter Octavia and that the
emperor adopted Nero, who was older than Claudius's natural son Britannicus
and would therefore stand a good chance of superseding him as emperor when
Claudius died. Ancient sources agree that Agrippina's shrewd (and at times
ruthless) acquisition of power as empress was considerable.

Claudius died in 54 CE (probably poisoned by Agrippina) and Nero became
emperor at the age of 17. Initially Agrippina maintained control over him but
it was inevitable that this would be resented by her teenage son who turned to
others for mentoring, in particular the moral philosopher and writer Seneca. The
sources covering the next five years are filled with speculation over the motives
behind Nero's final decision to kill his mother, whether this was motivated by his
mistress Poppaea Sabina who would ultimately become his wife (Tacitus, *Annals*

1.45) or the urging of others hostile to Agrippina. Before the end, rumours also circulated that he was committing incest with Agrippina (Tacitus, *Annals* 14.2; Suetonius, "Nero" 28.2; Cassius Dio, *Roman History* 61.11.3–4).

The final act was committed in 59 CE, and Tacitus' description is one of the most memorable vignettes in Latin literature. Nero chose as the setting a festival of Minerva celebrated at the resort town of Baiae on the Bay of Naples. He invited his mother to join him and welcomed her warmly. At the festival she occupied a seat of honour and the two feasted and embraced each other. After midnight they went to the shore where several vessels were moored, one decked out in honour of Agrippina. Nero had arranged for it to be outfitted with a device that would collapse the roof over his mother, break up the boat and drop her into the sea. When she was on board the device was activated but she survived. Nero panicked and sent soldiers to kill her, accusing her of conspiracy to kill him.

"The gods presented a night brilliant with starlight and the tranquility of a calm sea, as if for a demonstration of the crime. The vessel had not gone far, with two of her closest companions accompanying Agrippina. One of these, Crepereius Gallus, stood quite near the helm, with Acerronia at her feet while she lay back on her couch recalling with delight the repentant mood of her son and the recovery of her maternal influence.

At a given signal the ceiling of the place caved in, weighed down with a lot of lead; Crepereius was crushed and died immediately. Agrippina and Acerronia were saved by the projecting sides of the couch that were too strong to give under the weight. And the breakup of the boat did not follow; there was commotion among everyone and the majority who were unaware of what was going on stood in the way of those who were in on the plot. It seemed best to the rowers that they tip the boat on one side and thus sink the boat, but no agreement on an immediate plan was reached among them and others, by pressing for a contrary option, provided the opportunity for a gentler casting into the sea. Acerronia quite unwisely shouted the while that she was Agrippina and called for help for the emperor's mother; she was killed by poles and oars and what projectiles from the boat that fortune offered. Agrippina was silent and to that extent less recognized, although she received one wound on her shoulder. By swimming, then by meeting up with some small boats she was carried to the Lucrine Lake and was brought to her villa.

There she reflected how for this purpose she had been summoned by a deceptive letter and treated with a special tribute, and how it had occurred not far from shore, how the boat, not driven by winds nor dashed on the rocks, had been broken up in its upper part as if by a mechanism that was made on land. Thinking about the killing of Acerronia, as soon as she looked at her own wound she realized that the only remedy against the treachery was not to think about it. She sent her freedman Agerinus to report to her son that by the kindness of the gods and his good fortune she had avoided a grave disaster. She begged him to put off the duty to visit, although he might be alarmed at the danger posed to his mother. For the moment she needed rest. Meanwhile, pretending that she was safe she applied ointments to her wound and poultices to her body. She gave orders that Acerronia's will be found and her property to be sealed. And in this alone did she act without disguise.

Meanwhile, when the danger to Agrippina was broadcast as if it had happened by accident, everyone, as soon as each person heard of it, rushed to the shore. Some climbed on the projecting piers, others the nearby boats. Others, whose bodies allowed it, waded into the sea. Some reached out their arms. The whole shore was filled with lamentations, prayers and shouting – different in the questions asked or unclear in the answers given. An enormous crowd streamed to the place with torches, and when they realized that she was safe they hastened to congratulate her until they were dispersed by the sight of an armed and threatening force of men. Anicetus surrounded the villa with a stationed guard, and having broken down the door dragged off the slaves who were in his way until he came to the door of her bedroom. A few were standing there, while the others had been frightened away by terror at the break-in. A small lamp was in the chamber and one slave-girl. Agrippina grew more and more anxious because no one had come from her son, not even Agerinus. The appearance of things forebode other than a happy outcome: now solitude and then sudden uproarings and signs of the worst disaster. Exclaiming, when the slave-girl was leaving, 'Are you too deserting me?' she looked around and saw Anicetus, accompanied by Herculeius the captain of the trireme and Obaritus, a centurion with the fleet. If he had come in order to see her he should report that she had recovered, but if he was about to carry out a crime she did not believe it had anything to do with her son. He had not given orders to kill his parent.
The attackers stood around her couch and the captain of the trireme first struck her head with a cudgel. Then, to the centurion who reached out to kill her with his sword bared she cried 'Strike my womb,' and with many wounds she was slain."
(Tacitus, *Annals* 14.5–6, 8)

Nine years later, in 68 CE, Nero was faced with a revolt from within the military, was declared a public enemy by the Senate and beaten to death. Before the assassins arrived, he persuaded his private secretary to do the deed. With this the Julio-Claudian era reached its end.

20

The Latin elegiac poets

During the Principate of Augustus, a genre of personal love poetry flourished that had developed from Hellenistic forbears, composed in the elegiac metre hence referred to as Latin Love Elegy. Many of these poems were written in an autobiographical style, presenting a poet-lover smitten by a domineering mistress who is given a name, and readers ancient and modern have attempted to use the poetry as evidence for a new kind of woman in the first century CE, one that challenged the traditional constraints placed on *matronae*. They argue that this could help explain the severity of Augustus' legislation regarding marriage and adultery. More recent readings, however, argue for the poetic portraits of sophisticated, sexually liberated and controlling women as part of the poets' artifice. The ultimate focus in the poems, in this view, is not the presentation of a "New Woman" but the male poet himself, engaged in a literary dialogue with contemporary and previous poets and exploring the artistic potential of posturing as someone who is at the mercy of both a woman and Love itself.

PROPERTIUS

Propertius, born in the mid–first century BCE, composed four books of elegiac verse. In many of these poems his relationship with a woman called Cynthia is the focus. Her name appears as the first word in the first poem of the collection.

"Cynthia first imprisoned me, unhappy man, with her eyes;
　before then I had been infected with no passion.
But then Love subdued my look of stubborn pride
　and with feet planted firmly pressed my head down
until he taught me to disdain chaste girls –
　the shameless fellow – and to live my life without design."
(1.1.1–6)

The poem closes with advice to other lovers to avoid his tragic situation, one that he, however, will endure heroically.

In the seventh poem of his first book, Propertius is explicit about the potential for earning fame by composing poetry that draws its inspiration from pain imposed by a harsh mistress. He is addressing an epic poet named Ponticus.

"I am compelled to serve not so much my talent as my pain
    and to bewail the harshness of this time in my life.
This is the way of life that consumes me, this is my fame;
    from this I desire renown to come to my songs.
May they praise me for being the only one to have pleased a learned girl,
    Ponticus, and to have often borne her unjust threats."
(1.7.7–12)

In the second book of Propertius' elegies, we find the poet's literary eroticism still engaged in an effort to establish a legitimate position in a poetic tradition that reached back through his Hellenistic antecedents to epic poets like Hesiod. Simultaneously he was engaged in another dialogue, with contemporary Roman values that defined male heroism by a life of action, particularly through military engagement and success.

In the seventh poem of this book he is explicit about his choice not to pursue activism on the battlefield or traditional marriage.

"... but Caesar [Augustus] is great in military strength:
    conquered nations are worthless in the arena of love.
For sooner would I allow this head to be severed from its neck
    than I could quench the fires of passion because of the conduct of a bride,
or as a husband pass by your threshold closed to me
    looking back with tearful eyes at this threshold I had betrayed."
(2.7.5–10)

His position is unchanged in the poems of Book Three.

"Love is a god of peace; we lovers show reverence to peace.
    Let those rough battles with my mistress be enough for me."
(3.5.1–2)

In his fourth book, written several years after than the first three, Propertius announced that his poetic talent would now be placed in the service of Rome and several of the 11 poems are devoted to specifically "Roman" themes, including one commemorating the victory of Augustus at Actium. Cynthia reappears in two of the poems, however. In the seventh poem the lover-poet describes a visit from her as a ghost following her death. He pictures her bending over him as he sleeps, reproving him for neglect.

"Faithless one – not expected to be better with any other woman!
    Can sleep hold its power over you already?
By now our stolen pleasures in sleepless Suburra have escaped your memory
    and my window worn thin by our night-time deceptions,
that window through which I so often dangled, having let down a rope for your sake,
    coming hand-over-hand into your embrace!
Often at the cross-roads Venus' rites were undertaken, and with our breasts intermingled
    our battles made the roads grow warm."
(4.7.13–20)

After upbraiding him further, and raising the suspicion that her death had been the result of poisoning, she acknowledges the fact that she occupied a prominent place in his poetry. She also registers the claim that she had been faithful to him.

"Nonetheless I don't reproach you although you deserve it, Propertius:
    my sovereignty in your books was long-lasting.
I swear by the chanting of the Fates, a song that can never be un-spun,
    (and may the three-headed dog soften his barking for me)
that I kept my faithfulness to you. If I am making a false claim may a serpent
    hiss on my tomb and lie over my bones."
(4.7.49–54)

In the next poem in this book she is very much alive, breaking in upon him as he is making love with a pair of street-women. (The sequencing of these poems supports an understanding of Cynthia as a literary construct.)

A poem in the fourth book celebrating Rome's history is devoted to the legendary tale of Tarpeia, who betrayed her city to the Sabines during the kingship of Romulus because of her love for the Sabine king Tatius (pp. 10–11 above). Propertius' Tarpeia is a Vestal whose passion violates her vows. The poet explores both her desire and her guilt. In the words he gives her, she becomes at once traitor and sinner. By opening the gates to the Sabines hoping to gain the commander's love, she betrays not only Rome but all young women. She also betrays Vesta herself, in whose temple resided the Palladium (the statue of Athena believed to have been carried by Aeneas from Troy).

"Such great censure I will bring upon young Roman women,
    I the wicked one selected as servant for the virgin hearth!
If someone is surprised that the fires of Pallas Athena have been extinguished

let him pardon me; the altar is being sprinkled by my tears."
(4.4.43–6)

The poem ends with the death of Tarpeia after she bargained for marriage to
Tatius and enabled the Sabines to enter the citadel. The king ordered his troops
to crush her under their shields for, in Propertius' words, "even an enemy does
not bestow honour on a crime" (v. 89).

Far different is the portrait of a real Roman matron, Cornelia, who is the focus
of the last poem of the fourth book of Propertius' elegies. The stepdaughter of
Augustus (whose mother was Scribonia, p. 130 above), Cornelia married Lucius
Aemilius Paullus Lepidus, who served as both consul and censor in Rome. To him
she bore three children before her death in 16 BCE. The poem is a monologue in
the form of an address from the grave to her husband. In this it resembles funerary
epigrams, words inscribed on tombstones intended to be read by passers-by. Most of
the poem consists of Cornelia's defence of her exemplary life, delivered to the gods of
the Underworld. In this it can be compared/contrasted with the seventh poem, and
the claim of the dead Cynthia that she had been without reproach as a mistress.

"My life was consistent; all of it was without censure.
    Between the torches (of marriage and death) we lived an exemplary life.
Nature gave me the laws that arise from a blood-line,
    such that I could not have been more virtuous through fear of being judged.
Let any voting urn at my sentencing carry stern verdicts about me;
    there will be no woman who sullies her reputation by sitting with me in my defence."
(4.11.45–50)

Cornelia had no reservations about the quality of her relationship with her
parents.

"Nor, mother Scribonia, dear to my heart, did I bring injury to you;
    what would you want changed in me, apart from my fate?
I receive praise through the tears of my mother and the laments throughout the city;
    and my bones are vindicated by the sorrow of [Augustus] Caesar."
(4.11.55–8)

After a reference to her earning the Augustan garment of honour bestowed on a
mother who has given birth to three children, she addresses them, consoling herself
with the knowledge that her descendants will continue to add lustre to the family.

"Be a pillar to the family by carrying on the bloodline; the boat of death is setting
off

for me, willing to go since so many of my blood will add to the glory of my actions.
This is the supreme reward in a woman's triumph,
    when a public report free from fear praises her in death."
(4.11.69–72)
(Propertius, *Elegies*)

TIBULLUS

Another Latin love elegist, probably an older contemporary of Propertius, was Albius Tibullus. Not much is known about his life, apart from the fact that he was closely connected with his patron, Marcus Valerius Messalla Corvinus ("Messalla"), a Roman orator, soldier and statesman whom Tibullus accompanied on military campaigns. Ancient and modern readers have commented on Tibullus' refined style and his deep affection for the countryside and its agrarian rituals. Two books of his poems have come down to us. In the first one a woman named Delia is the subject of his erotic attention, although some other poems (4, 7 and 8) reflect upon the attraction and dangers of boy-love. In the first poem, Tibullus distances himself from his patron's life of activism, and uses the poetic image of the lover who is kept outside of the door of the beloved (the *exclusus amator*, a motif that had been used in Greek erotic poetry).

"For you it is appropriate to go to war by land and sea, Messalla,
    so that your house may display the spoils of the enemy.
The chains of a beautiful girl keep me tethered
    and I sit as a porter in front of her unyielding doors.
I don't care to have a good name, my Delia; as long as I am with you
    I beg to be called idle and lazy.
May I be looking at you when my last hour has come,
    may I be holding you in my failing arms as I am dying."
(1.1.53–60)

In the next poem the poet-lover laments the fact that Delia's door is firmly barred. He addresses the door itself and proposes some covert cooperation to reach her.

"A cruel guard is positioned over my girl
    and the solid door is shut, firmly barred.
You, obstinate door of your master, may the rains lash you,
    may the bolts hurled by the powers of Jupiter seek you out.
Door, open now only for me, being overcome by my complaints

and, as the hinge-pin is turned when you open, groan on the sly."
(1.2.5–10)

The poet then addresses Delia, encouraging her to enlist the help of Venus to slip out from under the control of her "man". (The Latin word *vir* can mean both "man" and "husband"; in some instances Tibullus is more explicit, using the term *coniunx*, "husband".)

"You too, Delia, trick the guard without holding back.
　　You must be bold! Venus herself assists those who are daring.
She herself shows her favours, whether some youth is attempting thresholds untried,
　　or a girl is unlatching a tightly-barred door.
She teaches how to steal out of a soft bed undetected
　　and how to place a foot down without a sound,
how nodding can carry on a conversation, right under her man's eyes
　　and how to keep words of seduction hidden, through pre-arranged signals."
(1.2.15–22)

In the fifth poem of this book, Delia has defected. The poet replays the fantasies that he had held earlier, of Delia engaged with him in activities in the countryside, looking after the flocks and attending to his needs. Conscious of the fact that this existed only in his imagination, he curses her.

"May she eat bloody banquets and with a gory mouth
　　drink dreary cups heavily diluted with gall.
May ghosts flit around her, lamenting their fate
　　constantly, and may a screech-owl sing of a violent fate from the rooftops.
Goaded by hunger, may she be driven mad and search for weeds on graves
　　and bones left behind by savage wolves.
May she run with her groin bared and scream through the city streets;
　　may a snapping herd of dogs behind her drive her from the crossroads.
Let it be so: a god gives the signal. There are guardian spirits for the lover;
　　Venus rages, abandoned by a law that is unfair."
(1.5.49–58)

As the next poem begins, the poet-lover berates Love itself for deceiving him, as he reflects upon Delia's promiscuity. He then addresses her husband (using the explicit term *coniunx*), urging him to be more vigilant.

"Love, you always present me with alluring looks so that I am cajoled;
　　later on, however, you are gloomy and harsh to wretched me.

What cruelty are you bestowing on me? Is it a great honour
    for a god to have laid snares for a man?
Snares have been set out for me, for now shrewd Delia on the sly
    caresses some man or other in the quiet of night.
She denies it, to be sure, over and over, but it is hard to believe her:
    in the same way she always denies her affair with me to her man.
I myself, poor fool, taught her with what bargaining she could toy
    with guards: alas, alas, I am put down by my own technique!
Now she has learned to contrive reasons for sleeping alone,
    and learned how doors can turn on silent hinges.
Back then I gave her extracts from herbs with which a skin-mark disappears,
    one that love-making causes from the imprint of reciprocal biting.
But you, oh heedless husband of a deceiving girl,
    watch out for my sake too – see that she does not go astray!"
(1.6.1–16)

In Tibullus' second book the love-object is a girl named Nemesis. We get the impression that Nemesis lives in an all-female household with no mention of an official father, husband, etc., and there are some new features. The poet uses his mistress' love of urban finery to reflect upon a general decline from an enjoyment of the simple life to a love of riches and the strife brought on by greed. In the third poem, addressed to his friend Cornutus (probably a pseudonym), he complains that Nemesis is off visiting a country villa and – after fantasizing that he could play the farmer with her – curses her host who ploughs his fields for profit. But he also plays with the idea of tolerating her love of riches and his even supplying these.

"Alas, alas, I see that girls delight in riches:
    now if Venus chooses wealth, let the spoils come on,
so that Nemesis may float in my wealth and proceed through the city
    to be gazed upon because of my gifts.
(2.3.49–52)

But he rejects this notion too, lamenting the loss of the truly "golden" age that preceded agriculture and its gains, interweaving this thought with the current inaccessibility of the mistress.

"Acorns fed our ancestors, and far and wide they made love continually;
    what harm was there in not having full-seeded furrows?
Back then, for those on whom Love breathed kindly, gentle Venus
    unreservedly granted delights in a shady vale.

There was no guard, no door to keep out the sad lovers;
　　if it is right, I pray that this way of life return!"
(2.3.69–74)

In the fifth poem of this book, the poet-lover is explicit about the vital role Nemesis played in his artistry.

"I celebrate Nemesis in my songs continually; without her none of my verses
　　can find words or appropriate rhythm."
(2.5.111–12)

SULPICIA

Attached to the manuscripts containing the poetry of Tibullus are six short poems ascribed to a female elegist, Sulpicia – a rare testimony to the literary activity of Roman women alluded to indirectly by male poets. The soldier and literary patron Messalla was Sulpicia's uncle and became her guardian after the death of her father. She was doubtless influenced by the poetic activity of others in Messalla's circle – not only Tibullus but Ovid. Her work has been admired for its straightforward simplicity and candour but also for its polish. Although like Propertius and Tibullus she is self-referential as both a lover and a poet, some elegies are framed as correspondence with her lover Cerinthus (likely a pseudonym) or as notes from a diary. The 45 verses that remain are assigned to the fourth book of some editions of the Tibullan collection (numbers 7–12, following a division of the third book in the 15th century), but the references below reflect their place in the third book, as used in the digital library Perseus and in the Loeb edition.

　　The following poem of Sulpicia's celebrates her new love affair, one that she is determined not to conceal, despite its violation of the norms expected of a young woman with her pedigree.

"At last love has come, such a love that a report that I had concealed it
　　would have brought me more shame than had I laid it bare to someone.
Venus, much entreated in my verses, has brought him
　　to my breast and laid him there.
Venus has kept her promise: let some person tell of my bliss
　　if s/he has had none of his/her own.
I could wish that I didn't [have to] send anything in sealed tablets
　　to avoid someone reading it before my lover.
But it delights me to have transgressed: to compose my appearance for a good name is offensive;

I will be spoken of as one who has been proper in taking a man equally
proper."
(3.13)

The next pair of poems appears to document some drama surrounding Sulpicia's
birthday, provoking the poet's resistance to her uncle's control.

"My detestable birthday is at hand, which must be spent in the stupid countryside,
    a miserable one without Cerinthus.
What is lovelier than the city? Is a country estate fit for a girl,
    or a chilly river on the Arrentine plain?
Now, Messalla, do relax. You are quite too solicitous for me;
    the roads are often not seasonable, uncle, for travelling.
If I am dragged away I leave behind my mind and my heart
    to the degree to which it cannot occur as I wish."
(3.14)

Sulpicia succeeds, and the companion poem is addressed to Cerinthus.

"Do you know that the journey has been lifted from your girl's morose heart?
    Now she can be in Rome for her birthday!
May that day of my birth be celebrated by us all,
    the event which now comes your way perhaps contrary to expectation."
(3.15)

The following poetic epistle to Cerinthus was composed in quite a different
mood, demonstrating a witty combination of fury and pride. (The word *toga*
here signifies the dress of a woman of low repute, one who like a prostitute was
obliged to wear this brief garment rather than the matron's *stola*.)

"Thanks, for permitting yourself to be completely unconcerned about me
    lest suddenly I tumble badly, in my silly way.
Let your attention be drawn rather to a toga, and a wench burdened with her wool
basket
    rather than for Sulpicia, daughter of Servius.
There are people worried about me, whose greatest cause for concern on our
account
    is that I might give way to a bed-mate of low account."
(3.16)

In the following elegy the poet is ill, and appeals to Cerinthus for attention.

"Is it in you, Cerinthus, to show due concern for your mistress
    since at this moment a fever agitates my feeble limbs?
I would not wish to get over miserable illnesses
    unless I thought that you too wished me to do so.
But what good would it do me to get over my sickness
    if you are able to put up with my troubles with an unfeeling heart?"
(3.17)

In the final poem of Sulpicia's that we possess, she takes some responsibility for a rift between them.

"Now, my darling, don't let me be such a passionate trouble for you
    as I feel myself to have been a few days ago.
If ever I have done anything foolish in my entire youth
    for which I might confess that I have had more cause to repent
it was the fact that last night I left you behind on your own,
    wanting to hide my ardent desire from you."
(3.18)
(Sulpicia, *Elegies* as transmitted through the poetic collection of Tibullus)

OVID

The poet who was regarded in antiquity as the last to compose Latin Love Elegy was Publius Ovidius Naso (Ovid). He adopted and adapted motifs of his forbears such as the narrator describing himself as a slave to both a domineering mistress and to love. For Ovid the mistress was Corinna, whose name (like Catullus' Lesbia) was derived from a female Greek poet. Often the lover-poet in Ovid's elegies appears to be deliberately adopting the passive, subordinate role, but contradictory poses within the same poem suggest that Ovid is exposing this as a rhetorical ruse. In some of the elegies we find a transparent invitation to the mistress to deceive her husband, and even a conversation with the husband about his potential to act as a pimp for his wife. This, together with other poems normalizing adultery, likely led to Ovid's incurring the resolute opposition of Augustus, who sent him into exile on the shores of the Black Sea in 8 CE. He died nine years later and was buried there, in modern Romania.

One of Ovid's elegies that addresses his mistress and encourages her to ignore the emperor's attempts to enforce marital fidelity is the fourth poem in the first book of his *Amores* ("Loves"), where the lover plans to be at a dinner-party with his mistress and her husband.

"Your husband is going to come to the same dinner as we are –
     may that be the last meal for that man of yours, I pray!
So am I to gaze at my beloved girl merely as a fellow dinner-guest?
     The one who has the pleasure of being touched – will it be another man?
Will you warm the breast of another, leaning close to him?
     Will that man throw his arm around your neck whenever he wants?"
(1.4.1–6)

He gives instructions to his mistress to give secret indications of her devotion
to him.

"Learn all the same what you must do, and don't give my words
     to the East Wind to be carried away, nor to the warm South Wind!
Come before your husband does – although I don't see what advantage there is
     if you arrive before him; nonetheless, come earlier.
When he lies down on the couch and you come as his companion with a modest
demeanour
     to lie beside him – secretly touch me with your foot!
Watch me and my nods and the words caught by my expression;
     catch my secret signals and return them yourself.
With my brows I will say words that speak without making a sound;
     you will read words traced by my fingers, words traced in wine.
When the wantonness of our love-play comes to your mind
     touch your flushed cheeks with your soft thumb.
If there is something about me of which you disapprove silently in your mind
     let your hand gently dangle near the tip of your ear.
When what I do or say pleases you, my darling,
     let your ring be twisted around and around with your finger."
(1.4.11–26)

In the fifth poem of the first book of the *Amores*, Ovid describes an afternoon of
lovemaking between the poet-lover and his mistress. The focus is on the narrator's desire, aroused by gazing upon various parts of her body.

"It was sultry, and the day had passed beyond its midpoint;
     I laid my limbs out to rest in the middle of my bed.
Part of my window was open, the other part closed;
     the light was almost like that commonly found in the woods,
like dusk glowing dimly when the sun is retiring,
     or when night has departed but day has not yet risen.
The light was such as should be offered to bashful girls

in which their timid modesty would hope to find cover.
Well! Corinna comes in, with the veiling of her tunic coming undone,
   her parted hair falling down over her white neck –
like famous Semiramis is said to have been as she went to her bridal chamber,
   and like Laïs, the one who was loved by many men.
I tore away at her tunic – and it did not do much injustice to her extraordinary features;
   she struggled to be covered nonetheless by the tunic.
Although she struggled thus, it was as one who did not want to win;
   she was beaten without difficulty, by her own betrayal.
As she stood before my eyes with her robe to one side
   there were no blemishes anywhere on her entire body.
What shoulders, what arms did I see and touch!
   The shape of her breasts – how perfect for being touched!
How smooth was her belly beneath her tight bosom!
   What a long and fine flank! How youthful her thigh!
Why do I recount each detail? Nothing did I see unworthy of praise
   and I held her naked body close to my own.
Who doesn't know the rest of the story? We both lay quiet, exhausted.
   May mid-days like this often come my way!"
(1.5.1–26)

In the seventh poem in this book, Ovid describes a repentant poet-lover who has been violent with his mistress.

"If there is some friend nearby put manacles on my hands –
   they have deserved chains – until all my madness disappears,
for madness drove my reckless arms against my mistress.
   My girlfriend is weeping, hurt by my reckless hand.
At that moment I could have laid hands on my dear parents
   or dealt savage blows even against the holy gods!"
(1.7.1–6)

After reflecting on some mythical examples of destructive madness, the narrator returns to self-reproach, in which there may be an element of pride in his manly aggression.

"Who did not say to me, 'Madman'! Who did not call me 'Barbarian'!
   She said nothing. Her tongue was checked by trembling fear
but her silent features uttered accusations nonetheless.
   She charged me with my guilt by her tears, although her mouth was silent.

I might have wished that my arms had fallen off their shoulders beforehand;
    I could have usefully done without a part of myself."
(1.7.19–24)

In several poems from the next two books of the *Amores* Ovid picks up the
scenario of adultery more directly, with a narrator who addresses the mistress'
husband. In the elegy that follows the poet-lover actually tries to persuade the
other man to keep a tighter rein on Corinna. Easy access to her makes the
exercise for him a boring one, and lessens his desire.

"Stupid man, if you don't feel the need to have the girl under guard for yourself
    still see that you guard her for my sake, so that I may want her myself all the more!
What one is allowed to do is tedious; what isn't allowed lights the flame more
passionately.
    He is made of iron, the fellow who is in love with what another man allows."
(2.19.1–4)

Just as the poet-lover had advised Corinna to use deception and feign disdain
for him to keep his desire alive, he continues his advice to the husband to bar
his way. The absurdity of using the loss of a lover's sexual desire as a threat to
Corinna's husband may actually be an indication that Ovid as poet is playing with
and undercutting his predecessors' use of the motif of the enslaved elegiac lover.

"Now I am giving you a warning in advance: unless you begin to keep an eye on
your girl
    she will start to cease being mine!
I have put up with a great deal for a long time. I often hoped that the time would
come
    when you would keep a close eye on her, so that I might talk circles around you.
You are a slow one, and put up with what no husband ought to endure;
    but for me it will be the end of love, when it is handed to me!"
(2.19.47–52)

Ovid completely reverses this position in another elegy, now presenting a lover
badgering a husband who is exerting tight control over his wife. This raises further
the question of how seriously he subscribes to any single model for the elegiac lover.

"Harsh man, you get nowhere by having placed a guard over your tender girl;
    each woman has to protect herself through her own character.
If a girl is chaste when her fear has been removed then in the final analysis she is
chaste.

The one who doesn't misbehave because it isn't allowed, she is the one who misbehaves!
It may be that you have kept close watch on her body; her mind is adulterous.
    There is no woman who can be confined so as not to want it."
(3.4.1–6)

Ovid closes the poem with mythical examples of Love's inevitable triumph over constraints, citing the parallel of Rome's founding heroes, Romulus and Remus, who were conceived illegitimately.

    In one of the later poems in his third book of the *Amores* Ovid makes it clear that Corinna was ultimately a fiction. As such a desirable mistress she became the common property of his male readers, conferring fame on the poet who acted as her literary pimp.

"The girl who recently was said to be mine, whom I alone began to love
    I fear must now belong to many, and not belong to me.
Am I mistaken, or is it through my books that she has become known?
    This is how it will be: she has become a prostitute because of my genius.
It serves me right! Why did I make a public declaration of her beauty?
    My mistress has been put up for sale through my own fault.
She pleases because I am her procurer; under my guidance a lover is brought in,
    through my handiwork the door has been opened."
(3.12.5–12)

Ovid composed another elegiac work in three books, his *Ars Amatoria* ("*The Art of Loving*"). Here he takes upon himself the role of instructor, guiding men in how to seduce and keep a mistress in the first two books and in the third book giving women advice on how to win over a male lover. As with his *Amores*, it is often difficult to determine the degree to which the poet is serious.

    In the following verses he instructs women on how to disguise their physical faults.

"Yet rare is the face that lacks a blemish. Conceal those faults
    by whatever means you can, hide your body's weak-points.
If you are short, sit down lest by standing you seem to be sitting;
    however small you are, lie down on your couch.
Here also, lest it be possible for a measurement to be taken as you are lying down
    see to it that your feet are out of sight with a robe thrown over them.
Let one who is too thin put on full-textured garments
    and let her robe fall loosely from her shoulders.
Let the pale woman cover her body with purple stripes;

let one who is dusky-hued have recourse to the Egyptian fish.
Always keep an ugly foot hidden in a white slipper;
   don't let shrivelled ankles out of their bonds.
Small shoulder-pads suit high shoulder-blades;
   keep a breast-band around a narrow chest.
Let her indicate with a small gesture whatever she has to say,
   the one whose fingers are fat and whose nail is rough.
The one whose mouth is foul-smelling – let her never speak when she is not eating,
   and let her always keep her distance from the face of her man."
(3.261–78)
(Ovid, *The Art of Loving*)

21

Women in the inscriptional record

AURELIA

A relationship between a man and woman quite different from that of the elegiac lovers is described on the following inscription, which comes from a tombstone commemorating a married couple, both former slaves. Produced early in the first century CE, it contains a relief portrait of the couple clasping their right hands; on either side of them are texts describing a relationship of mutual devotion and the faithful attentiveness of the wife.

(*Left side*) "Lucius Aurelius Hermia, freedman of Lucius, a butcher from the Viminal Hill.
She who has preceded me in death
with her chaste body, my only wife, possessed of a loving spirit,
lived faithful to her faithful husband with equal devotion
since she failed in her duty out of no avarice."
(*Right side*) "Aurelia Philematium, freedwoman of Lucius.
While alive I was named Aurelia Philematium,
chaste, modest, knowing nothing of crowds
faithful to my husband.
He too was a freedman to the same master,
a man from whom I am separated, alas.
He was to me in fact and in truth
more than and beyond a parent.
He took me to his breast at the age of seven years.
At the age of forty years I am stronger than death.
He flourished in everyone's opinion
because of my constant attention."
(*CIL* I².1221 = VI.9449 = *ILLRP* 793)

ALLIA POTESTAS

The following inscription, with fulsome praise for a freedwoman, may date to the late Augustan period (but possibly later). Composed in verse and erected by a patron who is distraught at her loss, it describes her virtues – which include sustaining a harmonious *ménage à trois* that likely included her patron.

"TO THE GODS OF THE DEAD: THE TOMB OF ALLIA POTESTAS, FREEDWOMAN OF AULUS
'Here is the resting-place of a woman of Perugia, than whom no woman was more precious;
compared with many others scarcely one or two seem more diligent.
Such a great woman, you are contained in a little urn.
Cruel ruler of Fate and harsh Persephone,
why do you snatch away the good and why do evils prevail?   5
This is asked by all. I am too weary now to reply;
they give me their tears, kindly indications of their disposition.
Courageous, irreproachable, resolute, pure, a most loyal guardian,
a good housekeeper, clean also outdoors, highly regarded by the populace,
she alone was able to face every task.   10
She remained blameless in small talk.
She was first to slip out of bed, and to that same bed she took herself
last of all, taking rest when affairs had been set in order.
Her wool never left her hands without cause;
no one was above her in showing compliance and in wholesome habits.   15
This woman was never satisfied with herself; never did she consider herself a free woman.
She was beautiful, with lovely eyes and golden hair.
An ivory sheen remained on her face
such as they say no mortal woman has ever had,
and on her snow-white breast the outline of her nipples was small.   20
And what of her legs? Her carriage itself was that of Atalanta on the comic stage.
She did not stay still when anxious, but moved her lithe limbs
beautiful in a body that was generous; her hair was checked out everywhere.
Perhaps you will find reason to disapprove of her on the grounds that her hands were rough:
nothing pleased her unless she had done it by and for herself.   25
There was no endeavour that she thought she knew well enough.
She remained without ill repute, because she had never accepted wrongdoing.
While she lived she so guided her two young lovers
that they became like the example of Pylades and Orestes:
one home contained them and one spirit belonged to both.   30
After her death now on the contrary they are both growing old separated from each other.
What one such woman erected now instants of time are defacing.

Consider Troy, and what a woman once did!
I pray that this may be fair – to use grand comparisons for an event on a small scale.
These verses your patron, weeping endlessly, gives to you   35
as a gift for one who has been lost – but never have you been taken from his heart.
These he thinks are being given as welcome ones for those who have been lost.
After you no woman has seemed good to him,
he who is living without you, he who detects his own death while he lives.
He carries your name in gold on his arm to and fro   40
where he can keep it: *Potestas* borne in gold.
As long as my published tribute holds its force, however,
you will live on in my little verses.
Instead of you I hold on to my image of you as consolation;
I look after it with reverence and many garlands are devoted to it.   45
When I come to you it will follow me as a companion-piece.
But in my despair, however, to whom would I entrust such solemn rites?
If on the other hand he comes forth, someone in whom I could place so much trust,
in this one thing perhaps I will be blessed, inasmuch as you have been lost to me.
Woe is me! You have won: my fate has become the same as yours.   50
Whoever does injury to this grave dares to harm the gods:
This woman, believe me, made famous by this inscription, has other-worldly power.' "
(*CIL* VI.37965)

FEMALE SERVANTS

Within upper-class and imperial households, female slaves and freedwomen were employed in a variety of occupations. We have little evidence for their lives apart from the short summary found on tombstones. Those quoted below are taken from the sixth volume of *CIL*.

Female attendants looked after the wife/mother of the household. Some were referred to on their tombstones as "dressers".

"Gemina, freedwoman, dresser of Augusta (Livia). Irene, freedwoman, gave her the funeral urn." 3994
"Iucunda, dresser of Agrippina. Comarus, a transcriber of books." (She shared her burial place, presumably with her partner/husband Comarus.) 8879
"Dresser of Agrippina, lived 22 years." (Her tomb is shared with Hermes, her fellow-slave) 8960

"For Paezusa, freedwoman of Octavia wife of Caesar Augustus [Nero], dresser, lived 18 years. Philetus, freedman of Octavia wife of Caesar Augustus, made it out of silver for his very dear wife." 5539

One tomb inscription for two women attendants came from a columbarium, a monument containing a number of funerary urns for the Volusii family. The columbarium has heen dated to between 40 and 60 CE. In this inscription the household slave "Spendo" has commemorated his two female partners who lived with him in *contubernium*, the common-law relationship permitted to slaves. Presumably Panope predeceased Phoebe and both waited on the *matrona* of this family, Torquata, wife of the consul of 56 CE.

"To the Shades of the Underworld. Panope, dresser of Torquata wife of Quintus Volusius who lived 22 years and Phoebe who held the mirror, and lived 30 years. Spendo made this for his *contubernales*, who were well-deserving, and for himself." 7297

Other women styled hair.

"Here lie the bones of Eros, a hairdresser." 6368

Some of these ladies-in-waiting were described as "foot-followers", who might follow their mistress when she went out, supplying both dignity and safety. The following tomb marker was for a follower of Livia.

"Dascylus, an attendant of Tiberius Augustus, [made] this burial place for Julia Nebris, foot-follower of Livia, his very dear wife, for himself and his family." 5200

Servants would accompany their mistresses to the baths, and were known as "anointers". (In like manner male anointers would accompany their masters.)

"Galene, anointer of Livia." 4045
"Chia, anointer of Antonia wife of Drusus." (This Drusus was the brother of Tiberius.) 9097

Tasks involving wool-working and the production and maintenance of clothing routinely fell to female servants in a Roman household, as elsewhere. Many such women worked in the production of cloth.

"Hedone the spinner lived 30 years." 6341
"Messia Dardana, spinner. Iacinthus Dardanus, anointer, made this." 6343

"The bones of Italia, weaver." 6362
"To the gods of the Underworld Irene, wool-weigher. She lived 28 years. Olympus made this for his well-deserving common-law partner." 9497

The following commemorates women making clothing in the household of Agrippina the Elder.

"Chrysaspis overseeing clothing for Agrippina. Heliconis wife of Narcissus of the house of Augustus; the daughter of Heliconis lived three years. Heliconis, clothing-maker for Agrippina lived 26 years. After three years she died on the same day as her daughter." 5206

Other household tasks for servant women included caring for the family's clothes – laundering, folding and putting them away, and mending them.

"Here lie the bones of Coca Silia, a woman who cared for clothing. She lived for 20 years. Acastus her fellow-slave made this for her in light of her poverty." 9980
"Fausta, freedwoman of Livia, clothes-mender." 9038
"Iucunda, clothes-mender for Livia lived 25 years. Plato the slave of the son of Nero Caesar made this [tomb-marker]." 5357

PROFESSIONAL WOMEN

Some women were engaged in non-domestic occupations. Doctors and midwives could be free agents or belong to privileged households, including that of the emperor. They would be employed to look after the slaves as well as the master and mistress and their children. The following inscriptions are found in *CIL* VI.

"Secunda, doctor of Livilla." 8711 (This Livilla was daughter of Drusus and Antonia or of Agrippina and Germanicus)
"Prima, midwife of Livia." 8948
"Hygia, freedwoman of Marcella, midwife." 4458 (Marcella was the daughter of Octavia and niece of Augustus.)

NURSES

Upper-class women frequently delegated the care of their babies to wet-nurses, slaves within the household who often retained a close bond with their wards through adulthood. (Nero, dying in disgrace, was buried by two of his nurses and a concubine.) These inscriptions are also found in *CIL* VI.

"Prima, freedwoman of Augustus and Livia, nurse of Julia daughter of Germanicus." 4352

"Julia Iucunda, nurse of Drusus and Drusilla." 5201 (These were children of Aprippina and Germanicus. Iucunda would have been a freed slave, taking the name "Julia" from the Julian family.)

"Valeria Hilara, nurse of Octavia daughter of Caesar Augustus [Claudius] lies here with her very dear husband Tiberius Claudius Fructus. Tiberius Claudius Primus and Tiberius Claudius Aster made this [tomb monument] for those richly deserving." 8943 (Messalina, wife of Claudius, needed a nurse for her daughter and was probably responsible for freeing Valeria Hilara.)

Some women had a certain amount of education, and worked in secretarial positions in houses or shops.

"The urn of Corinna, clerk of the storeroom." 3979

"Sciathis Magiae, clerk, lived 18 years. Eros, a chamber-servant of Publius Octavus, made [the tomb monument]. He made it for his wife and himself." 9301

The following woman would have been employed primarily as a personal secretary, writing letters (an *emanuensis*).

"Balb[i]lles Hermes made this [tomb monument] for his wife Tyche, an *emanuensis*, who was well deserving." 9541

Other women made a living as entertainers.

"For Demetria Actes, freed slave of Augustus, a Greek musical performer who lived 35 years. Trophimus, a chamber-servant [made this] for his fellow slave, well deserving. Sacred to the gods of the underworld." 8693

"For Cnisimus the shoemaker and Peloro the singer who lived 30 years." 9230

22

The housekeeper of the villa

Many wealthy Roman men during the first century CE kept country estates, some of considerable size, which were worked by slaves in the same manner as they were during the Republic, when the farm was under the supervision of a steward, in most cases a slave. His partner (a common-law wife in the case of slaves) was an essential part of the smooth functioning of the villa, according to the agricultural writer Columella (first century CE).

Columella mentions the importance of the *villica* (cf. Cato's *vilica*, p. 69 above) in both restraining excesses in her partner and being of help to him in certain matters (*On Agriculture*, 1.8.5). Subscribing to the traditional idea that men's work is outside and women's inside the house, Columella sets down the ideal characteristics of such a woman.

"The *villica* ought to be young ... of sound health and not ugly in her appearance, nor again extremely beautiful, for undiminished strength will be what is required for keeping watch and for other tasks, and ugliness will make her partner disdainful of her, while too fine an appearance will make him lazy. So we must take care that we not possess a *villicus* who wanders and is disaffected from his partner, nor one who settles down inside the house and fastens himself to the embraces of the woman. But these considerations that I have mentioned are not the only ones to be attended to in a *villica*. For in the first place one must consider whether she keeps herself very far from an attachment to wine, food, superstitions, sleepiness, and from men, and whether what she ought to keep in mind and what she ought to provide for the future occurs to her as important." (12.1.1–3)

Columella spells out some of the *villica's* responsibilities, a certain number of which will take her outside the house.

"Finally, it will be necessary for her to remain as little as possible in one place, for her tasks are not of a sedentary sort, but at one point she will have to go to the loom and, if she knows something better, to teach it. If she knows less, then she should learn further from the one who understands things better. Then she must supervise those who prepare food for the household. At another time she must see to the cleaning of the kitchen and the animal stalls and – no less important

– the mangers. The sick rooms, even if they are free of patients, she must open from time to time to clear them of dirt, so that when the situation demands they may be available as in good order and in a healthful state for the sick. She also ought to exercise her authority over the provisioners and the stewards when they are weighing out something; no less important is her being present when the shepherds are milking in the stables or giving the teats to lambs or the young of other herd animals. She most certainly should be present for their shearing, and observe the wool carefully, and count the fleeces in comparison with the number of sheep. Then she must urge the house-stewards to air the furnishings and clean and polish the bronze utensils and free them from tarnish, and the other things that need repairing she should hand over to the craftsmen for fixing." (12.3.8–9) (Columella, *On Agriculture*)

23

Religion and magic

The importance of women's roles in religious rites was a constant throughout Rome's history. Although the father of the household (the *pater familias*) conducted several private family rituals, women were engaged in a variety of public religious activities that also were aimed at safeguarding family life.

THE MATRONALIA

One of the important festivals in which *matronae* were the principal participants was the Matronalia, a festival that occurred on the old Roman New Year, on the first day of March. It honoured the goddess Juno Lucina in her capacity as patron of childbirth. Ovid, in his verse chronicle and description of Roman festivals, describes the participation of mothers who crowded Juno's temple.

"Bring flowers to the goddess; this goddess delights
    in flowering plants. Wreathe your head with fresh flowers,
and say 'You have given us light, Lucina.'
    Say 'You attend to our prayer for safe childbirth.'
If there is a woman with child let her pray with hair unbound,
    so that the goddess may gently loosen her womb."
(Ovid, *Fasti* 3.252–8)

In a tradition preserved by Macrobius (early fifth century CE), *matronae* at this festival hosted their slaves at a banquet.

"During this month (March) ... the *matronae* serve up dinners for their slaves, as the masters do at the Saturnalia. They do this so that at the beginning of the year with this honouring they might induce the slaves to show perfect obedience. The men do it to render thanks for the services they have rendered."
(Macrobius, *Saturnalia* 1.12.7)

There are indications that some *matronae* may have not always have treated their slaves well, hence the annual banquet may have served to help quiet unrest in the household (e.g. Ovid, *Ars Amatoria* 235–44, *Amores* 1.14.12–18).

THE FESTIVAL OF *FORTUNA VIRILIS*

Ovid describes women's activities at another annual festival, that of *Fortuna Virilis* ("Manly Fortune"). It occurred on the first day of April, when the women bathed the statue of the goddess and offered her incense, then bathed themselves. The goddess shared her cult with Venus *Verticordia* ("Changer-of-the-Heart"), and with the focus in the ritual placed upon women's beauty the goal would seem to have been at least in part to ensure that men continued to be as attracted to their wives as they had been when first married. Ovid's account indicates, however, that prostitutes (barred from wearing the *stola* of a Roman matron) would also benefit from the rituals, remaining attractive to their clients.

"Latin mothers and newly-wedded women, worship the goddess with proper ceremonies,
     and you to whom the fillet and the long robe are not appropriate.
Remove the golden necklaces from her marble neck.
     Take off her ornaments: the goddess must be bathed all over.
When her neck is dry put back the necklaces on her neck.
     Now other flowers, now a fresh rose must be given to her.
You too she orders to bathe, under the green myrtle.
     There is a clear reason why she bids this, and take heed.
She was naked, drying her dewy locks on the shore.
     Satyrs – a wanton lot – caught sight of the goddess.
She realized it and covered her exposed body with myrtle.
     She was safe, and bids you repeat this in what you do.
Now learn why you give incense to Fortuna Virilis,
     there where the place is damp with warm water.
That place welcomes all women when their clothing has been put aside
     and one sees every blemish on the naked body.
So that she may cover the blemish and hide it from the sight of men Fortuna Virilis
     offers her services and accomplishes this when requested, for a little incense.
Nor is poppy, ground with white milk an unwelcome gift to choose
     and liquid honey squeezed from the comb.
When Venus was first led to her eager spouse she drank this;
     from that moment she was married.
Propitiate her with prayers of petition: under her watch
     beauty and virtue and a good reputation are there to stay.

In times of our ancestors Rome had slipped away from chastity:
    Forefathers, you consulted the old woman [Sibyl] of Cumae.
She ordered a temple to be built for Venus, and when it was duly completed
    Venus from that moment took on the title 'Changer-of-the-Heart'.
Most beautiful one, always look upon the race of Aeneas with gentle regard
    and take care of the great number of your brides."
(Ovid, *Fasti* 4.133–62)

THE FESTIVAL FOR CARMENTIS

Ovid gives an explanation for the festival held on 15 February in honour of the goddess Carmentis, a prophetic Muse who was reported to have immigrated from Greece. The rites commemorate the success of Italic women who aborted their offspring as an act of resistance against Senatorial rule that prevented them from riding in carriages. Plutarch's account of this (*Moralia* 278B) adds the detail that they also held a sex strike until they obtained what they wanted.

"For long ago the Ausonian mothers drove in carriages,
    which I believe were also named from Evander's parent.
Abruptly the honour was taken away from them, and every matron decided
    not to renew the line of the ungrateful spouses with any offspring.
So that she would not give birth each boldly, with an unseen thrust,
    she would drive the growing burden out of her womb.
They said that the Senate rebuked the daring wives for their cruelty,
    but restored the right that had been snatched away from them.
They ordered twin festivals to occur in like manner for the Tegean (Arcadian) mother
    for the sake of producing boys and girls."
(Ovid, *Fasti* 1.619–28)

RITUALS FOR TACITA

In the following account Ovid describes the rituals undertaken by an old woman to avert hostile speech. The rites, with magical overtones, are in honour of a divine figure named Tacita ("Silent One").

"Lo, an old woman sitting in the midst of young girls
    accomplishes rituals for Tacita (although she herself does not remain silent).
With three fingers she puts three beads of incense under the threshold
    where a little mouse has made a secret path for itself.
Then she ties enchanted threads to dark lead

and turns over seven black beans inside her mouth.
She burns in a fire the head of a *maena* (a small sea-fish)
    which she has bound with pitch and pierced through with a bronze needle.
She also drops wine on it, and whatever wine is left
    either she or her companions drink – however, she gets the larger share.
'We have overcome hostile tongues and unfriendly mouths,' she says
    as the old lady, drunk, departs."
(Ovid, *Fasti* 2.571–82)

WITCHCRAFT

A distinction between religious and magical activity is often difficult to make, as is clear from the above excerpt. Under the dictator Sulla in 81 BCE a law was passed against assassins and poisoners (*Lex Cornelia de sicariis et veneficiis*), which punished those who were judged guilty by throwing them to the beasts, crucifying them, burning them alive or, if they belonged to the upper classes, with exile. Women were often accused of using magical means, particularly to gain control over a lover, or to seek vengeance for a love relationship that had failed.

During the reign of Tiberius it may have been this law that was invoked during an investigation into the suspected killing of his second wife by the praetor Plautius Silvanus. Tacitus describes the charge against Silvanus for having flung the woman headlong to her death. When her father brought Silvanus before the emperor the accused gave an incoherent reply. Tiberius referred the matter to the Senate, after going to the praetor's house himself and taking note of signs that there had been a struggle. Meanwhile, Livia and the grandmother of Silvanus got involved, then the first wife of the accused was charged with witchcraft, on the grounds that it could have accounted for Silvanus' deranged behaviour.

"He referred the case to the Senate, and when a judicial committee had been formed Urgulania, the grandmother of Silvanus, sent her grandson a dagger. This action, as one might expect, was considered more or less a warning from the Emperor, owing to the friendship between Livia and Urgulania. The accused, after an unsuccessful attempt with the weapon, arranged for his veins to be opened. Soon Numantina, his first wife, accused of having inflicted insanity upon her husband by means of spells and poisons, was judged innocent."
(Tacitus, *Annals* 4.22)

We are not told why Numantina was relieved of the charge of witchcraft.

Judging from writers like Horace, who constructed a fearsome witch-hag named Canidia in his poetry, there was still anxiety in the Julio-Claudian age about the magical powers of women to control men. Canidia appears in three of his epodes – satirical verses in the iambic tradition. In the fifth epode he describes the witch as having captured a young boy in order to use his innards as a love-charm to woo back her lover Varus.

"Canidia, her hair and dishevelled head
    wreathed with short vipers,
orders wild fig-trees to be uprooted
    from graves, funereal cypresses,
and eggs smeared with the blood of a filthy toad;
    and the feather of a night-owl
along with the herbs that Iolcos and Iberia,
    rich in poisons, sends,
and the bones snatched from the jaws of a starving dog
    to be burned in the magic flames." (15–24)

Canidia, supported by the rituals of other witches, appeals to Night and to the goddess Diana for help in retrieving Varus, whose indifference she assumes was the result of a spell cast by another witch.

"He lies asleep on perfumed couches
    forgetful of every mistress.
Ah! Ah! he walks freely, released
    by the spell of an enchantress more skilled.
It is not through ordinary potions, Varus,
    lover of mine about to weep copious tears,
that you will run back to me, nor will your attention
    resume through Marsian spells.
I will prepare a greater one, a stronger drink poured out
    for you since you are scorning me." (69–78)
(Horace, *Epodes* 5)

In his third epode (v. 8), Horace gives an exaggerated poetic account of the effects of a dish infused with an overly-generous dose of garlic and served to him by his patron Maecenas. He asks whether Canidia might have had a hand in the composition of the dish.

FURTHER READING

Ancona, R. and E. Greene. 2005. *Gendered Dynamics in Latin Love Poetry.* Baltimore

Barrett, A. A. 1996. *Agrippina. Mother of Nero* London

—2002. *Livia. First Lady of Imperial Rome.* New Haven, CT/London

Bartman, E. 1999. *Portraits of Livia. Imaging the Imperial Woman in Augustan Rome.* Cambridge

Bradley, K. R. 1991. *Discovering the Roman Family: Studies in Roman Social History.* Oxford

—1994. *Slavery and Society at Rome.* Cambridge

Dixon, S. 2001. *Reading Roman Women.* London

Dolansky, Fanny. 2011. "Reconsidering the Matronalia and Women's Rites". *Classical World* 104, 191–209

Evans-Grubbs, J. 2002. *Women and the Law in the Roman Empire. A Sourcebook on Marriage, Divorce, and Widowhood.* London/New York

Fantham, E. *et al.* 1994. "Women, Family, and Sexuality in the Age of Augustus and the Julio-Claudians", in *Women in the Classical World.* Oxford. 294–329

—2006. *Julia Augusti. The Emperor's Daughter.* London/New York

Freisenbruch, A. 2010. *The First Ladies of Rome: The Women Behind the Caesars.* London

Gardner, J. F. 1986. *Women in Roman Law and Society.* London/Sydney

—1998. *Family and* Familia *in Roman Law and Life.* Oxford

George, M. 2005. (ed.) *The Roman Family in the Empire. Rome, Italy and Beyond.* Oxford

Ginsburg, J. 2006. *Representing Agrippina: Constructions of Female Power in the Early Roman Empire.* Oxford/New York

Greene, E. 1998. *The Erotics of Domination. Male Desire and the Mistress in Latin Love Poetry.* Baltimore/London

Hallett, J. 1992. "Martial's Sulpicia and Propertius' Cynthia". *Classical World* 86.2, 99–123

Horsfall, N. 1985. "*CIL* VI 37965 = *CLE* 1988 (Epitaph of Allia Potestas): A Commentary". *ZPE* 61, 251–72

Johnson, M. and T. Ryan. 2005. *Sexuality in Greek and Roman Society and Literature. A Sourcebook.* London/New York

Joshel, S. R. 1992. *Work, Identity, and Legal Status at Rome: A Study of the Occupational Inscriptions.* Norman, OK

—1995. "Female Desire and the Discourse of Empire: Tacitus' Messalina". *Signs* 21.1, 50–82

—2010. *Slavery in the Roman World.* Cambridge

Kaplan, M. 1979. "Agrippina Semper Atrox: A Study in Tacitus' Characterization of Women," in C. Deroux (ed.) *Studies in Latin Literature and Roman History.* vol 1. Brussels. 410–17

Keith, A. 1997. "*Tandem venit amor.* A Roman Woman Speaks of Love", in M. Skinner and J. Hallett (eds) *Roman Sexualities* . Princeton, NJ. 295–310

—2008. *Propertius. Poet of Love and Leisure.* London

Kleiner, D. E. E. and S. B. Matheson 1996. (eds) *I Claudia. Women in Ancient Rome* I. Austin, TX

Kraemer, R. S. 2004. (ed.) *Women's Religions in the Greco-Roman World.* Oxford

L'Hoir, F. S. 1994. "Tacitus and Women's Usurpation of Power". *Classical World* 88, 5–25

McGinn, T. A. J. 1998. "Emperors, Jurists, and the *Lex Iulia et Papia*" and "The *Lex Iulia de Adulteriis Coercendis*", in *Prostitution, Sexuality, and the Law in Ancient Rome.* New York/Oxford. 105–215

—2004. *The Economy of Prostitution in the Roman World: A Study of Social History and the Brothel.* Ann Arbor, MI

Potter, D. S. and C. Damon. 1999. (eds) *The Senatus Consultum de Pisone Patre*. Text, Translation, Discussion. *American Journal of Philology* 120.1, Special Issue.

Purcell, N. 1986. "Livia and the Womanhood of Rome". *Proceedings of the Cambridge Philological Society* 32, 78–105

Rawson, B. 1986. (ed.) *The Family in Ancient Rome. New Perspectives*. Ithaca, NY

Treggiari, S. 1971. "Libertine Ladies". *Classical World* 64, 196–98

—1974. *Women in Domestic Service in the Early Roman Empire*. Cambridge, MA

—1979. "Lower Class Women in the Roman Economy". *Florilegium* 1, 65–86

—1991. *Roman Marriage.* Iusti Coniuges *from the Time of Cicero to the Time of Ulpian*. Oxford

Wood, S. E. 1999. *Imperial Women. A Study in Public Images 40 B.C.–A.D. 68*. Leiden/Boston

Wyke, M. 2002. *The Roman Mistress. Ancient and Modern Representations*. Oxford

PART 5

THE LATER EMPIRE

After the death of Nero, Rome experienced a succession of emperors whose tenure was not infrequently short (four followed Nero in a single year). The next 300 years are referred to here as "The Later Empire". During this period the Romans experienced a period of relative stability and prosperity under the Antonine emperors until c. 180 CE. when with the Severan dynasty turbulence and civil wars again returned. In 284 CE Diocletian became emperor and re-established security with administrative reforms throughout what had become an enormous empire. The rise of the cult of Christianity had been threatening this stability from within, however, and Diocletian undertook the most severe of repeated official persecutions against the sect, until the emperor Constantine gave it legitimate status in 313 CE.

As the empire expanded Roman women could be found not only in Rome and throughout the Italian peninsula but on the frontiers of the Empire – elite women who followed Roman magistrates or military officers to the provinces and army outposts, but also women attached to regular soldiers throughout the Empire. In addition, families were sent out from Italy to form Roman settlements, and as the army began to recruit infantry and cavalry from local communities and Roman soldiers were permitted to marry non-Roman women (by the late second century CE) the Empire was growing increasingly hybrid.

While this and other factors resulted in some substantial positive changes in the lives of Roman women, who were exposed to non-Roman customs and sometimes found themselves sufficiently wealthy to become benefactors, there persisted the ideal of the chaste but fertile *matrona* whose reputation was inseparable from, and expected to enhance, that of her husband. It is not surprising, then, that the promotion of this ideal can be found in the writings of such men of the elite class as the historian Tacitus (56–117 CE) and the lawyer, magistrate and letter-writer Pliny the Younger (61–112 CE).

24

Women of the Imperial households

DOMITIA DECIDIANA

In his historical account of the achievements of his father-in-law Agricola (the Roman general credited with much of the conquest of Britain), Tacitus praises the harmony between Agricola and his wife and credits the latter for this.

"From [Britain] he returned to Rome to take on public magistracies and married Domitia Decidiana, who had been born into an illustrious family. And this marriage lent distinction and authority to his striving for greater achievements. They lived in wonderful harmony, through mutual affection and through taking turns advancing the other's interests. A more considerable amount of praise is warranted in the case of a good wife, although more blame is deserved by a bad one."
(Tacitus, *Agricola* 6.1–2)

PLOTINA POMPEIA

Pliny the Younger, a friend of Tacitus and a prominent Roman who undertook a number of magistracies under the Emperor Trajan, composed a speech praising the emperor that was delivered in the Senate in 100 CE. In his panegyric he praises Trajan for his choice of Plotina as wife.

"For many distinguished men a wife was either chosen unadvisedly or retained with some degree of tolerance, to their disgrace. In this way domestic dishonour ruined men highly esteemed in the public sphere, and what prevented them from being regarded as citizens with the highest reputation was the fact that they were of poor repute as husbands. But in your case your wife falls into the category of prestige and eminence. What, then, is more inviolable than this, more in keeping with traditional values? If a chief priest must choose a wife, wouldn't he choose either her or a woman like her – but where is one of her type? Notice how she lays claim to nothing for herself out of your good fortune except her own pleasure; how invariably she holds you personally in the highest regard, rather than your power!"
(83.4–6)

He continues with more details about the ideal wife who is a credit to her husband.

"How simple she is in her attire, how discreet in the company she keeps, how refined in her deportment! This is the task for a husband, one who has given such instruction and training, for to obey is glory enough for a wife." (83.7)

In the same speech, Pliny praises Trajan's sister Marciana, and the fact that she and Plotina were able to live in harmony under the same roof.

"As for your sister, how she keeps in mind that she is your sister! How in her your own simplicity, your integrity, your straightforwardness are recognized! So that if one were to compare her to your wife one would be compelled to wonder whether it is more effective to have been well instructed or well born, when it comes to living a principled life. Nothing is more likely to provoke dissention than jealousy, especially among women, and this all the more particularly so when a woman is born into a life shared [with another] and nurtured with equal attention; then she becomes inflamed with jealousy, and the outcome of this is hatred. To this extent it must be considered all the more admirable that there is no strife, no rivalry, between the two women living in one house and with equal good fortune. They admire one another in turn, they give way to one another in turn, and since each loves you most effusively they think that it doesn't matter to them in the least which one you love more. They have the same goal, the same rule of life and there is nothing that would make you think they are two individuals." (84.1–4)
(Pliny the Younger, *Panegyric for Trajan*)

That Plotina was more than a demure wife in the shadow of the emperor, however, is indicated by a short historical summary of the Roman emperors written at the end of the fourth century called the *Epitome de Caesaribus*. In referring to wives whose advice helped their husbands, the writer mentions an intervention of Plotina's.

"Not to mention others, it is beyond words to say how much Pompeia Plotina enhanced the reputation of Trajan. When his procurators were stirring up the provinces with their malice to the extent that one of them was said to meet each rich man with 'Why are you wealthy?' and the other would reply 'Where did *you* get your riches?' while a third would say 'Lend at interest what you have,' Pompeia grabbed her husband and, upbraiding him on the grounds that he was being careless of his good name, delivered such a reproach that afterwards, hating shameless extortions he called the imperial treasury spiteful, because as it grew the rest of its extensions were wasting away."
(*Epitome de Caesaribus* 42.21)

Plotina and Trajan had no children, and it appears that the empress played a role in the selection of her husband's successor. According to the biography of Hadrian in the *Historia Augusta* (another fourth-century document compiling imperial "biographies" from the fourth century that often included anecdotal and unverifiable material), Plotina encouraged the marriage between Marciana's granddaughter Sabina and Hadrian, a cousin of the emperor for whom the imperial couple had acted as guardians after the death of his father. Trajan resisted the match at a time when the two men were at odds (2.10), but Plotina's will prevailed. Given that the couple had no children, Hadrian's marriage to Trajan's closest surviving female kin was significant, and the same source reports the belief that it was through the manoeuvring of Plotina that Trajan, when he realized he was dying, named Hadrian to succeed him as emperor (4.10).

Plotina's reputation for intervening in affairs calling for imperial decisions continued after Trajan's death in 117 CE. In a letter she wrote to Hadrian four years later, preserved on an inscription found in Athens, she launched a petition on behalf of the Epicureans, requesting that the emperor loosen the require- ments for becoming head of the philosophical school in order to ensure quality leadership. The letter begins diplomatically, with her address to the emperor as "master", but also indicates that she is on familiar terms with Epicureanism.

"Master, you know very well that I have an interest in the Epicurean school. You must help in the question of its succession, for because it is not permitted for a non-Roman to be named successor the ability to choose one is restricted. I am asking therefore in the name of Popillius Theotimus, who is the present officer in Athens, that he be permitted by you to give notice in Greek concerning the section of his dispensations that pertains to the orderly arrangement of successors, and that he be able to replace himself with a successor of non-Roman status, should he consider it an advantage for his public appearance. See that what you have conceded to Theotimus the future successors of the School of Epicurus will enjoy from now on, according to the same principle. This is all the more pertinent since it is noted that, whenever there has been a mistake made by the testator in the case of the election of a successor by common consent, a replacement is made by the disciples of this same sect – one who is the best man. This would be easier if he were selected from a larger group."
(*ILS*² 7784)

Hadrian's response follows this on the same inscription in the form of a letter confirming that new regulations will be put in place. A third letter was recorded on the inscription, Plotina's (in Greek) reporting with enthusiasm to the Epicurean community the imperial decision for which they owed gratitude to Hadrian.

When Plotina died (122/121 CE), Dio reports that Hadrian in his tribute to her acknowledged her strength and the success of her petitions to him.

"When Plotina died Hadrian praised her, saying 'she asked a great deal of me and was never disappointed'. By this he meant nothing other than that she asked such things as were not onerous for me, nor did she tolerate my refusal."
(Cassius Dio, *Roman History* 69.10.3)

MATIDIA

Shortly afterwards, Hadrian gave another eulogy, for Matidia, the mother of his wife Sabina. The speech is preserved (in a fragmentary state) on an inscription. In what survives the emperor refers to her as his "most beloved mother-in-law", and indicates that his own grief makes it difficult to do justice to her virtues, which were broadly known. He focuses on her fidelity to the husband who predeceased her, despite her relative youth, and on her family loyalty that supported his position as emperor.

"She lived as one beloved of her husband and after [his death] she was, during her long widowhood, in the peak flowering of her life and lived with the utmost chastity as one with supreme beauty in her appearance, most obedient to her own mother and herself a most generous mother, a most loyal kinswoman, helpful to everyone – a burden to no one and causing grief to nobody. As for her relationship with me ... such great discretion that she never requested anything from me because she did not ask for many things that I would have preferred be asked by my women-folk. With much good will and lengthy prayers ... She preferred to rejoice in my good fortune rather than to profit by it."
(*CIL* XIV.3579)

Matidia, Marciana (Trajan's sister and Matidia's aunt) and later Plotina were awarded the title of "Divine Augusta" by Hadrian, an honour first bestowed upon Livia.

SABINA

Sabina, Hadrian's wife, accompanied him to Egypt together with her friend Julia Balbilla, a Greek woman with poetic skill for whom Sabina may have acted as patron. (Hadrian's court was characterized by a hybrid cultural mix of Greek and Roman.) Julia Balbilla commemorated the Egyptian visit in epigrams that were inscribed on a statue of the Greek mythical hero Memnon at Thebes. The statue was (and still is) a "singing" statue, and the poem referred to the voice as one welcoming Sabina. Julia does not, however, miss an opportunity to have recorded in stone her own royal lineage and her authorship of the verses.

"Memnon, child of Dawn and revered Tithonus
   sitting before the Theban city of Zeus
or Amenoth, an Egyptian king, as they relate –
   the priests who are knowledgeable about ancient tales.
Hail! And by your utterance may you be earnest in welcoming her also,
   the revered wife of the lord Hadrian.

The poem then refers to the fact that the statue had been carved by the Persian king Cambyses, who had led an invasion of Egypt in the 6th century BCE, destroying statues of Egyptian gods. His impiety led to his eventual death, perhaps accidentally, by his own sword. In contrast to Cambyses, the statue will live on, as will the words of Julia Balbilla.

"But I do not reckon that this statue of yours would perish,
   and I am aware within that your soul shall be immortal.
For pious are my parents and pious were my grandparents,
   Balbillus the wise and King Antiochus –
Balbillus, sire of my royal mother
   and Antiochus the king, father of my father.
From their lineage I too have a share in blood that is royal
   and these written words are from me, Balbilla the pious.
(From Bernand, A. and E., no. 29)

Julia Balbilla's grandfather Antiochus was the last Hellenistic king of Commagene (modern Armenia); her other grandfather (Balbillus) had been a Roman prefect in Egypt.

   There are some indications that Sabina's marriage to Hadrian was not a harmonious one. In the *Historia Augusta* the author of the chapter on Hadrian mentions that the emperor dismissed some learned men for acting in too familiar a fashion with Sabina. (One of these was the biographer Suetonius.) This is followed by a comment on Sabina's ill humour.

"[Hadrian] installed successors to Septicius Clarus, the prefect of the praetorian guard, and Suetonius Tranquillus the overseer of imperial correspondence, and many others, because they had – without his consent – conducted themselves in Sabina's company in a more informal way than the dignity of the imperial court demanded. He would even have divorced his wife as he himself said, if he had been a private citizen, on the grounds that she was stubborn and bad-tempered."
(*Historia Augusta*, "Hadrian" 11.3)

Later in this same section (11.7) we are told that Hadrian was resented for committing adultery with married women and for homosexual liaisons. Despite all of this, coins and other public images of the imperial couple at the time stressed marital harmony; on one sculptural relief produced after her death, Sabina was depicted ascending to the heavens with an attentive Hadrian looking on.

FAUSTINA THE YOUNGER

Hadrian was succeeded by Antoninus Pius who married Annia Faustina. Like Hadrian, Antoninus found a male imperial heir through adoption. He married Marcus Aurelius to his daughter Faustina the Younger. The marriage was extremely fertile, and the symbolic association of imperial fecundity with political concord was exploited and projected through images in the public sphere. From the *Historia Augusta* we have the suggestion that this praise was even more sharply out of line with the nature of this marriage than was the case with Hadrian and Sabina.

"Some say, something that also appears close to the truth, that Commodus, Antoninus' successor and son, was not begotten by him but was the product of adultery. And such a story they connect with a popular rumour, that once Faustina, the daughter of Pius and wife of Marcus, when she saw some gladiators pass by, was inflamed with passion for one of them. When she was suffering from a lengthy illness she confessed her passion to her husband. When Marcus had related this to the Chaldeans their advice was this: once the gladiator was killed Faustina should bathe herself in his blood and in this state should sleep with her husband. When this had been accomplished her passion was indeed removed, but Commodus was born a gladiator, not an emperor." (19.1–5)

The author contends that the rumour is plausible, for Commodus had disreputable habits associated with the likes of gladiators. The text continues with the claim that Faustina's adultery was no secret.

"Many, however, have reported that Commodus was clearly born as the result of adultery, since it is generally agreed that Faustina had chosen as lovers for herself at Caieta both sailors and gladiators. When Marcus Antoninus was told about this, so that he might divorce her, if he did not kill her, he is reported to have said 'If I divorce my wife I would also return her dowry.' What, then, was regarded as her dowry? The Empire, because he had received it from his father-in-law after being adopted in accordance with Hadrian's wishes."(19.7–9)
(*Historia Augusta*, "M. Antoninus")

Like the empresses who immediately preceded her, Fautina The Younger received divine honours after her death, and was depicted (like Sabina) ascending to the heavens. Marcus Aurelius was shown at her side.

JULIA DOMNA

A mixed report is also given for Julia Domna who married Septimius Severus, a Roman from North Africa who seized power in 193 CE following a period of political turbulence. The empress was clearly a patron of literature and learning. The Greek sophist and writer Philostratus explained his debt to her, which included his receiving the papers of a Syrian scholar named Damis, a man who became his mentor.

"One of the kinsmen of Damis brought his notebooks containing his memoirs, previously unknown, to the attention of the empress Julia. Since I participated in the circle that gathered around her, for she admired and followed rhetorical discourse of all kinds, she assigned to me the transcribing of these treatises and to take care with their contents, since they were explained by the man from Ninos clearly but not so skilfully."
(Philostratus, *Life of Apollonius of Tyana* 1.3)

It was at the instigation of the empress that Philostratus embarked upon his biography of Apollonius, a Neo-Pythagorean philosopher. The negative reports about Julia Domna that have come down to us may be explained by evidence supplied by Dio about the undue influence wielded in the imperial household by the prefect of the Praetorian Guard, one Plautianus.

"In all sorts of ways did Plautianus have such control over [the emperor] that he did many terrible things to Julia Augusta, for he altogether hated her and he was always slandering her in front of Severus, making investigations into her conduct and extorting evidence from well-born women by torture. Because of this she began to study philosophy and spent her days with sophists."
(Cassius Dio, *Roman History* 75.15.6–7)

Dio is less concerned with protecting Julia's reputation when he passes on an anecdote that circulated about a conversation the empress had with a woman from the north of Britain.

"In connection with this (laws enacted by Severus against adultery) a very clever remark is reported to have been made by the wife of a certain Argentocoxus, a

Caledonian, to Julia Augusta. She [Julia] was teasing the woman after the treaty about their unrestricted sex with men. She replied, 'We fulfil the constraints of nature much better than you Roman women, for we keep company openly with the best men, while you are debauched in secret by the worst sort.'"
(Cassius Dio, *Roman History Epitome* 77.16.5)

Some of the negative reports of Julia's conduct are, predictably, transmitted by the *Historia Augusta*, whose entries are marked by a tendency to include details with sensational appeal.

"[Severus] was, however, less cautious at home; he restrained Julia, who was notorious for her adulteries, and was even guilty of conspiracy against him." (18.8)

Julia produced two sons, Caracalla and Geta. After Severus' death in 211 they ruled jointly until Caracalla had his brother murdered. The *Historia Augusta* implicates their mother in both the murder and incest.

"What could have been more fortunate for Septimius Severus than if he had not begotten Bassianus (Caracalla)? He was a man who immediately accused his brother of contriving plots against him, a murderous fiction, and killed him. He was a man who took as wife his own stepmother. What did I say, stepmother? On the contrary, I meant 'mother', on whose breast he had killed her son Geta." (21.6–8)
(*Historia Augusta*, "Severus")

Julia Domna committed suicide in 217 CE.

25

Women throughout the Empire

REFLECTIONS IN POETRY

Martial, a composer of epigrams from Spain who published his work in Rome in the late first century CE, frequently satirized Roman life, and women were not infrequently his target. He took advantage of the expansion of the frontiers of the Roman Empire in one of his poems to present in raw terms the array of foreign lovers available to a Roman girl away from the imperial city.

"You give yourself to the Parthians, you give yourself to the Germans, you give yourself to the Dacians, Caelia,
    and you do not disdain the couches of the Cilicians nor the Cappadocians;
and for you from his Egyptian city comes sailing the sex-driving Memphiticus,
    and the black Indian from the Red Sea.
Nor do you run from the groin of the circumcised Jews,
    and the Scythian on his Sarmatian horse does not pass you by.
For what reason do you do this – although you are a Roman girl –
    given that no Roman cock is pleasing to you?"
(Martial, *Epigrams* 7.30)

It is worth noting that Martial benefited from the patronage of a woman on the fringes of the Empire, his Spanish countrywoman Marcella who provided him with a house and estate where he could write far from the distractions of Rome (*Epigrams* 12.31). In one poem he praises her refinement.

"Who would think, Marcella, that you were a citizen of hardy Salo
    and were born in my homeland?
So rare, so sweet your good taste. The Palatine will claim
    that you are its own if they but hear you once,
nor will a girl born in the centre of Subura rival you
    or someone raised on the Capitoline Hill.
The glory of a foreign birth will not soon deride a woman
    who would be a more suitable Roman bride.
You bid my desire for my Mistress City be milder;

you alone make a Rome for me!"
(Martial, *Epigrams* 12.21)

Martial had a high opinion of another foreign woman, Sabina Ateste from Gaul, to such a degree that – presumably because of her own literary prowess – he arranged to place in her hands a fresh copy of some unpublished poetry. In *Epigrams* 10.93 he describes wrapping the manuscript in purple, perhaps indicating that she was a provincial patron. This is significant, not only because she was a non-Roman but because Martial, like his contemporary satirical poet Juvenal, was certainly capable of composing misogynistic verse.

Educated women were not always treated with respect by the poets. In his *Sixth Satire*, Juvenal takes on women who parade their learning.

"She is more disagreeable, however, the one who, when she begins to lie down at table
praises Vergil, pardons Dido when she is about to die,
takes on the poets and compares them, then holds up Vergil
on one side of the scale and Homer on the other.
The grammarians admit defeat, the rhetoricians are beaten;
the whole crowd is silenced, and neither the lawyer nor the herald would speak
nor another woman. Such a force of speech pours down
that you would say an equal number of bowls and bells were being beaten."
(Juvenal, *Satires* 6.434–42)

INTERACTIONS ON THE FRONTIER

Roman governors of the provinces throughout the Empire, together with a retinue that not infrequently included their wives, were sometimes impressed by the strength and effectiveness of the women in the tribes they were sent to conquer or rule. In his study of German tribes Tacitus says the following of the influence German women had over their men.

"It is recorded in their living memory that certain battles when they had been lost or were wavering were reversed by the women, through their unrelenting prayers and by bearing their breasts in front of them when captivity was shown to be close at hand, which they fear far more intensely for their women's sake." (8.1.1–5)

Tacitus adds the comment that taking young German women of high birth as hostages was effective for securing the loyalty of defeated tribes, then he adds another detail about features of the German women that commanded respect.

"But it's true that they think that in women is some sort of holiness and prophetic power, and they don't disdain their advice or disregard their responses." (8.2.1–3.1) (Tacitus, *Germania*)

By contrast with the Germans, who acknowledged their dependence upon women, Romans were somewhat reluctant to encourage wives from following their husbands into the field. In 21 CE, a motion had been passed in the Senate that provincial governors' wives should be prevented from accompanying their husbands. Tacitus explains why.

"With an entourage of women there were features that would delay the process of peace through their extravagance, or of warfare through their timidity, and would convert a Roman march into something resembling a barbarian procession. Not only is their sex frail and unequal to struggling, but if freedom to act as they please is available they become ferocious, ambitious, greedy for power." (Tacitus, *Annals* 3.33)

ROMAN BRITAIN

In Britain the Romans had faced the formidable female commander Boudica in 60/61 CE when Nero was emperor. Leading her tribe (the Iceni) in revolt against the Roman occupation in response to some treachery on the part of the occupiers, she had routed a Roman legion while the general was fighting on the nearby island of Anglesey, and spurred the Britons to fight.

"The whole island went to war under the command of Boudica, a woman of royal descent – for they do not make a distinction of sex in their rulers. Going after the (Roman) troops who had been scattered among the forts they captured the garrisons and invaded the colony (Colchester) that they saw as the seat of slavery. Their wrath and their victory overlooked no sort of savagery found among barbarians." (Tacitus, *Agricola* 16.1)

The Romans regrouped under their general upon his return and defeated the Britons, despite being heavily outnumbered. Boudica either took her own life or fell ill and died.

Twenty-five years after the defeat of Boudica, a Roman garrison was stationed on the northern frontier of Britain in Vindolanda, where Hadrian would later build a fortified wall across the island. Between 85 and 120 CE, the settlement of soldiers with wives, children and slaves carried on an active life together. Details of this have survived in part because some correspondence between the settlers was preserved on wooden writing tablets in anaerobic conditions. From these we can get a partial glimpse of the daily life of Roman women in this outpost. (The tablets can be read on both sides of the thin sheets of wood but there are gaps in the text.)

When men corresponded with one another they often included greetings to or from female relatives. Where individuals are addressed as "Sister" or "Brother", the term is probably being used as one of endearment within a small and isolated community, rather than indicating a biological relationship.

(Front) "Florus to his Titus, greetings ... Brother
(Back) Your daughter Ingenua greets you both."
(*Tab. Vindol.* III 643)

The prefect-commander of the garrison at Vindolanda was Flavius Cerialis and his wife was Sulpicia Lepidina. Sulpicia had a female friend named Claudia Severa, and the correspondence between the two women reflects their closeness. The following was written by Severa.

(Front) "... greetings, Sister. Just as I had spoken with you and promised that I would ask Brocchus and would come to you I made my request and he answered me that it was always with a ready heart that he permitted me to be able to come to you in company, in whatever way I can. For there are certain necessities which ... you will receive my letters in which you will know what I am about to do ... these things for us. I was and I will remain at Briga. Greet your Cerialis for me."
(Back) "Farewell, my very dear Sister and my longed-for soul-mate.
To Sulpicia Lepidina, wife of Cerialis, from Severa, wife of Brocchus."
(*Tab. Vindol.* II 292)

On one of the better known tablets we find Severa inviting Lepidina to join her for her birthday celebration.

"Claudia Severa to her Lepidina, greetings. On September 11th, Sister, for my birthday celebration I am asking you with pleasure to see that you come to us, to make the day more enjoyable for me by your coming, if you will do this ...
Greet your Cerialis. My Aelius and my little son send greetings ...
I shall expect you, Sister. Farewell, Sister, soul-mate, may I be in good health.
To Sulpicia Lepidina, wife of Cerialis, from Severa."
(*Tab. Vindol.* II 291)

Another tablet refers to a birthday celebration for Lepidina, one which a colleague of her husband felt obliged to attend.

(Front) "Clodius Super to his Cerialis. Greetings. I would have been with you most willingly, Brother, for your Lepidina's [birthday]. In any case ... that you ... reciprocate [?]. For may you know at least that every time we are together it is most delightful for me. For I did not think ... lest before ...
(Back) To Flavius Cerialis
(*Tab. Vindol.* III 629)

The following letter supplies evidence that women in Vindolanda directed petitions to Commander Cerialis through Lepidina.

"Valatta to her Cerialis. Greetings. I ask you, my master, by your posterity and through Lepidina, that you grant me what I ask."
(*Tab. Vindol.* II 257)

ROMAN EGYPT

Other direct textual evidence for the lives of women living at a distance from Rome comes from papyri in Egypt. In an affidavit from the fourth century CE that was read before a court, a woman complains about the extremely violent behaviour of her husband.

"A response to all the outrageous things he said about me:
He locked up his own slaves and mine, along with my foster-children and the administrator and his son for seven whole days in his cellar; he dealt violently with his slaves and my slave-girl Zoë, [nearly?] killing them with his beatings, and set fire to my foster-daughters, after stripping them naked, totally against the laws.
   He said to the same foster-daughters, 'Give me everything of hers,' and they said that they had received nothing from me. He said to the slaves as they were being beaten, 'What did she take from my house?' Under torture they said then, 'She took nothing of yours, but all your property is safe.'"
(*Pap. Oxy.* 903.1–11)

Further allegations emerge about their troubled marriage, including her husband's taking the keys from her, locking her out when she went to church and manipulating the accounts that were in her name. The statement closes with the woman's claim that he threatened to take a mistress.
   In keeping with the legislation first enacted under Augustus (pp. 127–8 above), a woman sent a petition to the Roman prefect for the right to act without a guardian because she has had the requisite number of children. The document seems to indicate that women in Egypt could strengthen the case

for conducting business on their own by claiming that they were literate. The papyrus is from the third century CE. The beginning is fragmented.

"[There are laws], most eminent Prefect, that grant to women who are honoured with the 'right of three children' the power to conduct their own affairs and to transact business without a guardian in household dealings that they negotiate, and much more so for those women who are literate.

Accordingly, in addition to this, having the fortune of being blessed with a good number of children and being literate and able to write with the greatest ease, I address you in full confidence, your Eminence, by this petition for the ability to carry out without impediment the household business that I conduct from now on."
(*Pap. Oxy.* 1467.1–21)

There is a sentence at the end of this text indicating that the application was filed in the prefect's office, presumably confirmation that the petition was successful.

POMPEII

From literary or historical texts we have only fictional or oblique textual references to the actual lives of working women. For sex-workers and waitresses, direct testimony comes from paintings uncovered in the brothels of Pompey and texts painted on the walls of shops and businesses (graffiti), discovered when the ash layer from the eruption of Mount Vesuvius in 79 CE was removed. From this evidence we learn, for example, that women worked in food and drink shops (*tabernae*) or inns (*cauponae*), where there was some expectation from the patrons that the women were available for sex.

"I screwed the maid at the *caupona*." (*CIL* IV.8442)
"Successus the weaver loves the serving-girl in the *caupona*. Her name is Hiris (= Iris), who doesn't care for him, however; when he asks she takes pity on him. His rival wrote this. Farewell." (*CIL* IV.8259)

A literary account of the *caupona* is found in the second-century novel of Apuleius, where the female wine-seller feeds, seduces then robs the principal character. (*Metamorphoses* 1.8)

Female barmaids and food servers played another role in Pompeii. Although they probably couldn't vote in local elections, their testimonies written on the doors, walls, ceilings, etc., of their places of work indicate that their preferences for certain candidates carried some weight with voters. On the walls of a *taberna* whose remains can be seen today we find the name "Asellina", who may be the owner. The names of other women are also recorded there – likely slaves/servants in the business – and the women register their support for local candidates who were campaigning for various public offices in the city.

"Asellina proposes Ceius Secundus as *duovir* for giving judgements." (*CIL* IV.7873)
"The Asellinae (sisters?), together with Smyrna, propose Gaius Lollius Fuscus as *duovir* for maintaining roads, temples and public buildings." (*CIL* IV.7863)
"Aegle proposes Gnaeus Helvius Sabinus as aedile, one worthy of the republic. I entreat you to make this happen." (*CIL* IV.7862)
"Maria proposes Cnaeus Helvius Sabinus." (*CIL* IV.7866)

With the following inscription on the outside wall of a building in Pompeii a woman urges voters to support her grandson as aedile.

"I, Taedia Secunda, earnestly entreat you to make Lucius Popidius Secundus aedile. His grandmother asks this and she made [the inscription]." (*CIL* IV.7469)

In the entrance room of Asellina's *taberna* was painted a greeting from one of her serving girls, who introduces herself as the "lovely Hedone" (her name is the Greek word for pleasure, which may signify her readiness to offer other services). In the inscription, Hedone lists the prices of her drinks in *asses*, a coin of small denomination.

"... Hedone says, 'for an *as* one can get a drink here; if you give two *asses* you will drink better, and if you give four you will drink Falernian wines." (*CIL* IV.1679)

Women also registered business deals on the walls of Pompeian eating/drinking establishments. A money-lender named Faustilla appears on a few such inscriptions. The following was found on the wall of a *taberna*.

"On the 10th of February Vettia loaned 30 *denarii* with monthly interest of 12 *asses*. On the 3rd of November Faustilla loaned 25 *denarii* with monthly interest of 9 *asses*." (*CIL* IV.4528)

(A *denarius* at this time was worth 16 *asses*, roughly equivalent to the daily wage for a common soldier or unskilled labourer).

26

Wealthy women

EUMACHIA

From other inscriptions we learn that certain women of the Late Empire were benefactors of their cities, and some of these were from Pompeii. Eumachia was a wealthy priestess and patron of the guild of Pompeian wool-cleaners (fullers), and according to the inscription funded a large and prominent public building, perhaps donating it (at least in part) for the fullers' use.

"Eumachia, public priestess, daughter of Lucius, in her own name and in the name of her son Marcus Numistrius Fronto had made with her own money a basilica chamber, the crypt and the colonnade, and dedicated these same constructions in honour of Concord and Augustan Piety." (*CIL* X.810)

The fullers demonstrated their gratitude to Eumachia by paying for a statue of her to be placed in the building. The statue and its dedicatory inscription have survived (*CIL* X.813).

JULIA FELIX

Another wealthy Pompeian woman was Julia Felix, who advertised through a graffito that parts of her estate were available for rent by an up-scale clientele. The translation of some terms in the following inscription is uncertain.

"On the property of Julia Felix, daughter of Spurius, are leased: Baths Venerium et Nongentum ('of Venus and Nine Hundred'?), taverns, shops, dining rooms/ upper-storey apartments. Available from the first August 13th until the sixth August 13th, renewable for five years. If the five years pass, the lease will be by agreement only." (*CIL* IV.1136)

The building with this bath complex can still be seen in Pompeii.

UMMIDIA QUADRATILLA

In Casinum, a town south-east of Rome (at the base of Monte Casino), was found an inscription for a woman named Ummidia Quadratilla, who presented her town with large public structures.

"Ummidia Quadratilla daughter of Gaius funded with her own money an amphitheatre and temple for the people of Casinum." (CIL X.5813)

Ummidia was the grandmother of Ummidius, who had been mentored by Pliny the Younger. In a letter written after the woman's death, just before her 80th birthday, Pliny applauded her careful upbringing of her grandson, while taking a dim view of the pastimes from which she shielded him.

"He lived an austere but deferential life in the household of his grandmother who was addicted to pleasure. She kept a troupe of pantomime actors and indulged them more freely than suited a woman of rank. Quadratus did not watch them either in the theatre or at home, and she did not require him to. When she was entrusting the education of her grandson to me I heard her say that as one of those women of leisure she was in the habit of relaxing her spirit with a game of dice and watching her pantomime performers, but when she was about to do one or the other of these things she had always given instructions to her grandson to go away and devote himself to his studies. This seemed to me to come from her affection no less than her respect for him."
(Pliny, *Epistles* 7.24.3–5)

CORELLIA

Pliny possessed a large family estate bordering Lake Comum (modern Lago di Como in Lombardy). He agreed to sell part of it to Corellia, a woman who had been a close friend of his mother's. His negotiations with her reflect the fact that she conducted financial transactions with ease and confidence. The following letter, written by Pliny to his wife's grandfather who lived near this estate, tried to justify his settling on a price lower than the going rate.

"You are surprised that my freedman Hermes disposed of land that I had inherited to Corellia without putting it up for auction, land that I had ordered to be sold at auction, at 700,000 *sesterces* – 5/12 of my estate. You figure that they could have yielded 900,000 and you are all the more curious whether I shall confirm what he has done as unalterable. I am confirming it for certain. Take heed of my reasons, for

I wish for you to approve and that it be forgiven by my fellow heirs, because I am disassociating myself from them out of obedience to a higher duty.

I am fond of Corellia, holding her in the highest esteem, first as the sister of Corellius Rufus (whose memory is most sacred to me) and also because she was a very close friend of my mother's. There are long-standing ties between me and her husband, Minicius Iustus, an excellent man, and likewise the strongest ties with her son – so much so that he presided over the games held during my praetorship. When I was last in the vicinity she indicated to me that she wished to possess something around our house at Lake Comum. I offered her any one of my estates that she wanted, for the price she wanted – with the exception of what I inherited from my parents. Even to Corellia I cannot concede this. So when the inheritance came my way, in which those farms are included, I wrote to tell her they would be sold. Hermes carried her this letter and when she urged him to transfer my share to her at once, he complied.

You see how I am bound to confirm the action that my freedman conducted in accordance with my own wishes. It remains for my co-heirs to bear with equanimity the fact that I had sold separately what was not permitted to sell at all. They are not compelled to follow my example; they do not have the same ties with Corellia. They can therefore look after their own interests, in place of which for my part was friendship. Farewell." (7.11)

In another letter Pliny wrote to Corellia directly, when she had indicated that she was prepared to pay the (higher) assessed price.

"You are most generous in asking so earnestly and insisting that I give orders that the price to be paid by you for my lands not be fixed at 700,000 *sesterces* (the price levied by my freedman) but at 900,000, the value on which you paid the 20th per cent inheritance tax to the tax-farmers. I ask and insist for my part that you consider not only what suits you but also what suits me and that you permit me to resist you on this one occasion, in the same spirit in which I usually comply with all our agreements." (7.14)

(Pliny, *Epistles*)

27

Lower-class women

Tomb inscriptions throughout Italy tell us of a variety of occupations in which freedwomen and slave-women were engaged. The inscriptions cannot be dated with certainty, beyond ranging from the Late Republic to the second century CE. The following are all found in *CIL* VI.

Some freedwomen were teachers (*paedagogae*), probably in all cases of girls.

"Statilia Tyrannis, freedwoman of Titus, teacher of Statilia." (6331)

Literate women could also function as secretaries.

"Sacred to the gods of the Dead. For Hapate (= "Hypate"), secretary, a Greek woman who lived 25 years, Pittosus erected this for his sweetest wife." (33892)

Skilled freedwomen could also find employment as seamstresses. Because freed slaves at this time could contract a legal marriage, Titus Savius could speak of Matia Prima as his wife.

"Titus Thoranius Savius, freedman of Titus, erected this for himself and for Matia Prima, his wife, freedwoman of Gaia, dressmaker from the Six Altars (an area of Rome). She lived 46 years." (9884)

Other freedwomen worked in food markets. Freedmen erecting their tombs referred to themselves as the women's patrons, and in some cases also their husbands.

"Aurelia Nais, freedwoman of Gaius, a fishmonger in the warehouses of Galba (emperor 68–69 CE). Gaius Aurelius Phileros, freedman of Gaius, her patron, and Lucius Valerius Secundus, freedman of Lucius. (9801)
"To the gods of the Dead. For Abudia Megiste, freedwoman of Marcus, most dutiful. Marcus Abudius Luminaris, her patron and also her husband, erected this for a well-deserving dealer in grains and vegetables from the Middle Staircase. [He erected it] for himself and for his freedmen and freedwomen and descendants and for Marcus Abudius his son of the senior contingent of the Esquiline tribe who lived 8 years." (9683)

For unskilled women, wool-weighing was an occupation. That Irene in the following inscription is referred to as a *contubernalis* rather than a wife suggests that she and Olympus were slaves.

"To the gods of the Dead. [The tomb] of Irene a wool-weigher. She lived 28 years. Olympus erected this for his well-deserving partner." (9497)

Certain Roman writers of this time period refer to other occupations in which women were engaged. Consistent with earlier practice, nurses were introduced to the household to help with childrearing, and often the attachment lasted beyond the age of dependence. Pliny the Younger, who owned several estates, felt close enough to his nurse to give her a farm. In the following letter he thanks his friend Verus for improving its condition and increasing its value for her.

"Thank you for undertaking to tend to that little farm I gave to my nurse. It was worth 100,000 *sesterces* when I gave it to her but later, when the returns decreased, its value shrunk. Now, under your care, it will recover. You just remember to keep your attention focused not only on my trees and the land, although I include these too, but on my little gift. That it become as fruitful as possible is not more important to her who receives it than that it is mine, as it is I who gave it."
(Pliny, *Epistles* 6.3)

Another occupation that was critical to the functioning of the Roman family was the midwife. Her tasks naturally included assisting a mother in childbirth, but would also involve supplying some general medical attention to women who might feel more comfortable confiding in her than in a male physician. The medical writer Soranus (late first/early second century CE) listed the requirements he regarded as essential for the Roman midwife.

"It is necessary to enumerate a full list of the qualities which make for the best midwife, so that the best ones recognize themselves and the beginners focus on them as their models. In addition, this is so the public knows whom to call when in need. In general we say that the one is accomplished who merely succeeds in carrying out the complete range of medical tasks, but the best one is she who, having acquired some techniques beyond this medical competence, is broadly experienced in theoretical approaches. More particularly, we say that the best midwife is she who is trained in all therapeutic areas (for some cases must be treated by diet, others by surgery, and still others with drugs). This midwife is able to supply instructions and is able to see both the broad picture and the particulars, and to gather from this what is expedient – not from the causes of the illness nor from repeated assessments of symptoms that occur generally or a single one of these.

Now with regard to detail she will not change her method according to changes in the symptoms, but will supply a remedy in accordance with the development of the illness. She will remain calm, unperturbed in critical moments; she will be able to give a clear justification for her remedies, providing encouragement for the patients and sympathy. She need not in all cases to have borne children, as some allege, in order for her to have compassion for the mothers because of the common experience of childbirth pains (for this sympathy is not felt more by someone who has given birth). She must be robust because of her duties and not in all cases young, as some allege, for a young woman can be weak and, on the contrary, an older person can be strong. She will be disciplined and sober on every occasion because of the uncertainty about when she will be summoned for women in danger. She must have a quiet demeanor, for she will be called upon to share many secrets of life. She must not be fond of money lest, wickedly, she give an abortive for payment. She is not to be superstitious, thanks to which she does not neglect a beneficial remedy because of a dream or an omen or some common and popular secret rite. Let her preserve the softness of her hands, avoiding wool-working that can harden them; she may have acquired the softness through the use of ointments if this is not present naturally. The best midwife must be of such a sort."

(Soranus, *Gynecology* 1.4 = CMG IV pp. 5–6)

28

The female body

In the second century BCE, Herophilus, a Greek physician working in Alexandria, had determined through dissection that in women's bodies the uterus was attached within the abdomen by membranes. Despite this, a belief persisted for many centuries that the womb moved throughout the body seeking moisture, a cause of illness and instability in women. This popular belief had been reflected in the treatises of the Hippocratics, and was repeated by Plato and Aristotle as well as medical writers of the Roman period.

ARETAEUS

Aretaeus was a physician from Cappadocia in Asia Minor practising in the first century CE. Like Plato he likened the uterus to a living thing, moving in response to smells. Like his predecessors he recommended a dramatic form of aromatherapy to alleviate the distress caused by the roving uterus.

"In the middle of the flanks of women lies the uterus, a female inner organ most like something living, for on its own it moves here and there toward the flanks. But it also moves upward in a direct line to below the cartilage of the thorax, and obliquely to the right or left, either to the liver or the spleen. It also becomes more inclined to prolapse downward, and in a word it is entirely erratic. It also takes delight in pleasant smells and rushes toward them, but is irritated by foul smells and flees from them. All in all, the uterus in a woman is like some living being within a living being.

If, then, it is suddenly carried upwards and remains there for a length of time and compresses the viscera then the woman experiences a choking sensation, akin to epilepsy but without the seizures. For the liver, the diaphragm, the lungs and the heart are quickly crowded in a narrow space. A loss of breathing seems to occur, along with a loss of speech."

After a description of other symptoms that follow the womb's upward movement through the body (including death), Aretaeus turns to recommended therapies for this condition.

"... the [symptoms] originating with the uterus are helped by foul smells, and the application of fragrant things to the female parts."

The treatise repeats the long-held belief that women's bodies are more moist than male bodies. This was particularly the case with young women, in whom the fluidity apparently could interfere with their ability to reason.

"... for the uterus is buoyant, and its membranes are moist. The place where the uterus lies is also humid. In addition, it both flees and is drawn to smells, toward pleasant ones and away from unpleasant ones. It easily plunges here and there like a block of wood, and floats up and down. Because of this the affliction occurs in young women, but least of all in old women. In the former their youth and their way of life and their judgement is more unpredictable, and their uterus is also unsteady." (63K)
(Aretaeus, *On the Causes and Symptoms of Acute Diseases* 2.11 = CMG II, pp. 32–3)

GALEN

Galen was a prominent Greek physician and philosopher born in Pergamum (in modern Turkey) in 129 CE. He received medical training in Smyrna, Corinth and Alexandria, and dissected animals, writing extensively on human anatomy and physiology. His understanding of the human body was adopted by European physicians until the Early Modern period. In Rome he was employed as the physician for several emperors, including Marcus Aurelius.

His understanding of the female reproductive system was affected by the Aristotelian belief that women possessed less heat than men. Although he saw the structure of the reproductive systems of men and women as analogous, he read the latter as inferior.

"The female is therefore less perfected than the male, and the first reason is the fact that she is colder. For if among animals the warm type is more active the colder one would be less perfected than the warmer one. In respect to the second reason, this is revealed by dissection."

In Galen's view, the structure of the female reproductive organs was the inverse of the male, with the components confined to the inside of a woman's body through lack of heat.

"All the parts that are found in men – these are there to be seen in women too. In only one way is there a difference between them, which must be kept fully in mind during the whole discussion, namely how the parts are located inside women but on the outside of men, originating in the area called the perineum."

Arguing that the ovaries are parallel to the male testes and the uterus to the scrotum, Galen describes their formation in the female embryo.

"Just as human is the most perfected of animals so in the same way is a man more perfected than a woman. The cause of this perfection is the superiority of his heat, for this is the first instrument of Nature. For those in whom it [heat] is defective the created being has to be less perfected. So it is not surprising that the female is less perfected than the male, to the degree that she is colder."
(Galen, *On the Usefulness of Parts of the Body* 14.6 = Kühn IV, pp. 158–62)

SORANUS

Soranus (pp. 192–3 above) was a Greek physician from Ephesus in Asia Minor, who had also practised medicine in Alexandria before working in Rome during the reigns of Trajan and Hadrian. He published four books on gynecology, and in comparison with his predecessors and contemporaries demonstrated a more mechanical understanding of women's physiology, pathologies and therapies.

Although Soranus accepted a connection between a woman's experiencing sensations of suffocation and a disorder of the uterus, he explained the problem not by likening the womb to a living being but by hypothesizing a constriction of the membranes that attached it to the surrounding organs. This was in keeping with the "methodist" school of medicine, which regarded a healthy state as one produced by a balance between constriction and looseness of body parts.

"The uterus is attached by fine membranes to the bladder on the upper side, on the underside to the rectum, on the sides and back to the projections of hip-joints and the sacrum. So when these membranes are constricted by an inflammation, the uterus is drawn up and tilted to one side, but when they are loosened and relaxed, the uterus prolapses. It is not so because it is a living creature, as some believe, but because it has, much like other living organisms, a tactile sense and because of this it is constricted by cooling agents and relaxed by loosening ones." (1.8 = CMG IV, p. 7)

For the discomfort suffered by the woman whose uterus had shifted, Soranus recommended gentler therapies than those used by his forbears.

"When the onset occurs one should lay the patient down in a room which is moderately warm and bright and, without disturbing her, rouse her from the collapsed state by moving the jaw, placing warm compresses all over the middle of her body, gently stretching out the entire cramped part, supporting each of the extremities, and through touching with the bare hands warming all the cool parts. Then one should wipe the face with a sponge soaked in warm water, for sponging the face has a vitalizing effect." (3.28.2–3 = CMG IV, p. 110)

Whereas earlier medical writers had focused on the need to regularize women's menstrual cycles, often by methods that were painful and put the patient at risk (such as urging marriage and intercourse as soon as girls reached puberty), Soranus advised a gentler approach.

"That menstruation is approaching has to be inferred by the difficulty in movement at the appointed time of the period. It is followed by a heaviness in the loins; sometimes there is pain as well, and sluggishness and constant yawning and tension of the limbs. Sometimes there is a ruddiness in the cheeks that either remains or is dispersed and after an interval shows itself again. In some cases it may be inferred also from the fact that there is nausea in the stomach and a loss of appetite. Menstruation occurring for the first time can be inferred both from these indications but in particular from the growth of the breasts, which broadly occurs during the fourteenth year, and from the heaviness around the abdomen along with the irritation of the onset of puberty. It happens that women forced to have intercourse suffer this. (1.24 = CMG IV, p. 16)

Soranus advised a regimen for women experienced in menstruation that may include some exercise.

"When menstruation begins for the first time, accompanied by the discomfort that we have described, rest is most often helpful.
    ... But in the case of women who have already menstruated often, each must be allowed to do what is her usual practice. For some are accustomed to taking a rest, while others continue with moderate activities. But it is safer to rest and not to bathe, especially on the first day." (1.26.1–2 = CMG IV, pp. 16–17)

When women were about to give birth, Soranus recommended that there be three women to assist in addition to the midwife (2.5), and that attention be given to keeping the woman warm and comfortable.

"For normal childbirth one must prepare in advance: olive oil, warm water, hot compresses, soft sea-sponges, wool, bandages, a pillow, a midwife's stool or chair, two beds and a proper room; oil for injections and cleansing, warm water for the washing of the places involved, hot compresses for the alleviation of pains and

sponges for wiping her off; pieces of wool to cover the woman's parts; bandages for swaddling the newborn and a pillow so that the infant may be placed on it below the woman giving birth until the after-birth has been carried away; things to smell such as pennyroyal, a clod of earth, barley-meal, quince, and if the season is right citron, melon, cucumber and everything like these, for the recovery of the woman in labour." (2.2–3 = CMG IV, pp. 50–1)
(Soranus, *Gynecology*)

A MISCARRIAGE

Death in childbirth was all too common in the Greco-Roman world, attested by tombstone inscriptions. Many of these inscriptions indicate that these women were adolescents, girls urged to marry as soon as they reached puberty. One young wife who faced this precarious situation was married to Pliny the Younger (61–c. 112 CE). At the age of about 40, after the death of two wives and hopeful of having children, he married Calpurnia Hispulla, probably only 14 or 15 years of age, a girl from his native town of Comum whose grandfather managed his estates there. From the letters he wrote her when they were separated, it is clear that there was a very strong bond between them. His desire for her to become a mother was offset by his anxiety when her life was endangered by a miscarriage, as he communicates in letters to Calpurnia's grandfather.

"As much as you wish to see a great-grandchild born to us you will be all the more sorry to learn that your granddaughter has had a miscarriage. In her youthfulness she did not realize that she was pregnant, and because of this she omitted certain precautions that need to be taken by pregnant women, and did certain things she ought to have left undone. She has paid for this by learning a severe lesson, in having been placed in the greatest danger.

So, although you must experience it as grievous that your old age is robbed now of a descendant, one that was on the way, yet you ought to thank the gods because, while they denied you great-grandchildren for the present they spared your granddaughter. They will grant us children, for whom she herself makes us firmer in our hopes, although her fertility has been proven in too unfortunate a manner."
(Pliny, *Epistle* 8.1)

Pliny was to be disappointed in these hopes, for Calpurnia did not produce children. Nonetheless, from their correspondence we can see the strength of the attachment between them. He wrote the following letter during one of the times when she was away from home. He understands the plight of the elegiac lover.

"It is unbelievable, how I am a captive of desire for you. In the first place the reason for this is my love for you, then because we are not accustomed to being apart. The result is that I spend a good part of the nights awake with your image before me, and then during the day, in the hours I was accustomed to seeing you, my feet of their own accord (to use an expression that is so true) take me to your room. Then finally, reluctant and sorrowful – like the locked-out lover – finding it empty I turn back. The one time I am spared these torments is when I am wearing myself out in the Forum and with the lawsuits of my friends. Judge then what life is like for me, when my rest is found in work and my consolation is found in my unhappiness and anxieties. Farewell."
(Pliny, *Epistles* 7.5)

29

Adultery and prostitution

A message that was conveyed to Romans throughout their history maintained that respectable women who engaged in sexual activity outside marriage were threatening not only the family but the harmony and health of the state. (See, for example, the words of the poet Horace above, p. 128) The attempt to draw a sharp line between the conduct of the chaste *matrona* and that of the prostitute was not always successful, according to the poets, however.

JUVENAL'S SIXTH SATIRE

Women's decadent behaviour was the subject of a poem composed by Juvenal, one of his 16 Satires composed in the late first and early second centuries CE during the reigns of Trajan and Hadrian (p. 182 above). These were poetic reflections on the social customs of Rome marked by hyperbole, and in the case of this poem comedic effect is produced for the audience by a variety of misogynistic comments.

"Eppia, a senator's wife, accompanied a gladiator
to Pharos and the Nile and the famous fortifications of Lagus,
while Canopus condemned the outrageous morals of our city.
That woman wasn't giving a thought to home and husband and sister,
nor was she devoted to her fatherland; shameless, she abandoned her weeping children,
and – you would be even more amazed at this – she deserted Paris and the games."
(82–7)

Claudius' wife Messalina is presented as an example of this type of behaviour.

"Why should you give a thought to a private house, to what Eppia did?
Turn your attention to those who rival the gods (deified emperors); listen
to what Claudius endured. When his wife had perceived that her husband was asleep
this woman, daring to prefer a rush mat to a couch on the Palatine,
the harlot Augusta daring to wear a hooded robe of the night

left home with no more than a single handmaid accompanying her.
Hiding her black hair under a blond wig
she entered a brothel seething with its well-worn quilts
and entered the empty cubicle reserved for her, then naked
with her nipples gilded she stood forth taking on the false name of Lycisca
and exposed the womb that bore you, Britannicus of noble birth. (114–24)
With flattering words she receives those who come in and demands her fee;
soon, when the brothel-keeper is already dismissing the girls
she leaves, reluctantly and – the most she can do, however – she closes her cubicle
last of all, even now burning hot with the lechery in her stiffened womb.
Exhausted by men but not yet having had her fill she goes back.
Grimy with dirty cheeks and the smoke of the lantern
she carried the filthy scent of the whorehouse to the imperial pillow." (125–32)
(Juvenal, *Satires* 6)

LUCIAN

Prostitutes and brothels were readily available for Roman men (indicated by the central location of the brothels that can be seen in Pompeii today). What was the life of a courtesan like? A fictional account is given by Lucian, another composer of satirical verse (c. 125–180 CE), who lived in the Roman province of Syria. Among the many works attributed to him were comic dialogues, including 15 purported conversations between courtesans. The fifth dialogue, between Leaena and Clonarium, conveys details of a sexual relationship between women (one of whom was from Lesbos) that purportedly took place at a party organized by two rich married women who were living like married partners. When Clonarium asks for some details about the party, Leaena reveals that she had been seduced by one of the women.

(Clonarium) "Leaena, we have been hearing strange things about you, that the rich Lesbian woman Megilla is in love with you just like a man and that you have sex, doing heaven knows what with each other. What is this? Are you blushing? Tell me if this is true."
(Leaena) "It is true, Clonarium. I am ashamed of it, for it is abnormal." (289)

When Leaena describes her Lesbian lover as man-like, Clonarium presses her for details about their love-making.

(Leaena) "She herself and Demonassa from Corinth, another rich woman who practises the same art as Megilla, organized a drinking-party. They took me along

to play the cithara for them; when I had played my music and it was late and time to sleep and they were drunk Megilla said 'Come, Leaena, it's now a perfect time for bed. Sleep here with us, in the middle between us.'"
(Clonarium) "Did you go to sleep? What happened after this?"
(Leaena) "At first they were kissing me just like men, not only bringing their lips to mine but opening their mouth and embracing me and rubbing my breasts. Demonassa even bit me the while. I didn't know how to make sense of what was going on. After a time Megilla, being by now quite heated, pulled the wig off her head, which was like real hair and close-fitting; it revealed the skin of her head, which was shaved close, just like the most manly of athletes. When I saw this I was taken aback. But she said, 'Leaena, have you ever seen such a handsome young man?' 'But I don't see a young man here, Megilla,' I said. 'Don't make a woman out of me,' she said, 'for I am telling you that I am Megillus and have been married for a long time to this woman Demonassa and she is my wife.' I laughed at this, Clonarium, and said, 'Then, Megillus, you concealed from us the fact that you were a man, just as they say Achilles was concealed among the girls, and you have all the manly equipment and do to Demonassa just what men do?' She said, 'Leaena, I don't possess that. I have absolutely no need of it. You will see that I have to hand a much more pleasing method of my own.'" (290–1)

Leaena, bewildered, asks Clonarium whether she is a hermaphrodite and possesses both male and female body parts. The latter assures her that she is physically a woman but has the mind and desires of a man, and can satisfy any woman. Leaena reports on the progress of the seduction.

(Leaena) "She said, 'If you don't believe me, Leaena, just co-operate and you will realize that I am lacking nothing that men possess, for I have a substitute for the masculine equipment. Just submit to me, and you will see.' I gave in, Clonarium, when she begged me over and over again and gave me a necklace, an expensive one, and linen of the finest weave. Then I embraced her just like a man and she went ahead and made love to me and panted and seemed to be enjoying herself to the extreme.'" (292)

Clonarium wants to know the technique her lover used, but Leaena resists.

(Leaena) "Don't ask me the exact details, for it is embarrassing, so by Heavenly Aphrodite I would not tell you!" (292)
(Lucian, *Dialogues of the Courtesans* 5)

The view of lesbian sex as abnormal but titillating could be explained by the poem's male author (and audience?).

30

Religion

Regular religious activity of Roman women continued throughout the imperial period. With the exposure to new cults that came with the expansion of the Empire, several of these were added to the array of traditional cults, something that was facilitated by the polytheistic nature of Roman religion. Tensions were inevitable, however, with the incorporation and development of the Christian cult, which was both monotheistic and exclusive.

WOMEN AND TRADITIONAL CULTS

That the Matronalia was still celebrated by women of the Late Empire is attested by a (fragmentary) tablet from Vindolanda mentioning the fact that, as in Rome, it occurred on the first of March (*Tab. Vindol.* III 581).

On a prominent tomb monument of the fourth century CE was inscribed a lengthy text recording significant details about a prominent Roman couple. It includes a list of the initiatory experiences and roles played by Fabia Aconia Paulina, daughter of a consul and wife of Praetextus, a prefect, consul elect, augur and priest. She credits her husband with her introduction to mystery cults. The following verse inscription was recorded on the back of the monument.

"You as a pious initiate keep hidden with secrecy of mind the revelations of the mysteries
and as a man of learning you acknowledge the many-faceted sacred power of the gods.
You include in your generosity your wife as a partner in the rituals,
a woman who has a joint understanding of men and gods, and is faithful to you.
What might I say of the honours or powers
and the pleasures to be sought through the prayers of men,
which you always assert to be destined to vanish and of little significance –
you who as priest of the gods with fillets of priestly office are called eminent?
You, my husband, through the advantage of your learning,
release me from the allotted destiny of death;
you introduce me to the temples and dedicate me as an attendant of the gods.

With you acting as my witness I am inducted into all the mysteries.
You, my pious consort, honour me as presiding priestess
of Cybele and Attis with their bull-mysteries;
you school me as an attendant of Hecate in her threefold secret rituals
and you prepare me to be worthy of the rites of Greek Ceres.
Because of you everyone celebrates me as blessed, as pious,
since you spread the word throughout the entire world that I am pious."
(*CIL* VI.1779.13–32)

Another inscription mentions the same Paulina, inscribed on a statue that she dedicated to the chief Vestal, Coelia Concordia, a woman who had previously erected a statue in honour of Paulina's husband.

"For Coelia Concordia, the Chief Vestal Virgin, Fabia Paulina daughter of Gaius has arranged for a statue to be made and erected, both on account of her distinguished chastity and her eminent purity in respect to the divine cult, and because this woman had earlier put in place a statue for her husband Vettius Agorius Praetextus, an extraordinary man most illustrious in all respects, and deserving of being honoured even by virgins and priests of this rank."
(*CIL* VI.2145)

VESTALS

Some Vestals had fared much worse than Coelia Concordia, particularly under Domitian, during his purge of "immorality" after he came to the imperial throne in 81 CE. Suetonius reports on the fate of three of them, including the Chief Vestal.

"The unchastity of the Vestal Virgins, overlooked by his father and brother, he curbed in various ways and severely, initially by capital punishment then later in the ancient way. For although he had permitted the Oculata sisters and Varronilla freedom of choice in their death and banished their seducers he then ordered soon afterward that Cornelia be buried alive – a Chief Vestal who had at one time been acquitted but then after a long interval again charged and found guilty. He ordered the Virgin's seducers to be beaten to death in the Comitium, with the exception of a man of praetorian rank, to whom he granted exile, since although he confessed his guilt the case was still not clear after the inconclusive examination and the torture of witnesses."
(Suetonius, "Domitian" 8.3–4)

THE CULT OF ISIS

In addition to her many other religious activities, Fabia Paulina was a priestess of Isis (*CIL* VI.1780). This cult, known to Greeks in Egypt from the Hellenistic period, spread to Italy with merchants. Frescoes in Pompeii and Herculaneum attest to its popularity in Campania, but in Rome the history of the cult was a troubled one. The broad appeal to women and the lower classes of this foreign cult fuelled fears of subversion at critical moments such as during the alliance of Cleopatra and Antony. Its operations were increasingly stabilized after Augustus, as emperors sought to justify absolute (and divine) rule by following the example of the Ptolemies. It reached the height of its legitimacy under Caracalla (emperor 198–217), and even survived for several decades after the legalization of Christianity by Constantine in 313 CE. Its broad appeal can be explained by the range of human needs and emotions encompassed by Isis. The fear and grief that accompany death were acknowledged in the myth and rituals of Isis' distress over the killing of her brother/consort Osiris, while her resurrection of his body offered the hope of an afterlife. Her presentation as archetype of wife and mother, as healer, goddess of fertility (within marriage), dispenser of justice, queen of heaven, land and sea, and above all her compassion, account for the longevity of the cult, from the fourth century BCE to the fourth century CE. The inscriptional record throughout Italy and the Roman provinces indicates the participation of women such as Paulina, who became initiates, priestesses or lay devotees. The open participation of women in the cult is reflected by the fact that Plutarch, in his essay "On Isis and Osiris", dedicates the work to Clea, a priestess at Delphi whose parents had initiated her into the Isis/Osiris rituals (*Moralia* 364E).

One of the best-known accounts of the cult is to be found in the novel of Apuleius (c. 125–180 CE), popularly known as *The Golden Ass* but officially as *Metamorphoses*. In it the roguish hero Lucius experiments with magic and is turned into a donkey, but in the process undergoes initiation into the cult of Isis. He describes a ritual procession in which women participated.

"Women clothed in white were resplendent, rejoicing in the various objects they carried and abloom with crowns of spring blossoms; they spread the ground with petals from the folds of their robes throughout the route where the sacred retinue was passing. There were other women who, with shining mirrors held behind their backs, turned toward the goddess as she came, and showed to her the devotion of those who were in her path. There were those who, carrying ivory combs, with a gesture of their arms and a bend of their fingers, modelled the combing and adorning of the queen's hair. There were also those who grouped together and spread the streets with various ointments and precious balsam, breaking it off drop by drop. Beyond this there was a great number of both sexes with lanterns,

torches, candles and other kinds of artificial lights, propitiating the daughter of the heavenly stars."
(Apuleius, *Metamorphoses* 11.9)

From Nîmes, in the Roman province of *Gallia Narbonensis* (modern Provence), came an inscription from the second century CE attesting to the participation of women in arranging the hair and dressing the statue of Isis in her shrine, at a considerable distance from Rome.

"Tita Savinis, dresser at the shrine of Isis, releases her vow freely, as is deserved."
(*CIL* XII.3061)

Another function that women performed in the cult was to identify with the grieving Isis by wearing black clothing, serving as "*melanophores*" (lit. "those wearing black"). From the following inscription found in Rome (cited in part) we learn that the freed-woman Marcia Salvia played this role along with a fellow freedman.

"Gaius Pomponius Sergia son of Gaius, *melanophore*; Marcia Salvia freedwoman of Lucius, *melanophore*; Gaius Publilius Trupho freedman of Gaius, *melanophore*."
(*CIL* VI.24627)

The elegiac lover-poets of the Augustan period (pp. 141–8 above) lamented the fact that the obligations of the Isis cult kept them from their mistresses, for the women were to observe sexual abstinence in preparation for her festival. Propertius refers to the goddess as a bitter one, keeping his Cynthia at bay.

"Once more those dismal ceremonies are revisiting us;
    Cynthia has been carrying out the rites for ten days.
And I wish they would perish, those rituals that the daughter of Inachus
    sent from the warm Nile to the matrons of Italy!
This is the goddess who has often divided such passionate lovers;
    whoever she has been she was always bitter to them."
(Propertius, *Elegies* 2.33.1–6)

WOMEN AND CHRISTIANITY

Women and the Apostle Paul

Ritual chastity was also a hallmark of the Christian cult, which eventually supplanted that of Isis in its appeal to a broad sector of the Roman population.

A leading founder of the establishment of communities of Christians was Paul (5–67 CE), a converted Jew from the city of Tarsus (in south-central modern Turkey). Writing to a group of believers in Corinth, he recommended adopting the celibate life he had chosen, with marriage a tolerable second option.

"I say to the unwedded and to the widows, it is better for them if they remain as I am. But if they cannot exert self-control over themselves let them marry, for it is better to marry than to burn with desire. To those who have married I proclaim – no, it is not I but the Lord – that a wife should not be independent of her husband. If she is independent let her remain unmarried or be reconciled with her husband, and the husband must not divorce his wife." (7.8–11)

Many couples during this time contracted a mixed marriage, in which only one partner was a Christian believer. Paul instructed them thus, using the terms "Brother" and "Sister", like the community at Vindolanda (p. 184 above).

"To the rest of you I say (not the Lord's words): if a Brother has an unbelieving wife and she consents to live with him, let him not divorce her. And whatever wife has an unbelieving husband and he consents to live with her, let her not divorce her husband. For the unbelieving man has been sanctified by living with his wife, and the wife who is an unbeliever has been sanctified by living with the Brother. Since your children are unclean now, you see, they are sanctified." (7.12–14)

Paul cautioned virgins about the trials of marriage, and encouraged sexual abstinence in marriage. (The expectation of the early Christians that the end of the world was near raised questions about the value of having children, and left room for them to design a reconfiguration of family structure.)

"If a virgin marries she is not committing a sin. But such people will have a burden in the flesh, and I am sparing you this. I say this, Brothers, the time is growing short. For the remainder of it let those who have wives live as if they do not. Let those who are weeping live as if they are not, and those who are rejoicing as if they were not rejoicing, and those who are buying up possessions live as if they had nothing, and those who take advantage of the world live as if they did not benefit from it. For the appearance of the world is passing away. I wish you to be free of care." (7.28–32)

Paul advised that the same domestic hierarchy of the married couple in a Roman household be retained among Christians.

"I want you to know that the head of each man is Christ, and the head of the wife is her husband; the head of Christ is God. Every man who prays or prophesies with his hair down over his head disgraces his head. And every woman who prays or prophesies with her head uncovered disgraces her head, for it is one and the same thing if she had her head shaven." (11.3–5)

A little later Paul appears to restrict even further women's performance in the early church.

"In all the churches of the sanctified let women keep silent, for it is not entrusted to them to speak aloud. But let them be kept in line, as the law states. If they want to learn something let them ask their own husbands at home, for it is shameful for a woman to talk aloud in church." (14.34–5)
(*First Letter of Paul to the Corinthians*)

In the *Acts of the Apostles*, the book in the New Testament that records events in the early formation of the Christian church, there is a record of Paul's removing the prophetic powers of a slave-girl in Philippi, a city in northern Greece (modern Macedonia). The event is narrated by one of the followers accompanying Paul.

"It happened as we where headed for a place of prayer that a slave-girl who possessed the spirit of divination met us. She was providing her masters with a considerable income when she offered prophecies. She was following Paul and called out to us, saying 'These men are servants of the highest God, who are proclaiming the path of salvation.' She did this for several days. Paul was annoyed and turning to the spirit said 'I order you in the name of Jesus Christ to depart from her.' And it left her at that moment."
(*Acts of the Apostles* 16.16–18)

The slave-girl, according to the narrator, became a Christian follower, but the event caused a local uproar, as non-adherents supported the slave-master, who stood to lose income from the girl, and they feared the powers demonstrated by Paul. The Christian group was tortured and thrown in prison. The authorities, however, had a change of heart and escorted them out of the city (*Acts of the Apostles* 16.18–40).

There are other accounts of Paul's actions as an apostle, some clearly fictional such as that found in a text likely composed in the second century CE and widely disseminated as the *Acts of Paul and Thecla*. The work has been described as a "religious romance", similar to Greek novels that appeared at this time. This fictional account did not of course make its way into the New Testament canon, but highlights the importance of chastity that Paul urged upon the early church communities, while at the same time suggesting an erotic attachment felt by women attracted to the cult's leaders. (The tensions that this aroused in families who didn't convert produced other narratives of virgin martyrs in the early centuries of the Common Era.) In this story, Paul was preaching in a house-church in Iconium (in modern Turkey) when he was overheard by a young virgin.

"While Paul was saying these things in the middle of the church gathering in the house of Onesiphorus a virgin named Thecla, whose mother was Theocleia and who had been betrothed to Thamyris, was seated in the window of a nearby house and listened night and day to the words spoken by Paul about holiness. She did not turn away from the window but rejoiced greatly and was drawn to this through her faith. Then when she also saw many women and virgins making their way toward Paul she was filled with yearning to be deemed worthy to stand also face-to-face with Paul and hear the word of Christ. For she had not yet seen the face of Paul, but had only heard what he said. (7)

Thecla's mother, who could not persuade her daughter to leave the window, sent for her betrothed, Thamyris, and expressed her alarm at the seductive power of Paul over her daughter. Thamyris, aware of the uproar in town resulting from the effects of Paul's teaching, got information from a couple of men about what was happening.

"Demas and Hermogenes said to him, 'Who this man is we don't know. But he is depriving the young men of wives and the young women of husbands, saying 'otherwise there will be no resurrection for you if you do not remain pure – only if you do not defile your flesh but remain vigilant over your chastity.'" (12)

Thamyris promised to feast the men in return for this information, and proceeded to arrange for Paul to be put in prison. Thecla visited him there, bribing the guards to let her in.

"That night Thecla, removing her bracelets, gave them to the gate-keeper and when the door was opened for her she went into the prison. She gave a silver mirror to the guard and went to Paul. Seated at his feet she listened to the mighty works of God. Paul was not frightened but because of the freedom to speak that came from God he conversed openly. Her faith increased, and she kissed his chains." (18)

Thamyris learned of Thecla's whereabouts from a fellow-slave of the doorkeeper, and gathered a crowd to present the case to the Roman governor. Paul was driven out of town and Thecla condemned to be burnt at the stake. When the crowd gathered in the theatre to watch as the fire was lit, Thecla didn't burn; an earth-quake followed by a miraculous storm quenched the flames (19–22). Thecla then found Paul preaching outside the city and begged to become his follower.

"Thecla said to Paul, 'I will cut off my hair and follow you wherever you go.' But he said, 'The timing is awkward, and you are very beautiful. I fear lest another temptation take hold of you worse than the first, and you will not stand firm but will be weakened by fear.' And Thecla said, 'Only give me the seal of Christ and temptation will not touch me.' Paul replied 'Thecla be of strong heart and baptism will be in your grasp.'" (25) (*Acts of Paul and Thecla*)

Paul took Thecla to Antioch, where she was pursued by a Syrian man named Alexander, who tried to bribe Paul to obtain her. Paul denied knowing her. Thecla was once again presented to a Roman governor and this time she was sentenced to be thrown to the wild beasts. In the arena she prayed, leapt into a basin of water and baptized herself. The beasts left her alone and a cloud of fire covered her nakedness (31–4).

Thecla was then taken into the home of a local woman but still longed for Paul. Dressing like a man, she travelled to find him. She told her story then returned to her home-town of Iconium to spread the gospel (40–1).

Perpetua

Another narrative of a Christian woman that is more historically grounded is that of Perpetua, found in the *Acts of the Christian Martyrs*, a compendium of stories of varying authenticity that circulated in the early centuries CE among Christian communities. Perpetua's story, an eye-witness account, is regarded as more reliable than some others. A woman of noble birth whose mother and two brothers were Christians but whose father was not, Perpetua was martyred at the age of 22 in 203 CE in Carthage (North Africa) in a wave of persecution under the Emperor Septimius Severus. Four other Christians were arrested with her. Most of the account is delivered in Perpetua's own voice.

"While we were still under arrest, she said, my father attempted to change my mind by his words and kept trying to dislodge me from my conviction out of his love for me. 'Father,' I said, 'for the sake of argument do you see this vase lying here, or this water-pot, or whatever?' and he said, 'I see it.' Then I said to him, 'Could it be called by any other name than what it is?' and he said 'No.' 'Well, just so I too cannot be called anything other than what I am, a Christian.' Then my father, provoked by this word, threw himself on me as if he would pluck out my eyes. But he only shook me, and left defeated, along with his devilish arguments. Then a few days later I gave thanks to the Lord for being parted from my father and I cooled down because of his absence. In the space of a few days we were baptized, and the Spirit directed me not to ask for anything else from the water except endurance of the flesh.

After a few days we were admitted to prison, and I was terrified because I had never experienced such darkness. What a day of horror! The heat was overwhelming because of the crowds, and there was rough treatment by the soldiers. The worst of all was the fact that I was tormented by anxiety for my baby there. Then Tertius and Pomponius, those blessed deacons who were trying to look after us, made an arrangement through a bribe so that we could get some calm in a better part of the prison for a few hours. Then everyone went out of the prison and left us to ourselves. I nursed my baby, who was faint for lack of food. In my anxious state I spoke to my mother on his behalf and tried to comfort my brother and commended my son to their care. I was consumed with distress for the reason that I saw they were upset out of concern for me. Such were the trials I endured for many days. Then I obtained leave for my baby to stay with me in prison. I gained strength immediately, relieved of my trouble and distress over my baby, and the prison was transformed suddenly into a palace for me, so that I preferred to be there than anywhere else." (3.1–5)

At her brother's bidding she asked to have a vision, and that night dreamt of climbing a ladder equipped with spikes and guarded by a dragon. Eventually she reached heaven where she was greeted by a man in shepherd's dress who was milking sheep. Surrounded by others dressed in white she drank the sweet milk he offered. The next day she related the dream to her brother and they agreed that this indicated that there was no more hope for their life on earth. Her father made another appeal, this time weeping and throwing himself before her. Once again he was unsuccessful.

When the prisoners were summoned to the Forum for a hearing, her father made one more attempt, holding her infant son and trying to drag her away from the prisoner's dock to offer a sacrifice for the emperor in honour of his birthday. But at the governor's questioning she confessed to being a Christian, and her father's last intervention led to his being thrown to the ground and beaten. All prisoners were condemned to death in a contest with wild beasts in the arena. The day before the contest, Perpetua had another vision, one in which she was in the arena but set to fight with a vicious-looking Egyptian. Her clothes were stripped off and her body was suddenly that of a man. She was successful in the fight and identified her opponent with the Devil.

In the actual contest she was wounded but not killed by the mad heifer chosen to attack her, and stood ready to be dispatched by the sword of a gladiator, as was customary. The narrator describes her final moments.

"Perpetua, however, had to taste more pain. She cried aloud when she was pierced between her bones, then took the wavering right hand of the young gladiator and guided it to her own throat. Perhaps it was that such a brave woman, who was

feared by an unclean spirit, could not be killed otherwise than if she herself were willing." (21.8)
(*Acts of the Christian Martyrs: of Perpetua and Felicitas*)

Perpetua was made a saint and her feast day is March 6th. There were other Christian women of the time who were canonized such as Macrina, daughter of a prominent and wealthy Christian family in Asia Minor who led an ascetic and celibate life and founded a monastic community on the family estate. For many centuries "biographies" (varying considerably in their authenticity) circulated among Christian communities and were widely popular. A number of the women whose stories were repeated had gained from their fathers and husbands independence from the traditional bonds of marriage and motherhood. One of these was Constantina, daughter of the Emperor Constantine.

HYPATIA

Tensions between this expanding monotheistic cult and traditional polytheistic religions ran high in the early centuries of the Common Era, and Christians were not the only martyrs. Hypatia was a brilliant Greek philosopher and mathematician in Alexandria whose body was torn apart by a gang of Christians who resented her influence with the Roman governor Orestes. The following account was given by one of the early Church Fathers, Socrates of Constantinople.

"There was a woman in Alexandria by the name of Hypatia. She was the daughter of the philosopher Theon. She advanced so far in her education that she outdid the philosophers around her and, leading the Neo-Platonic school that developed from Plotinus, she passed on all the philosophical learning to those who wanted to acquire it. For this reason people from everywhere wanting to study philosophy, hastened to her. Because of the seriousness attached to her through her teaching she began to speak openly with the rulers, face-to-face with moderation. And there was no awkwardness in her being present in the midst of men, for everyone respected her more because of her extraordinary chastity and they were amazed at her.

Then, following from this, envy of her grew. Since she oftentimes happened to be with Orestes this stirred up slander against her among the laity of the church, as if she was the one who stood in the way of Orestes developing a friendship with the bishop. Some men who were hot-headed agreed with this, men whom a man called Peter the Reader was leading. They were on the lookout for the woman when she was returning to her home from somewhere. Throwing her out of the carriage they dragged her to the church that was named Caesarion. They tore off her clothing and killed her with potsherds. They tore her apart limb from limb and gathered up the pieces to a place called Cinaron and burned them up.

This produced no small amount of disgrace for Cyril and for the church at Alexandria. For murder and fighting and things of this sort are completely alien to those who are believers in the Christian doctrine."
(Socrates, *Historia Ecclesiastica* 7.15 = *PG* vol 67, columns 768–9)

Socrates adds that the date for the murder was 415 CE. Hypatia's story is the subject of the recently produced film *Agora*.

FURTHER READING

Allason-Jones, L. 1989. *Women in Roman Britain.* London

d'Ambrosio, A. 2001. *Women and Beauty in Pompeii.* Los Angeles

Bagnall, R. S. 2006. *Women's Letters from Ancient Egypt. 300B.C.–A.D.800.* Ann Arbor, MI

Bernand, A. and E. 1960. *Les Inscriptions grecques et latines du Colosse de Memnon.* Paris

Bowie, E. L. 1990. "Greek Poetry in the Antonine Age", in D. A. Russell (ed.) *Antonine Literature.* Oxford. 53–90

Bradley, K. R. 1991. "The Social Role of the Nurse in the Roman World", in *Discovering the Roman Family. Studies in Roman Social History.* New York/Oxford. 13–36

Clark, G. 1993. *Women in Late Antiquity. Pagan and Christian Life-Styles.* Oxford/New York

Dixon, S. 1988. *The Roman Mother.* Norman, OK

—2001. *Reading Roman Women.* London/New York

Duncan, A. 2006. "Infamous Performers: Comic Actors and Female Prostitutes in Rome", in C. A. Faraone and L. K. McClure (eds) *Prostitutes and Courtesans in the Ancient World.* Madison, WI. 252–73

Edwards, C. 1997. "Unspeakable Professions: Public Performance and Prostitution in Ancient Rome", in M. Skinner and J. Hallett (eds) *Roman Sexualities.* Princeton, NJ. 66–95

Evans-Grubbs, J. 2002. *Women and the Law in the Roman Empire. A Sourcebook on Marriage, Divorce, and Widowhood.* London/New York

Flemming, R. 1999. "*Quae corpore quaestum fecit.* The Sexual Economy of Female Prostitution in the Roman Empire". *Journal of Roman Studies* 89, 38–61

Freisenbruch, A. 2010. *The First Ladies of Rome. The Women Behind the Caesars.* London

George, M. 2005 (ed.). *The Roman Family in the Empire. Rome, Italy and Beyond.* Oxford

Gilhuly, K. 2006. "The Phallic Lesbian: Philosophy, Comedy, and Social Inversion in Lucian's *Dialogue of the Courtesans*", in C. A. Faraone and L. K. McClure (eds) *Prostitutes and Courtesans in the Ancient World.* Madison, WI. 274–91

Greene, E. M. 2013. "Female Networks in Military Communities in the Roman West: A View from the Vindolanda Tablets", in E. Himelrijk and G. Woolf (eds) *Gender and the City: Women and Civic Life in Italy and the Western Provinces.* Leiden (forthcoming)

Hanson, A. E. 1990. "The Medical Writers' Woman", in D. M. Halperin, J. J. Winkler and F. I. Zeitlin (eds) *Before Sexuality. The Construction of Erotic Experience in the Ancient Greek World.* Princeton, NJ. 309–38

Heine, S. 1988. *Women and Early Christianity.* A Reappraisal. (transl. from the German edition of 1987). Minneapolis, MN

Hemelrijk, E. A. 1999. *Matrona Docta. Educated Women in the Roman Élite from Cornelia to Julia Domna*. London/New York

Heyob, S. K. 1975. *The Cult of Isis Among Women in the Greco-Roman World*. Leiden

Kampen, N. 1981. *Image and Status. Roman Working Women in Ostia*. Berlin

Kraemer, R. S. 2004. *Women's Religions in the Greco-Roman World. A Sourcebook*. Oxford

Lefkowitz, M. R. *et al.* 1992 (eds). *Women's Life in Greece & Rome* (1st edn 1982). Chapter IX, "Medicine and Anatomy", pp. 225–64; Ch. X, "Religion (Christianity)". Baltimore/London, pp. 307–34.

MacMullen, R. 1980. "Women in Public in the Roman Empire". *Historia* 29, 208–18

Marshall, A. J. 1975. "Roman Women and the Provinces". *Ancient Society* 6, 109–27

McGinn, T. A. J. 2004. *The Economy of Prostitution in the Roman World. A Study of Social History and the Brothel*. Ann Arbor, MI

—2006. "Zoning Shame in the Roman City", in C. A. Faraone and L. K. McClure (eds) *Prostitutes and Courtesans in the Ancient World*. Madison, WI. 161–76

McGinn, T. *et al.* 2002 (eds). *Pompeian Brothels, Pompeii's Ancient History, Mirrors and Mysteries, Art and Nature at Oplontis and the Herculaneum Basilica*. Portsmouth, RI

Olson, K. 2006. "*Matrona* and Whore: Clothing and Definition in Roman Antiquity", in C. A. Faraone and L. K. McClure (eds) *Prostitutes and Courtesans in the Ancient World*. Madison, WI. 186–204

Salisbury, J. E. *Church Fathers, Independent Virgins*. New York/London

Shelton, J. 2012. *The Women of Pliny's Letters*. New York

Temkin, O. 1991. *Soranus' Gynecology* (1st edition 1956). Baltimore/London

Treggiari, S. 1976. "Jobs for Women," *American Journal of Ancient History* 1, 76–104

—1979. "Lower Class Women in the Roman Economy". *Florilegium* 1, 65–86

General bibliography

Balsdon, J. P. V. D. 1962. *Roman Women. Their History and Habits.* London

Beard, M., J. North and S. Price. 1998a. *Religions of Rome I. A History.* Cambridge

—1998b. *Religions of Rome II. A Sourcebook.* Cambridge

Bradley, K. R. 1991. *Discovering the Roman Family. Studies in Roman Social History.* New York/Oxford

D'Ambra, Eve. 2007. *Roman Women.* Cambridge/New York

Dixon, S. 2001a. *Reading Roman Women. Sources, Genres and Real Life.* London

—(ed.). 2001b. *Childhood, Class and Kin in the Roman World.* London/New York

—1992. *The Roman Family.* Baltimore, MD

—1988. *The Roman Mother.* Norman, OK

Fantham, E. 2011. *Roman Readings.* Berlin

Fantham, E., H. P. Foley, N. B. Kampen, S. Pomeroy and A. Shapiro. 1994. (eds) *Women in the Classical World.* New York/Oxford

Frier, B. W. and T. A. J. McGinn. 2004. *A Casebook on Roman Family Law.* Oxford

Gardner, J. F. 1986. *Women in Roman Law and Society.* London/Sydney

—1998. *Family and Familia in Roman Law and Life.* Oxford

Gardner, J. and T. Wiedemann. 1991. (eds) *The Roman Household. A Sourcebook.* London/New York

Hallett, J. P. 1984. *Fathers and Daughters in Roman Society. Women and the Elite Family.* Princeton, NJ

—1999. "Women in the Ancient Roman World" in B. Vivante (ed.) *Women's Roles in Ancient Civilizations. A Reference Guide.* Westport, CT. 257–89.

—and M. B. Skinner 1997. (eds) *Roman Sexualities.* Princeton, NJ

Hemelrijk, E. A. 1999. *Matrona Docta. Educated Women in the Roman Élite from Cornelia to Julia Domna.* London/New York

Johnson, M. and T. Ryan. 2005. *Sexuality in Greek and Roman Society and Literature.* London/New York

Joshel, S. R. 2010. *Slavery in the Roman World.* Cambridge

—and S. Murnaghan (eds) 1998. Women and Slaves in Greco-Roman Culture. *Differential Equations.* London/New York. 92–108

Keegan, P. 2004. "Boudica, Cartimandua, Messalina and Agrippina the Younger: Independent Women of Power and the Gendered Rhetoric of Roman History," *Ancient History* 34, 99–148

Kleiner, D. E. E. and S. B. Matheson 1996. (eds) *I Claudia. Women in Ancient Rome.* Austin, TX

—(eds). 2000. *I Claudia II. Women in Roman Art and Society.* Austin, TX

Kraemer, R. S. 2004. *Women's Religions in the Greco-Roman World. A Sourcebook.* Oxford

Laes, C. 2011. *Children in the Roman Empire. Outsiders Within.* Cambridge

Lefkowitz, M. and M. Fant. 2005. *Women's Life in Greece and Rome. A Source-Book in Translation* (revised edition). Baltimore, MD

Olson, K. 2002. "*Matrona* and Whore. The Clothing of Women in Roman Antiquity". *Fashion Theory* 6.4, 387–420. Reprinted 2006 in *Prostitutes and Courtesans in the Ancient World*. (eds) C. A. Faraone and L. K. McClure. Madison, WI. 186–204

—2008. *Dress and the Roman Woman. Self-Presentation and Society*. Abingdon, NY

Pälvi, S. and L. Savunen. 1999. *Female Networks and the Public Sphere in Roman Society*. Rome

Rawson, B. and T. A. J. McGinn. 1991. (eds) *Marriage, Divorce and Children in Ancient Rome*. Oxford/New York

Richlin, A. 1983. *The Garden of Priapus. Sexuality and Aggression in Roman Humour*. New Haven, CT/London

Schultz, C. E. 2006. *Women's Religious Activity in the Roman Republic*. Chapel Hill, NC

Setälä, P. and Savunen, L. 1999. *Female Networks and the Public Sphere in Roman Society*. Rome

Skinner, M. B. 2005. *Sexuality in Greek and Roman Culture*. Malden, MA/Oxford/ Victoria, Australia

Treggiari, S. 1979. "Lower Class Women in the Roman Economy". *Florilegium* 1, 65–86

—1991. *Roman Marriage. Iusti Coniuges from the Time of Cicero to the Time of Ulpian*. Oxford

Warrior, V. 2002. *Roman Religion. A Sourcebook*. Newburyport, MA

Index of ancient authors and texts

General index